TURKISH COAST
Through Writers' Eyes

TURKISH COAST

Through Writers' Eyes
The South-Western Shore

Edited by
RUPERT SCOTT

ELAND

First published by Eland Publishing Ltd
61 Exmouth Market, London ECIR 4QL in 2008

Editorial content © Rupert Scott

All extracts © of the authors, as attributed
in the text and acknowledgments

ISBN 978 1 906011 09 3

Cover design by Nick Randall
Typesetting by Antony Gray
Cover image Kaputas Bay © Grand Tour/Corbis
Text edited by Rose Baring & Fran Sandham
Map by Reginald Piggot
Printed in Spain by GraphyCems, Navarra

Contents

Map   10

Foreword   13

Introduction   19

Chapter One: The Sea
page 23

Travels in Various Countries of Europe, Asia and Africa
  by Dr Edward D. Clarke   23

'The Isles of Greece' by Lord Byron   24

Odyssey by Homer   26

'Sailing Weather' by Hesiod   28

The Travels of Lord Charlemont in Greece and Turkey,
  edited by W. B Stanford   29

Travels in Southern Europe & The Levant, by C. Cockerell   31

The Mediterranean Pilot by Captain Thomas Spratt   31

The Companion Guide to the Greek Islands
  by Ernle Bradford   31

Karamania by Captain Francis Beaufort   32

A Journal written during an excursion in Asia Minor
  by Charles Fellows   33

'A Masterpiece from the Sea' by George E. Bean.   34

'Thirty-three centuries under the sea' by Peter Throckmorton   35

The Ancient Mariners by Lionel Casson   38

The Bellstone by Michael Kalafatas   40

Travels in Lycia by T. Spratt and E. Forbes   40

Bus Stop Symi by William Travis   41

The Bellstone by Michael Kalafatas   43

Europa Minor by Patrick Kinross   44

Chapter Two: Turkish Pleasures
page 46

Bread and Velvet Turkish Delights by Lesley Blanch   46
Turkish Cooking by Irfan Orga   49
Turkey on $5 a Day by Tom Brosnahan   53
Life in a Turkish Village by Joe Pierce   56
Welcome the Wayfarer by Nancy Phelan   60

Chapter Three: Turtles, Lions and Lilies:
the Flora and Fauna of the South Aegean Coast
page 63

Kaptan June and the Turtles by June Haimoff   64
Travels in Lycia by T. Spratt and E. Forbes   72
A Journal written during an excursion in Asia Minor
   by Charles Fellows   73
Sport & Travel, East & West by Frederick C. Selous   75
George Maranz in *The American Weekly*   78
Cornucopia 1996   81
'The Travel Journals of Dr John Sibthorp'
   quoted in *The Magnificent Flora Graeca* by Stephen Harris   84
'A Journey in South-West Anatolia' by P. H. Davis in
   Journal of the RHS, April 1949   85
Remarkable Trees of the World by Thomas Pakenham   90
Turkey Beyond the Maeander by George E. Bean   91
Travels in Lycia by T. Spratt and E. Forbes   91

Chapter Four: An Ancient Coast
page 92

The Voyage of Argo by Apollonius of Rhodes   93
The Ship, or the Wishes – a Dialogue by Lucian of Samosata   95
The Ancient Mariners by Lionel Casson   97
Travel in the Ancient World by Lionel Casson   98
The Loves – a dialogue by Lucian of Samosata   99

Historia Naturalis by Pliny   101
A History of Lycia by Polycharmus   101
Lycian Turkey by George E. Bean   101
'Aegean Odyssey' by Barnaby Rogerson   102
Travels in Asia Minor 1764–5 by Richard Chandler,
    edited by Edith Clay   103
South from Ephesus by Brian Sewell   105
Greek Anthology by Antipater of Sidon   106
Ionia: A Quest by Freya Stark   106
Europa Minor by Patrick Kinross   107
Karamania by Captain Francis Beaufort   109
Travels in Various Countries of Europe, Asia and Africa
    by Dr Edward D. Clarke   110
Turkey's Southern Shore by George E. Bean   110

Chapter Five: Travellers in the Nineteenth Century
page 112

Anastasius by Thomas Hope   112
A Visit to the Seven Churches of Asia
    by Rev. Francis Arundell   118
'Remarks for the Guidance of Travellers' in *Journal written
    during an excursion in Asia Minor* by C. Fellows   119
Eothen by William Kinglake   121
Murray's *Handbook for Travellers in Turkey*   123
The Cruise of the Vanadis by Edith Wharton   124

Chapter Six: Twentieth-Century Travellers
page 125

The Caravan Moves On by Irfan Orga   126
The Blue Exile (Mavi Sürgün) by Cevat Şakir Kabaağaçlı   130
Cornucopia by Barnaby Rogerson   131
The Lycian Shore by Freya Stark   135
The Western Shores of Turkey by John Freely   136

Dinner of Herbs by Carla Grissmann   137
Welcome the Wayfarer by Nancy Phelan   138
Some Talk of Alexander: The Letters of Freya Stark   144
Europa Minor by Patrick Kinross   147
Bus Stop Symi by William Travis   148
Mermaids Singing by Charmian Clift   150
A Fez of the Heart by Jeremy Seal   150
A Fez of the Heart by Jeremy Seal   152
Breakfasts with Kaptan June by June Haimoff   153
Turkish Reflections by Mary Lee Settle   155

Chapter Seven: Ottoman Episodes
page 158

Assedio e conquista di Rodi nel 1522, secondo le relazioni
edite e inedite dei Turchi by E. Rossi   159
The Two Sieges of Rhodes by Eric Brockman   160
Bodrum, a town in the Aegean by Fatma Mansur   162
The unpublished letters of Bertram Thesiger   165
Smyrna 1922 by Marjorie Housepian   167
Daily Mail, September 1922   168
I was sent to Athens by Henry Morgenthau   169
Twice a Stranger by Bruce Clark   170
Birds without Wings by Louis de Bernieres   171
Public Record Office, Kew   175
He Who Dares, David Sutherland   176
Raiders from the Sea by John Lodwick   178
Europa Minor by Patrick Kinross   179

Chapter Eight: Expeditions, Archaeologists and Discoveries
page 180

Karamania by Captain Francis Beaufort   180
Travels in Southern Europe & The Levant
by Charles Cockerell   184

Contents   9

Journal Written in Asia Minor by Charles Fellows   185
Travels and Researches in Asia Minor
    by Sir Charles Fellows   187
Travels in Lycia by T. Spratt and E. Forbes   188
Travels and Researches in Asia Minor by Sir Charles Fellows 189
Travels in Lycia by T. Spratt and E. Forbes   190
Travels & Discoveries in the Levant by Charles Newton   192
FO Papers, Public Record Office, Kew   197
Travels & Discoveries in the Levant by Charles Newton   198

The Historical Appendices
page 201

Appendix A – Daily Life in the Ancient Cities
    by Ffiona Gilmore Eaves   203

Appendix B – Ancient Lycia 'The First Republic'
    by Barnaby Rogerson   235

Acknowledgements   241

Works & Writers mentioned in the text   243

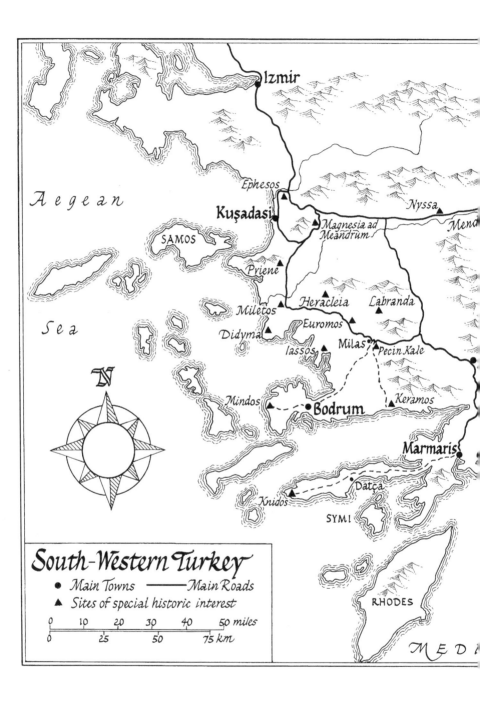

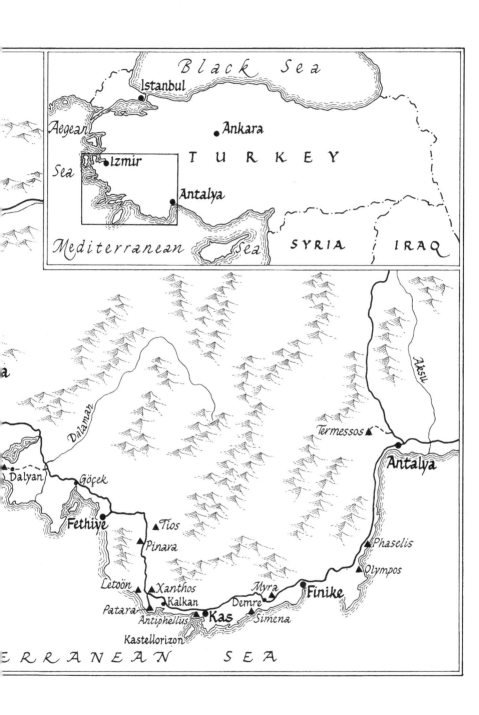

Foreword

Imagine anchoring in the gin-clear strait between the thickly forested Turkish mainland and the islet of St Nicholas on the eastern edge of Fethiye Bay where the only settlements in view are the shack cafés on Gemiler Beach. Snorkel from the *gulet* over the starfish-strewn remains of submerged Byzantine cisterns before putting ashore to potter among the island ruins of fifth-century basilicas. Leave the children searching for wild tortoises or crickets as you climb to the summit, with its grand views over Baba Dağ (Father Mountain). Descend by the impressive remains of a once-grand covered walkway, whose precise function in early-Christian ceremonial even today can only be guessed at. Return to the *gulet's* awning-covered rear deck, running the gauntlet of the circling ice-cream boats vying for the attention of the children, for lunch: freshly prepared *biber dolma* (stuffed peppers), *patlican salata* (aubergine salad), *sigara börek* (crumbly white cheese and herbs in filo pastry), and perhaps even squid lately sourced by the captain after a foray with the *gulet's* own speargun, all washed down with a glass or two of Turkish wine or Efes beer. And so to the sundeck for the afternoon. Or you might come over all reckless, and even find yourself asking the crew to saddle up the *gulet's* windsurfer. The crew will be kind, even encouraging. They always are, and they will always come to retrieve you and the lousy, dysfunctional board should your confidence proved misplaced.

The afternoon draws on and, in the established rhythm of *gulet* living, the captain proposes the shortest of hops to that night's anchorage. Not that the guests need lift a finger as the crew bustle in preparation for departure. Most *gulet* were motor-cruisers until recently. Now, however, increasing numbers are responding to demand and rigged to sail when conditions allow. On such occasions, a thrilling beat may take the *gulet* deep into the recesses of Fethiye Bay. Oregano, thyme and pine – the scents of spice rack and bathroom

– fill the nostrils as the *gulet* noses into Batikhamam (Sunken Baths) Bay. The crew moors in the time-honoured fashion, anchor from the bow, stern landline around a sturdy pine. You don the masks again to explore the submerged remains of what local lore has down as an Ottoman bathhouse. You have your doubts, thinking it more likely to have been a timber warehouse or a local customs post. Not that it matters, as shoals of striped fish flit between the submerged stone arches with your children in pursuit.

The sunken ruin is all alone except for a ramshackle houseboat ablaze with geraniums potted in rusting olive-oil cans. It functions as a café. Currently. The place has the stamp of impermanence, which is the way you like it. And the way it must be on these remote shores where business is so fickle. Who can say, for example, whether Hasan's place, a picture of simplicity serving cold beer, a shepherd's salad of onions, parsley, tomato and lemon, and a plate of grilled *barbunya* (red mullet) will open this season to serve those *gulet's* lucky enough to have discovered the divine solitude of Dirsek Buku near Bozburun? So you drink tea from tulip-shaped glasses beneath the houseboat's faded awning and marvel at museum-quality chunks of fluted marble; these remnants from 2,000-year-old columns are casually embedded in the terrace walls at the foot of this remote and lovely hillside.

Early evening draws on, so it's back to the *gulet* to the comfort of wood-panelled cabins, with hot showers and not a confusing stop-cock in sight. There is backgammon and raki, moonlight and the soft slap of water against the *gulet*. Over dinner, there is general agreement that this is a life you could live forever.

Whatever the vessel – traditional timber *gulet*, flotilla yacht or even tour boat on a day out of Kaş, Bodrum or Fethiye – the enchantment of immersion in these ruin-strewn lands is as rich as any in history, culture and natural beauty. There is something almost Hebridean, with the heat turned up, in these indented shores, at least as far as the mountain-backed bays and little inlets, islets and sudden, spectacular beaches go. Other draws, rather less Scottish ones, are the weather and the comparative calmness of these essentially inshore waters. Breezes can get up, not least the gusty *meltem*, but they tend to be refreshingly welcome rather than the cause of any serious queasiness.

These coasts are as reminiscent of the Norfolk Broads – I'm thinking particularly of the reed-fringed indents at the head of the Gulf of Gokova – as of the Solent.

These shores, home to the fire-breathing Chimera and to St Nicholas, are liberally scattered with the fig- and olive-tangled ruins of the Byzantines and Romans, and with the ubiquitous stone sarcophagi, like capsized ships, of the Lycians. For those who like their ruins abundant, unimproved and atmospheric there are no coasts quite like those of ancient Caria and Lycia. Nor is there a better way of accessing them than by *gulet* (from the French *goulette*, or coasting vessel), as much the signature craft of south-west Turkey as the felucca is to the Nile or the dhow to Zanzibar. These ketches, with their high-windowed galleon sterns, twin masts and prominent bowsprits, once carried cargoes of lemons and mandarins to Izmir or Antalya. They were put out of work by the gradual extension of the regional road network from the 1960s, but have since been refitted and reinvented as the most congenial and civilised of small-group cruising craft; floating holiday villas for bare-foot but fair-weather boating types.

The truth is you could see much of this coast in a month, but it's unlikely you'll have that long. So it's as well to have an idea of the highlights. The most memorable of the ancient sites? Knidos, at the tip of the Datça Peninsula, with its shoreside theatre and its harbours where triremes once sheltered beneath the bulk of Cape Crio. Patara, birthplace both of St Nicholas and of successive generations of endangered loggerhead turtles, hard up against the dunes of what must be the Mediterranean's prime unspoilt beach. Olympos, with its tangled riverbank atmosphere and the subterranean monstrous Chimera, where volcanic gases vent from a hillside in perpetual flame.

You're also sure to take in a modern port or two. The amount you're consuming, the crew need opportunities to re-provision. Besides, the usual convention is that they get granted the odd night off. This is your opportunity to take in a proper bar and shop for tat, or even a genuinely lovely kelim, in the hibiscus-festooned arcades of Kaş or Kalkan. But push instead for Fethiye, not so much for the town itself as its proximity to the haunting ruins at Kaya some twenty minutes' drive inland. Organise a taxi at the quayside and you'll soon be among the olive groves and orchards of a hillside town which has stood abandoned since its Greek-speaking Christian citizens were deported from Turkey in the population exchanges of the 1920s. Kaya is a moving memorial to this ethnic reshuffle, which uprooted hundreds of thousands of people and marked the end of the Christian presence in Anatolia after almost 2,000 years. Wander among the churches and chapels where martins nest. Follow the cobbled lanes between the hundreds of houses, their interiors choked with pine trees and walls faded to a faint blue. Eat under the mulberry trees at one of the al fresco restaurants that hem these mournful but enchanting ruins before returning to your *gulet* for the night.

At the aptly named Balikasiran, or Fish Leap, south-west Turkey narrows to a pine-clad isthmus. This rocky waist of just 250 metres is all that connects the rest of the country with the Datça Peninsula, a high-spined, heavily wooded finger of land which was rarely visited until substantial improvements were recently made to the one access road. Datça people are widely known for their distinct character. In a country decidedly short on islands they almost pass as Turkey's islanders, tending towards the raffish, maverick and creative, not to mention boozy. All of which explains why the more conformist 'mainland' Turks tend to see the 'Fish Leap' as something of a psychological Rubicon. To cross, they warn, is to risk mental and perhaps moral degeneration, rather in keeping with the local topography's own descent into a confusing scatter, even by the region's mazy standards, of gulfs, bays, capes, coves, headlands and adjacent Greek islands such as Symi and Kos.

I have been to the Datça Peninsula a number of times. And never have I felt the local madness conjured by those urbane mainlanders, with index fingers twirling at the temples, who would rather I demonstrated a preference for the concrete barscapes, with their lewdly named cocktails, of Marmaris or Bodrum. I have often arrived on the compact little car ferry from bustling Bodrum, crossing the Gulf of Gokova with dolphins on the bow wave to the ruinous beauty – a single minaret, abandoned windmills – of the peninsula's sub-tropical north shore. I have also come by land in recent years, crossing the 'Fish Leap' following improvements to the appalling road in 2005. Mostly, however, I have arrived by *gulet*, just as I have arrived at any number of places along this concertina coastline. Then there is the Dalyan delta where your *gulet* can't go, but with more than enough attractions – wildlife, ruins, freshwater Lake Köyceğiz, the fabulous river-mouth beach and even a sulphur-smelling mud bath – to keep everybody entertained. Ask your captain to arrange a local caique for the day. Shelter beneath the sun awning as the boat threads its way through the delta's reed-lined channels, with flocks of bee-eaters overhead, to the ruins of ancient Caunus. Olive trees have pushed between the stepped tiers of masonry blocks in the theatre. Kingfishers flash across the long-silted harbour. Onwards, past the Lycian rock tombs which announce the town of Dalyan, with its bustle of spice shops and carpet sellers, to swim in the lake while a lunch of chicken kebabs cooks on the caique's stern-mounted barbecue. Then it's back downstream, taking in a messy visit to a sulphurous mudhole, to the beach where you wash off the face packs your children have so thoughtfully provided in the rolling surf. But you are out of time. The last night is hot. Some of you abandon your cabins and take to the deck in search of cooling breezes. And so to the classic *gulet* cameo – simple and romantic – of parents and children star-gazing while frogs chorus from the shoreline marshes.

JEREMY SEAL

Introduction

This book concerns itself with only a small part of Turkey's vast shoreline, known as Caria and Lycia by antiquarians or remembered by thousands of holiday-makers as 'The Turquoise Coast'. This name is a fairly recent but highly convenient invention to describe the area between Antalya and Bodrum. It is a coast of limitless fascination and astonishing beauty. The landscape is in places huge and dramatic. Mountains such as the Baba Dağ above Ölü Deniz rise to over 2,000 metres, almost directly from the shore. Rocky headlands alternate with idyllic beaches and sheltered bays. There are literally hundreds of these, and often they are not accessible by road. Huge stretches of the coast are barely inhabited. In summer there is something almost ethereal about the intensity of the light and the colour of the sea.

What we like about this coast nowadays is its emptiness – the wonderful reality that it is still possible in the twenty-first century to sail from empty bay to empty bay, to swim, to see Homer's 'rosy-fingered dawn' and the sunset more or less undisturbed by others. But if we had come here 2,000 years ago we would have been struck, I think, by how busy this coast seemed. This was the epicentre of the Hellenic-Roman world, and since there were few roads on land, virtually all goods and people went by sea. There were at least thirty cities, some large, others quite small, on or near the coast between Bodrum and Antalya and there would have been many boats plying between them, and also out to the myriad islands. On those boats there would have been tourists from all over the Empire visiting the great 'sights' of the ancient world – like Praxiteles' famous statue of Aphrodite in Knidos, or the temples and oracles on the coast, or the Colossus of Rhodes. Some of these cities had large populations – there were perhaps 70,000 people in Knidos at its height. Many of the bays that are now empty would have been farmed. And in many of them, if you look carefully enough, you will find some lingering hint of ancient occupation – pieces of cut stone reused in walls, or broken terracotta handles of amphorae. And if you look up into the hills you can sometimes see the terracing of what were Roman vineyards. Amphorae carrying the exports of the cities along this coast have been found all over the Mediterranean and the Black Sea.

A combination of piracy, invasions, and the general breakdown of peace, saw the complete ruination of this world. What had been the most visited part of the Mediterranean became the least visited. It is not an outrageous generalisation to say that from the waning of Byzantium to the Age of Enlightenment, from the ninth century to the nineteenth century, the Turquoise Coast was virtually unvisited by foreign travellers. But there were exceptions, and these accounts are all the more fascinating for their rarity. Visitors to this coast almost invariably came with a purpose – they were botanists like John Sibthorp, gathering specimens for the 'Flora Graeca', or cartographers like Captain Beaufort making charts for the Royal Navy, or antiquarians and archaeologists trying to locate ancient cities or excavate their remains. They were zoologists and geologists and even hunters of big game. This coast remained a frontier and a challenge until very late. To quote Captain Beaufort: 'It does appear somewhat strange that while the spirit of modern discovery has explored the most remote extremities of the globe . . . this portion of the Mediterranean has remained undescribed and unknown.'

By the early twentieth century the Turquoise Coast was more settled and more prosperous, but it did not entirely escape Turkey's brutal experience during the years from 1914 to 1924. There was an Italian occupation from 1919 to 1922, and in 1924 came the Exchange of Populations. By the terms of the Treaty of Lausanne of 1923, which formally ended the Greek-Turkish War, the Orthodox population of Turkey was exchanged with the Moslem population of Greece. Some three million individuals were involved in this exchange. This must have been traumatic for the individuals involved and for the economic life of the communities they left behind. Some parts of this coast lost a third of their population. And with the Exchange there ended the harmonious cohabitation of this coast by Greek and Turk that had lasted more than five hundred years.

From 1948, when the Dodecanese Islands became part of Greece (from 1912 to 1943 they had been Italian), the separation between the islands and the mainland became complete. It became almost impossible for Turks on the mainland and Greeks on the islands to visit each other. Only in the last few years have relations between Greece and Turkey improved, but in the intervening decades the people on the islands and the people on the mainland have grown apart. But despite this modern separation of peoples, this coast retains a blend of East and West – it as much Europa Minor as it is Asia Minor.

The first writer to draw attention to the delights of sailing on this coast was Cevat Şakir, the 'Fisherman of Hallicarnassus', who was exiled to Bodrum in 1926. He invented the expression *mavi yolculuk* (blue cruise) for his expeditions of discovery in small boats along the coast in summer. Like Homer, he would pull his boat up on to the beach at night, and sleep on the shore. His books and stories describing his experiences were well known in Turkey, and in the 1950s there was a sudden rush of foreign imitators – two British writers, Freya Stark and Patrick Kinross, made the *mavi yolculuk* on the same small *gulet*, the *Elfin*, in successive years. Freya Stark sailed west-to-east and Patrick Kinross sailed east-to-west. Both wrote charming books about their journeys. Freya Stark wrote that 'there are not many places left where magic reigns without interruption and of all of those I know, the coast of Lycia was the most magical'.

Although the popularity of the blue cruise steadily increased, most of the Turquoise Coast remained undisturbed until surprisingly late. In 1975 June Haimoff (later to become famous as the environmental campaigner, who saved İstuzu Beach near Dalyan) brought her *gulet*, *Bouboulina*, into Turkish waters. She was amazed at the sheer emptiness of Dalyan beach which, when first seen from the boat, 'stretched away in a flawless white arc, losing itself in the far distance under a summer haze – serene, solitary and mysterious'.

The last twenty-five years have brought huge changes. Some areas have been developed very fast and with little sensitivity. From an aesthetic point of view it is difficult to find very much to admire in the towns that have appeared out of almost nothing – like Marmaris,

Datça, or Fethiye. But at the same time vast areas of the coast remain remarkably unspoilt – almost all the north and south sides of the Datça peninsula, all of Bozburun and most of the Lycian coast. Encouragingly, there are signs that the protection of the shore and of the sea is now being given a much higher priority by the Turkish government.

CHAPTER ONE

The Sea

There can be very few parts of the sea anywhere in the world that have been sailed on for longer than the Turkish Aegean. For thousands of years before Homer ships were making their way along the coast of the mainland and between the islands. Nowadays there is little commercial traffic, but great numbers of yachts and *gulets* with human cargoes that delight in the sheer pleasure of living on the sea in a warm climate, of moving from bay to bay, of swimming in clear water, and perhaps of rising early to catch a sight of Homer's 'rosy-fingered dawn' or to gaze at the stars from the deck at night. But this association of the sea with pleasure, and this rugged coast with beauty, is historically very recent. For thousands of years sailors have associated the sea with danger and the coast with fear. And with good reason, for in all seasons sudden and terrifying storms can rise without warning.

Dr Edward Clarke, an intrepid traveller in the eastern Mediterranean during the early nineteenth century, whose many adventures included a month on a Turkish warship, was one of the first writers to describe the magnificence of the scenery in the Turkish Aegean:

The appearance of all the south of Asia Minor from the sea is fearfully grand, and perhaps no part of it possesses more eminently those sources of the sublime which Burke has instructed us to find in vastness and terror, than the entrance to the gulph into which we were now sailing . . .

From the eastern coast of Rhodes, our Captain stood over once more towards the coast of Lycia and the Seven Capes. In the morning of October the second, we found ourselves in the midst of islands and promontories placed upon the bright expanse, as it were, of a mirror. It is quite impossible to afford by description, any ideas of such scenery. The impression made upon our minds, who had beheld these sights before, was new again. The immensity of the objects; the varied nature of the territory over all the southern shores of Asia Minor; the prodigious effect of light and shade, in masses extending for leagues; the sublime effulgence and the ineffable whiteness of the snow-clad summits, contrasted with the dark chasms on the sides of the mountains; the bold precipices, and the groups of numerous islands; the glorious brightness and the intensity of colour diffused over the horizon; these, indeed, may be enumerated, but they cannot be described. We continued surveying them, as if we had then seen them for the first time. The Turkish practice of keeping near the shore, when land is in sight, enabled us to view the whole coast of Lycia and of Caria. As we proceeded towards Doris, the eye commanded, in one prospect, the whole of that part of Asia Minor, even to the Triopian Promontary, or Cape Crio, together with the islands of Rhodes, Syme, Sicklia, Telo, and even Scarpanto lying at a distance of thirty leagues in the Carpathian Sea.

FROM *Travels in Various Countries of Europe, Asia and Africa*
by Dr Edward D. Clarke

As Clarke suggests, it is partly the intensity and clarity of the light and colour that make the views of the coast and the islands so dramatic, and also the sheer scale of the mountains, which rise in places to 3,000 metres. Perhaps it was partly the brilliant light that inspired Byron to pen these famous stanzas:

> The isles of Greece! the isles of Greece!
> Where burning Sappho loved and sung,
> Where grew the arts of war and peace,
> Where Delos rose and Phoebus sprung!
> Eternal summer gilds them yet,
> But all, except their sun, is set.

> The Scian and the Teian muse,
> The hero's harp, the lover's lute,
> Have found the fame your shores refuse;

Their place of birth alone is mute
To sounds which echo further west
Than your sires' 'Islands of the Blest'.

The mountains look on Marathon
And Marathon looks on the sea;
And musing there an hour alone,
I dream'd that Greece might yet be free
For, standing on the Persians' grave,
I could not deem myself a slave.

A king sat on the rocky brow
Which looks on sea-born Salamis;
And ships, by thousands, lay below,
And men in nations; all were his!
He counted them at break of day
And when the sun set, where were they?

And where are they? and where art thou,
My country? On thy voiceless shore
The heroic lay is tuneless now
The heroic bosom beats no more!
And must thy lyre, so long divine,
Degenerate into hands like mine?

'Tis something, in the dearth of fame,
Though link'd among a fetter'd race,
To feel at least a patriot's shame,
Even as I sing, suffuse my face;
For what is left the poet here?
For Greeks a blush – for Greece a tear

FROM 'The Isles of Greece' by Lord Byron

WINDS, STORMS AND CURRENTS

The Aegean is a surprisingly dangerous sea. Very strong winds can rise quite suddenly and apparently from nowhere, whipping up frenzied waves from a previously tranquil sea, and driving boats on to the rocks. This was an ever-present danger for small ships in the Ancient World, which tended to keep close to shore. It is perhaps not surprising that such storms were seen as the whimsical creations of Poseidon, the terrifying god of the Sea.

Perhaps the greatest description of an Aegean storm is in Homer's *Odyssey*. Odysseus, during his long return journey to Ithaca from Troy, escapes from the beautiful nymph Calypso on a raft. But out at sea he is struck by a terrifying wind sent by Poseidon, that destroys his rigging then capsizes his raft.

> So spake he, and the clouds at this command
> Gathered, and with the trident in his hand
> He stirred the sea and roused the hurricane
> Of all the winds, and blotted sea and land
>
> With clouds: night swept across the firmament:
> East wind and south, and west athwart them sent,
> Clashed, and the crystal-cradled northern blast
> Rolling a mighty wave before him went.
>
> Trembled Odysseus then in heart and knee,
> And to his mighty spirit inwardly
> Grieving he spoke: 'O miserable man!
> Is this the end? What shall become of me?
>
> 'I fear lest all was true the Goddess said,
> How on the deep, ere yet my land I tread,
> I must fill up the measure of my woes:
> Now to the word is all accomplishèd.
>
> 'With such enveloping clouds the breadth of sky
> Zeus covers, and the sea runs mountains high,
> And all the hurricanes of all the wind
> Burst round me: now as good as dead am I.
>
> 'Thrice of our host and four times happy they
> Who in wide Troy of old were cast away,
> Serving the sons of Atreus! Would to God
> I too had died then and fulfilled my day,

'When the bronze spears of Trojans many a one
Struck nigh me round the corpse of Peleus' son!
Then fame and funeral I had earned, nor here
Had perished by this dismal death undone.'

Even as he spoke, a monstrous wave abaft
Came towering up, and crashed into the raft:
And the raft heeled, and off it far he fell,
And from his hand shot out the rudder-shaft.

And in one whirling gust the hurricane
Snapped the mast midway; far into the main
Fell top and rigging: and beneath the surge
He sank, nor for a while his head again

Out of the overwhelming wave could lift:
For now the raiment, bright Calypso's gift,
Weighed heavy on him: but at last he rose,
And with abundant-streaming head made shift

Out of his mouth to spit the salty spray.
Yet withal marking where the wrecked raft lay,
He plunged amid the waves and caught at it,
And crouched amidships, keeping death at bay:

While the raft helpless on the tideway spun,
As down the plain when Autumn is begun,
Before the north wind tufts of thistledown
Entangled close together twirling run;

So him across the sea in furious race
Hither and thither the winds bore apace:
And now south wind to north its plaything tossed,
And now east wind to west gave up the chase.

FROM the *Odyssey* in
Oxford Book of Greek Verse in Translation

Eventually Odysseus is thrown into the sea, but he lands safely on Scherie, home of the Phaeacians, though he is nearly dashed against the rocks at the first attempt.

The ancient Greek poet Hesiod, who may have lived in the same century as Homer, describes the right time for sailing:

The best time for making a voyage is during the fifty days that follow upon the solstice, when summer is drawing to a close. You will not wreck your ship at that season, nor will the sea drown your men, unless Neptune, Lord of the earthquake sets himself to wreck you, or Jove, King of the immortals compasses your destruction, for the issues of good and evil are in their hands. At that season the winds are steady and the sea safe; you can therefore draw your ship into the water in confidence, relying upon the winds, and get your cargo duly within her, but come again as fast as you can; do not wait for new wine, not for the autumn rain and the beginning of winter with the great gales that the South wind raises when it begins to blow after heavy rain the autumn, and makes the sea dangerous. There is also a time in spring when men make voyages; as soon as the buds begin to show on the twigs of a fig tree about as large as the print of a crow's foot, the sea is fit for sailing, but a voyage at this season is dangerous; I do not advise it, I do not approve of it, for the voyage will be a snatched one, and you will hardly escape trouble of some sort. Nevertheless, men are foolish enough to go on voyages even then, for money is the life and soul of us poor mortals, but drowning is a horrible death. I bid you, therefore, think well over all that I have been saying to you. And again, do not put all your substance on to a single ship; leave the greater part behind, and put the smaller half on board. It is a sad thing for a man to meet with a mishap on the high seas; and it is a sad thing if you have overloaded your waggon, so that the axle breaks and your load is damaged; use moderation in all things and let everything be done in due season.

FROM 'Sailing Weather' in Hesiod's *Works and Days*,
in *Oxford Book of Greek Verse in Translation*,
translated by Samuel Butler

This is a terrifying description of a storm from the diary of Lord Charlemont, a young Grand Tourist sailing from Rhodes to Athens in November 1750:

Monday, November 17th 1750 – The wind growing favourable about
nine in the morning, we set sail. Already we had made with a fine
fair gale ten leagues of our short course, and were gaining the
channel between the islands . . . when on a sudden the sky was
overcast. The horizon was covered with black clouds streaked with
a treacherous gleamy light. Thunder rolling all around us with its
horrid growl and boding voice foretold an approaching tempest,
and quick lightnings flashing from every side made the gloom more
dreadful. The black waves rising in heaps with their hollow roar
seemed to imitate the thunder, and, in their colour, the lowering
black of the clouds . . . All things conspired to assure us of a most
violent and, still worse, of a contrary wind. The Captain roared out
his commands. The seamen bustled. Our pilot himself, though a
Greek and well acquainted with these seas, seemed astonished.
Every circumstance now concurred to warn us of our approaching
danger, and to persuade us to get as soon as possible into the port of
Thermia which was to the leeward, and which our Palinurus [the
pilot of Aeneas's ship in *Aeneid*] assured us was perfectly secure,
telling us at the same time that a violent *fortuna*, the common name
in these parts for a storm, was at hand.

Changing then our course we stood in directly for the port, and
with some difficulty were able to make it; but here we soon found
that we had gotten from Scylla to Charybdis, for the pilot, ignorant
of its situation, suffered us to pass by the secure anchorage, and
steered us in so close to the land, that we were within less than ten
feet of being dashed against the rocks; and, this danger luckily past,
we found ourselves in a situation equally perilous, being compelled
to lie so near the shore, and so exposed to the sea, that it depended
entirely upon the winds changing a few points to break our cables,
which were none of the best, in which case we must necessarily
either run ashore, or be driven against the rocks. We now en-
deavoured to recover that safe creek, which we had unfortunately
passed, striving against the wind with our utmost efforts. But all was
in vain. The gale grew stronger and stronger. A point of land alone
defended us, and the slightest change of wind would infallibly
deprive us of that protection, and we were compelled to lie all night

in this anxious situation, depending for our safety on the constancy of the inconstant wind.

Tuesday – The elements did not threaten in vain, for last night a most violent tempest at n.n.-east arose, and continued for three days without intermission.

Wednesday – It raged with the utmost fury, the sea being so agitated even in the harbour that the Captain could not venture to lower his boat lest she should be stove to pieces, so that there was no possibility of getting ashore, and we were forced to remain on board in the utmost peril, tantalized by the sight of land within a few yards of us. The waves were driven against the rocks with such a violence that the spray flew more than a hundred feet high. We now dropped our sheet anchor and thus we lay with all our anchors and cables out, in anxious doubt of our safety, but expecting the worst, dreading every instant to part our cables, and to be dashed to atoms against those rocks upon which we would have given the world to have set our feet, and which we viewed at once with looks of fear and of desire!

Thursday – The storm seemed to abate, and the sea being somewhat less turbulent, with much difficulty we got out our boat, and rowed ashore, experiencing a sensation of delight upon our first setting our feet upon firm ground much more easy to be conceived than expressed. As no transition can be more sudden from sickness to health, from terror to confidence, from danger to safety, so is there, I am confident, no circumstance of life which affects the mind with equal pleasure to that which is afforded by the first feel of land after a long and perilous storm at sea.

FROM *The Travels of Lord Charlemont in Greece and Turkey*
edited by W. B Stanford

Charles Cockerell describes a sudden storm between Kuşadasi and Samos in 1811. Cockerell was twenty-four years old at the time, and like other young Grand Tourists was travelling in Greece and Asia Minor because the Napoleonic Wars made the more conventional journey to Italy impossible.

I rode from Aisaluck [now Ayvaluk] to Scala Nuova, which is only four hours off, and from thence I took a passage for Samos on a Maltese brig of twelve hands and six guns and set sail the following morning (March 25th); but when we had made half the passage, which is by rights only about two hours, we met a furious wind which obliged us to put back. I went ashore again, and as the wind rose to the force of a hurricane I watched out of my window no less than eighteen boats and vessels of various sizes blown ashore and wrecked under my very eyes. It was a scene of incredible destruction. The shore was strewn with wreckage and cargoes which had been thrown overboard, oranges, corn, barrels of all sorts of goods, while the sailors, ruined, although thankful to have escaped with their lives, sat round fires in some sheds by the port, the pictures of dejection.

FROM *Travels in Southern Europe & The Levant* by C. Cockerell

Captain Thomas Spratt, a naval officer who served for thirty years on the Admiralty's Mediterranean Survey, and whose maps are still in use today, writes of the Aegean north wind, the dreaded '*Meltemi*'. He observes that the wind:

. . . generally rises very suddenly, without any clouds to warn the navigator, some few mountains only being capped by them as monitors of its coming to the experienced local mariner. It is especially dreaded for the violence of its squalls on the leeward side of all high land; for they have the character of what nautical men call 'white squalls' from giving little or no warning until felt, and are truly 'typhonic' in effect, from the whirling columns of wind and spray that they lift from the surface of the sea.

FROM *The Mediterranean Pilot*

For Ernle Bradford, a sailor-writer in the 1960s and 1970s, it was the wind that made the Aegean unique:

It is the *Meltemi* which gives the Aegean its unique quality. Every day they begin to blow at dawn, reaching their maximum round about noon, and usually dropping off at sunset. It is their cool invigorating rush which dissipates that bugbear of so many Mediterranean islands – the noonday lassitude and high humidity which curb thought and action alike. At midday, in an Aegean island, one can stand on a rocky peak or sit in a quayside taverna and feel, in a shade heat of 90 degrees, the stimulating wind that helped to make Aegean civilization . . .

FROM *The Companion Guide to the Greek Islands*
by Ernle Bradford

The eastern Mediterranean has surprisingly strong currents. This was something first observed in 1812 by Captain Beaufort (who would later give his name to the famous Beaufort Scale of wind speeds). He measured a strong current running from east to west, and he could see no logical explanation for this in a sea without tidal movement:

> From Syria to the Archipelago there is a constant current to the westward, slightly felt at sea, but very perceptible near the shore, along this part of which it runs with considerable but irregular velocity: between Adratchan Cape and the small adjacent island we found it one day almost three miles an hour; and the next, without any assignable cause for such a change, not half that quantity. The configuration of the coast will perhaps account for the superior strength of the current about here: the great body of water, as it moves to the westward, is intercepted by the western coast of the Gulf of Adalia; thus pent up and accumulated, it rushes with augmented violence towards Cape Khelidonia, where, diffusing itself in the open sea, it again becomes equalized.

FROM *Karamania* by Captain Francis Beaufort

Captain Beaufort had observed something that would not really be understood for at least another 150 years. It is now thought that this current exists due to the formation in winter of the Levantine Intermediate Water (LIW) in the sea between Rhodes and Cyprus. Cold, dry winter winds blowing from Anatolia make the surface of the sea colder and more saline, and therefore denser. As the water becomes more dense it sinks to a depth of 200–600 metres, and its vertical circulation causes a violent mixing of the sea. This initiates the strong currents of the eastern Mediterranean. 'New' water, that is less dense and less saline, flows into the sea above the Levantine Intermediate Water, which itself flows east and west. These complex thermal motors in the Mediterranean explain how a landlocked sea manages to remain surprisingly well oxygenated.

The mid-nineteenth century traveller Charles Fellows observed freshwater springs in the sea – these can still be seen in many places on the Turquoise Coast. The springs come from underground rivers and aquifers:

> A curious effect is produced by strong springs of fresh water rising in the sea at a distance of a few yards from the shore, causing an appearance like that seen on mixing syrup or spirit with water; the sea being so clear that the bursting of the fresh water from among the stones at the bottom, although at a great depth, is distinctly visible.
>
> FROM *A Journal written during an excursion in Asia Minor*
> by Charles Fellows

SHIPWRECKS AND UNDERWATER ARCHAEOLOGY

On the seabed around the south Aegean coast are umpteen wrecks of boats from four millennia. Many of these were known to fishermen and to sponge divers, but it was only in the second half of the twentieth century that anyone began to take much interest in them, perhaps because the technology of diving had made such rapid advances. The aqualung was developed in the 1940s by Captain Jacques Cousteau, and the first serious attempts at scientific underwater archaeology soon followed. Bodrum became and remains the centre of Turkish marine archaeology, and the results of the various summer underwater 'campaigns' on this coast since 1960 are gathered in Bodrum Castle, in the Museum of Underwater Archaeology. This is well worth a visit.

Dozens of wrecks have been located and excavated around the coast of south-west Turkey. In places wrecks lie on top of wrecks. Around a single submerged reef to the south of Bodrum peninsula there are fifteen different wrecks, dating from the fifth century BC to the eighteenth century, when the reef claimed an Ottoman warship. While there has been no discovery quite as sensational as that of the exquisite *Bronzi di Riace* (found in 1972 off the coast of Riace, near Reggio di Calabria in Italy), the discoveries off this part of Turkey's coast, from an archaeological perspective, have been fascinating. In 1953 a sponge-fishing boat made a remarkable catch – a bronze statue of Demeter from the fourth century BC. The archaeologist George Bean was in Turkey at the time, heard about the find, and travelled to the village of Bitez near Bodrum, where he found the bronze lying on the beach where it had been landed. It is now in the Archaeological Museum in Izmir. George Bean describes the discovery:

On August 9th 1953, some Turkish sponge-fishers brought to the village of Bitez, near Bodrum, the upper part of a bronze statue. There, four days later, I was fortunate to be the first person to see it, apart from a few local inhabitants. It had come up in their nets, they said, from deep water; not however, in the immediate neighbourhood, but round the next cape to the south . . .

The statue is agreed by all experts who have until now seen it or its photograph to be a work of the full classical period of Greek art, almost certainly an original of the fourth century BC. It represents a veiled woman, with bent head, perhaps the mourning Demeter, most familiar at present from the marble Demeter of Knidos now in the British Museum. The sponge-fishers' strange catch seems likely, therefore, to rank among the most remarkable artistic finds of recent years. Ancient bronze statues of any kind are quite rare, since, owing to the value of the metal when melted down, they rarely escaped destruction in the Middle Ages. Most of the few existing life-size bronzes have been recovered either, like ours, from the sea, or from deep excavations at Pompeii and Herculaneum. When to this general rarity we add the obviously superb quality of the new Demeter, we have clearly a discovery of the first importance . . .

FROM 'A Masterpiece from the Sea' by George E. Bean,
Illustrated London News, November 1953

Peter Throckmorton, a young American journalist, visited Bodrum in 1958 in the hope of finding and exploring underwater wrecks. He made friends with a tough old sponge diver called Kemal Aras and obtained permission to spend a month surveying wreck sites aboard the latter's rickety old sponge-boat called the *Mandalinci*. Over six weeks he identified some twenty wrecks for study. But it was at the very end of the trip that he got the 'lead' to the Cape Gelidonya shipwreck.

He describes his experiences on *Mandalinci*, and the conversation that led to his important discovery:

> When night fell, we would anchor in a cove or behind an ancient breakwater such as the one at Knidos, where the ruins of a city that once sheltered thousands of people lay around the harbor. The sail would be spread on *Mandalinci*'s foredeck, and we'd roll up in our blankets in some corner. Or we would sleep ashore on a sandy beach.
>
> We seldom saw another boat or another human being. The coast we cruised along was beautiful with great mountains that loomed sheer out of the sea and deserted valleys where grew wild figs that we sometimes picked on trips ashore in the dinghy. It was a life like that which must have been led by the sea raiders of Homer's time – raiders who may have hauled their black-hulled ships onto the very beaches where we slept.
>
> So the days went by, pleasantly and profitably. In addition to several well-preserved wrecks we found many sites worth further investigation someday. And our notebooks were full of jottings about other wrecks, on other parts of the coast, gleaned in evening talks around the mast or campfires ashore.
>
> For we were accepted now as divers, not tourists. We had proved we could pick sponges and live on a sponge boat. Divers along the coast gave us information, even though they might think our search for broken pots and sea-rotted pieces of wood was crazy. Some even became interested in archeology themselves – a tribute to the stories, cribbed from Homer, which Mustafa had told around our campfires.

When our month's cruise was over and we were back in Bodrum, Mustafa and I were invited to spend an evening with Kemal and a sea captain friend of his from Istanbul. The talk turned to dynamite and its use in salvage jobs. I was sitting half asleep, unable to follow much of the conversation. Then I was snapped alert by the word bakir, Turkish for copper.

'What was he talking about?' I asked Mustafa.

'Some things they found in the sea.'

'What things?'

'Bronze things. He found some pieces of bronze, stuck to the rock.'

After ten minutes of confused questioning the story came out. The season before, Kemal had been diving near Finike, at a place called Cape Gelidonya. He found about two tons of bronze objects – 'big bars of metal, but flat, and stuck together on the rock in 15 fathoms of water'. Amca Seytan had taken some pieces and sold them for scrap. But the price was poor, very poor, because the metal was so corroded and rotten.

I lost interest. Big bars of metal; ingots, no doubt. Sounded modern, probably from an 18th- or 19th-century merchant ship. But something about the story bothered me.

That night, thinking it over in my hotel room, I decided what it was.

Kemal had said that the bronze was rotten and corroded. Now, I had seen plenty of bronze from wrecked 18th-century ships and it almost never was so badly corroded that it could be called 'rotten'. The only bronze I had seen that badly decayed had been from classical times. I began to speculate about the bars. Where had I heard that flat ingots were traded by the Kefti, a seafaring people who lived in the Aegean during the Bronze Age?

Next morning I went through my books and found a repro-duction of a painting from an Egyptian tomb of about 1500 BC, which showed the Kefti bringing tribute to the Pharaoh. Part of the tribute was, unmistakably, flat ingots with leglike handles, looking for all the world like an animal hide.

It was weeks before I got a chance to bring up the subject again with Kemal and his men of the *Mandalinci*. Did any of them remember the bronze stuff in the sea near Finike? Yes, one of them did; he had taken two bronze boxes from the place, hoping that they would be full of gold. Instead, they held some black, greasy stuff, and were so corroded he had thrown them away in the sea.

I knew I was on the right track when Devil scratched his head and said he had picked up some pieces to sell for scrap. He remembered there had been three of them.

'One was like a spear point. And there was a knife. And a thing like a sword. All of bronze.'

'Who bought them?'

'Oh, some junkman: I don't remember.'

Kemal broke in – 'Don't worry, Peter. Next year when we dynamite the stuff for salvage I'll save you a piece.'

On an impulse I turned to Kemal. 'Promise me you won't touch the bronze wreck until I get to see it,' I blurted. 'I'll pay you double the scrap value by weight, of everything we recover from her.'

Where I'd get the money I didn't know. Nor had I any idea, at the moment, how I'd be able to promote the expedition to hunt for the underwater wreck.

He returned the next year, on board a seventy-foot ketch called *Little Vigilant*, loaned to the expedition by its wealthy American owner. The wreck was in one of the wildest parts of the Lycian coast, a jagged peninsula called the 'Five Islands'.

We arrived at the five islands on 17th July 1959 and found them forbidding and savage. There is no water. In most places the cliffs are perpendicular and it is difficult to land on the brittle rock which has been worn into fangs by the erosion of wind and water. It is impossible to walk barefoot anywhere on the islands and in most places hard to walk at all, even with heavy boots . . .

Two days were spent searching without success. The bottom was a mass of huge boulders, some the size of an automobile, some as large as *Little Vigilant*.

We were preparing to leave when we went for a last dive, and quite by chance, discovered the wreck. We managed to chip off two

lumps containing bronze and, when cleaned, these proved to be a
ploughshare and a bronze double axe . . .

FROM 'Thirty-three centuries under the sea'
by Peter Throckmorton,
National Geographic, May 1960

When excavated the next year, the wreck turned out to be a small
freighter, from about 1200 BC, perhaps thirty feet long. Its principal
cargoes were copper and bronze ingots shaped like oxhides. A number
of objects found make it almost certain that the ship either touched at
or operated from the ports of the Levant. The excavation was led by
the University of Pennsylvania, and was the first scientific underwater
'dig' of a wreck anywhere in the Mediterranean.

An even older wreck with a much more valuable cargo was discovered in 1982, off Ulu Burun, south of Kaş (and west of Cape
Gelidonya). This ship dates from about 1350 BC, and is a veritable
treasure trove. Its cargo gives a vivid picture of the trade and life of
the time:

The ship off Gelidonya was a tramp freighter shuttling along the
coast with a cargo of metals. The Ulu Burun ship, to judge from the
nature of the cargo, very likely was carrying a royal consignment.
The major component was a batch of sixty-pound ingots of copper,
some 200 of them, carefully stored in rows deep in the hull. There
were also dozens of ingots of tin; the smiths who would ultimately
receive the shipment would mix the two to manufacture bronze.
The second largest component was terebinth resin, perhaps a ton
of it, packed in amphoras; such resin was used in making perfume.
Then there was a collection of scrap metal intended for re-use – not
mere copper or tin but fragments of gold and silver jewelry. There
was a beautiful cup, in mint condition, made of solid gold. There
were pieces of raw ivory, some hippopotamus teeth, ingots of raw
glass, logs of African ebony, a consignment of Cypriot ceramics,
eighteen pieces in all, carefully packed in a huge clay jar. The cargo
reveals graphically how international was the trade of this period:
the copper and ceramics came from Cyprus, the resin and glass

from the Near East, the ebony and hippopotamus teeth from Egypt. Individual objects that were found underline the same point: Near Eastern cylinder seals, Egyptian scarabs, a Mycenaean seal, and pieces of Mycenaean pottery.

The ship had loaded on the resin at some port on the Levantine coast. It may have also taken on here the Egyptian goods or it may have made a stop at Egypt itself for these. It loaded the copper and ceramics at some port on Cyprus, and most likely was on its way farther westward from there, to the west coast of Asia Minor or the Aegean islands or even Crete, when it went down. At least one Mycenaean was aboard, the owner of the seal, but this does not mean that the ship was Mycenaean; he may have been a passenger, not the owner. The vessel could just as well have been the property of a businessman or a consortium of businessmen from some port along the Levant.

FROM The Ancient Mariners by Lionel Casson

Other important wrecks excavated on this coast, now exhibited in Bodrum Castle, include the 'Glass Wreck'. This was discovered in the 1970s at Serçe Limanı, a natural harbour on the eastern side of Bozburun. This was an early medieval merchant ship mainly carrying glass.There were many intact glass cups and bottles in a variety of patterns and colours, but the greater part of the cargo seems to have been broken glass shards – over a million fragments – being transported to a place where they would be recycled. The ship was also heavily armed, with fifty-two javelins, eleven spears and one sword on board.

SPONGE DIVERS

Since antiquity this coast and the Greek islands of the Dodecanese have been famous for sponge-fishermen, who would dive to collect sponges from the sea-floor. Sponges, then as now, had great value. This is an explanation of how sponges are cured, whitened, etc, by George Kalafatas, an American academic whose grandfather was a sponge-fisherman in Symi:

The natural sponge, as we see it on store counters, is the cleaned skeleton of an animal that grows in the sea, attached to the sea-bottom. The skeleton is a network of fibres made up of spongin, a substance similar to that found in our own hair and fingernails and the hoofs of animals. A dark, slimy mass of cells envelops the sponge, which must be thoroughly cleaned and washed until only 'the golden fleece' remains.

Like black, curly haired heads, sponges were tossed up by the surf onto the beaches of the Aegean and the Mediterranean. The ancient Greeks . . . cleaned them and found them useful in every day life. While the Egyptians and Phoenicians were actually the first to discover and use sponges their writings make reference to a sponge industry . . . The superior skill gained by the ancient divers is the reason that diving was introduced into the Olympic Games.

Because of the wide diversity of uses for the natural sponge, a far flung commerce in sponges sprang up in classical times and has continued into the present. Always it has involved the Dodecanese. Pliny reported that the finest sponges could be fished from waters off the island of Rhodes . . .

FROM *The Bellstone* by Michael Kalafatas

An indication of how highly prized sponges were (and still are), is that when Sultan Süleyman took the Dodecanese from the Knights of St John in 1522 it was stipulated that some islands should, in lieu of tax, produce an annual consignment of 4,000 sponges for the Ottoman court. The Symiots were regarded as the greatest of sponge-divers. Symian boats ranged as far as Tripoli, Cyprus, Syria and Tunisia in search of sponges. The sponge divers worked shallow depths, which they reached with a diving 'bellstone' to which they clung. These stones were prized possessions, passing from father to son.

In the 1840s the sponge fishery still continued much as it had for thousands of years, and was observed by Lieutenant Thomas Spratt:

The sponge divers are mostly people from the islands off the Carian coast; from Calymnos and the islands between Calymnos and Rhodes. They go in little fleets of caiques, each of six or seven tons of burthen and manned by six or eight men. The season for this fishery lasts from May until September. All the men dive in turn. They remain under water from one to three minutes. They descend to the bottom at various depths between five fathoms and twenty or even, though rarely, thirty. Very few of the Archipelago divers can descend so deep as the last-named depth, and it is doubtful whether they can work, in such case, when down. . . . In deep water a rope weighed by a stone is let down, by which the divers ascend when they have gathered the sponges. They carry nothing about their persons except a netted bag, which is attached to a hoop suspended around their necks; in this they place the sponges. In a good locality a diver may bring up fifty okes of sponges in a day. A very large sponge may weigh two okes. The weight is calculated from the sponges when they are dried. A sponge is dried in the sun, after being cleaned in seawater . . . They are sold at 25 drachmae an oke, the chief markets for them being Smyrna, Rhodes and Napoli.

FROM *Travels in Lycia*
by T. Spratt and E. Forbes

However, change was imminent. Augustus Siebe had invented the enclosed diving suit in 1819. In 1863 Siebe's invention was first used in Symi, and quickly revolutionised the industry. For it hugely magnified a diver's yield, by allowing him to see much better, by allowing him to remain underwater for indefinite periods, and by making accessible depths previously unobtainable.

Inevitably, the south Aegean was soon 'fished out' of sponges. But before that happened the sponge-diving centres, like Symi, became very rich.

Between 1880 and 1890 the township [Symi] grew to become one of the wealthiest sea-ports in the Mediterranean – for its size, the wealthiest of all. In a single season a Symiot merchant-captain could earn himself a fortune and, at this time, most of the captains were their own merchants and each waterfront house was a little factory with the master's sponge-boats discharging their precious loads directly into ground-floor warehouses where the women of the family beat, cleaned, rinsed and finally packed the sponges for export. These were the 'good old days' of Symi when every fourth house was a taverna; when musicians in their dozens set up their little three-piece bands under the tamarisk tree; when oxen, sheep and pigs were roasted whole along the waterfront and meat was free for all; when half of the harbour space was reserved for caiques bringing goods from Turkish ports to satisfy the roistering all-consuming appetite of the populace and when the sea seemed an inexhaustible gold-mine which only Symiots were allowed to work. This was the era of the great house – the painted, perspective ceilings, the grand marble staircases hewed not from mere Paxian stone but cut and carried from distant Carrara. And all this built upon the ever-growing demand – the demand for soft, luxurious sponges. Sponges to be shipped to London, Paris and Vienna; sponges for New York, Milan and Berlin; sponges for wherever the new era of industry created new markets for de luxe goods amongst the newly-rich.

And these new markets meant bigger sponge-boats, more divers and better pumps but as the sponge-yield increased so too were the sponge-beds destroyed, the rate of cropping exceeding the natural rate of re-growth. The era developed into a vicious economic race – with merchants demanding more sponges from their divers and the divers demanding more sponges of themselves so that they could keep pace with their families' growing needs in this plentiful age; an age that supplied silks and satins, Italian marble and French furniture, family portraits and exotic foodstuffs. The known sponge-beds thinned, were wiped out. There was but one way, the way down. Down beyond the hundred-and-fifty-foot level, down past two hundred feet where even Aegean daylight grows dim and faint, down to the darkness of forty fathoms that their new diving suits made possible for them. Down and down until they died . . .

Neither shark, nor octopus nor yet angry sea-god killed them, but something small, invisible, and against which they had not even the protection of foreknowledge – gas. The life-gas they breathed, the fresh sea air their pumps delivered to them and without which they could not survive, was the unseen enemy for, under pressures in excess of the normal, a proportion of the nitrogen content of the air held within the lungs is absorbed directly into the blood-stream. Here the inert gas circulates throughout the body without harm to the system as long as the pressure remains constant and does not exceed certain limits. When these limits are passed, however, the nitrogen-saturated blood produces an effect upon the nervous system known nowadays as Nitrogen Narcosis, whose symptoms include loss of physical co-ordination, inability to concentrate, depression and other nervous disorders.

FROM Bus Stop Symi by William Travis

'Nitrogen narcosis' is a technical description for 'the bends', an affliction that took a terrible toll of the Dodecanese divers:

The new diving suit brought not only a dramatic change in productivity but also a fundamental change in the physiology of diving. The naked diver took one, long, all-engulfing breath of sea air at one atmosphere before he plunged to the bottom. Using the Siebe-designed suit, the diver was now breathing compressed air, in effect multiples of air, at depth. Since normal air is 78 percent nitrogen, a diver in compressed air – as Jacques Cousteau pointed out – is also breathing multiples of nitrogen, an inert gas that does not entirely pass away in a diver's exhalations. At one atmosphere, at sea level, the nitrogen is inhaled and exhaled with no effect on the body; but in multiples, at more than one atmosphere of pressure, it goes into supersaturated solution in the blood and soft tissue of the body. When the diver rises abruptly into lesser pressure, the nitrogen quickly escapes the blood in bubbles – it 'boils' or froths – similar to what happens when a bottle of warm beer is opened too quickly. In mild cases the froth gives the diver pains in the joints, but in severe cases the nitrogen bubbles can clog veins, cause nerve damage, cut off the spinal ganglia, or cause instant death by heart embolism. If a diver stays at depth too long, or ascends from depth too rapidly – or even if the interval between his dives is too brief he risks death or paralysis from 'the bends'.

FROM The Bellstone by Michael Kalafatas

An understanding of what caused 'the bends' came very late to the sponge fishery. It was normal practice, if a diver got into trouble on the sea-floor, to pull him up as fast as possible. This, of course, was the worst possible thing to do. Between 1866 and 1896, on the island of Kalymnos alone, three hundred young men died of the bends and six hundred more were paralysed. Travellers to the Dodecanese in the 1950s and 1960s describe the pitiful sight of broken, incontinent old divers, whose health had been ruined on the sponge fleet.

For some islands in the Dodecanese sponges remained the main source of income until at least 1960. In 1984 blight struck the remaining Mediterranean sponge-beds, and ended the sponge-fishing altogether.

But let us leave the sea on a lighter note, in the company of Patrick Kinross, whose biography of Atatürk remains prominently displayed in every English language bookshop in Turkey. His travel book on western Turkey contains an enchanting description of sailing under the light of the stars.

After a final bathe in the naval harbour, we sailed out into the velvet night beneath a voluminous skull-cap of stars. The two lighthouses winked across at each other, with punctilious monotony: two flashes from Knidos, one flash from Kos, their beams sweeping low over the sea. Five brighter stars, strung out in a line, shone on the water itself – the acetylene lamps of the Greek fishermen, who had just put out from the harbour. We coasted close to the shore of the island, so close indeed that we almost ran aground, in rapidly shallowing water. Disengaging ourselves, to my faint regret, we saw ahead of us a broader bar of light, the electric street-lamps of Halicarnassus. Punctually at midnight they went out. The town was asleep when we glided into the harbour and anchored beneath the walls of the massive medieval castle.

Here, in the same lucid prose, he describes the pleasures of swimming in the sea:

Following our usual habit, we anchored for the afternoon in the shade of a cliff. Before a *raki* and luncheon I dived down in goggles into the ultra-violet submarine world, tracing the rock to its foundations amid rounded boulders and pits like a giant's footprints. Here was a life of weeds with waving tresses, of roving fish with a rainbow gleam, of colonies of sea-urchins, purple and treacherous, cushioning the smooth white rocks.

FROM *Europa Minor* by Patrick Kinross

CHAPTER TWO

Turkish Pleasures

Visitors to this coast over the last few centuries have given widely different accounts of just about everything, but they seem to have been united in their unstinting praise of its food. In the 1950s and 1960s, when many parts of the south-west were still without electricity, travellers were often astounded at the sophistication of food that emerged from simple kitchens without fridges or cookers. Nowadays there is electricity everywhere and every kitchen has a fridge and a cooker, but fortunately the traditional attitudes to cookery remain unimpaired. The food, with remarkably few exceptions, remains one of the joys of this coast.

Lesley Blanch, author of *The Wilder Shores of Love* and such other great travel books as *Journey into the Mind's Eye*, was also an accomplished writer on cooking. She dedicated *From Wilder Shores*, a book about exotic food, 'to my digestion, which has nobly supported so many surprises, trials and unwise indulgence throughout our long years of travel together'.

Here she allows her imagination to run on the origins of Turkey's marvellous cuisine:

The Turkish cuisine is said to be one of the world's finest, along with the Chinese and French, but it is its amalgam of other ages and far horizons, central Asian, or Arabic, reflecting the ways of both nomadic and sedentary races, that gives it so special a quality. It is a flavour the Turks imposed on conquered lands – and flavours acquired from the lands they conquered. Indeed, the haute cuisine of France can be challenged, in Turkey, by recipes still in use, which date from the court cuisine of the Baghdad caliphs and other remote splendours.

Around the Turkish table I see shades of Byzantine emperors and Ottoman sultans gathered beside shepherds, Seljuk warriors or Mongol tribesmen. A sumptuous dish such as *tavuk göğsü* (breast of chicken pounded smooth with cream and cinnamon), the acme of sophistication, may derive from the kitchens of an Osmanli padishah at Topkapı Serai, while another dish, equally delicious in more rustic terms, may have originated at the primitive hearth of a caravanserai deep in the wilds of Anatolia. Likewise the prevalence of yoghourt in so many Turkish recipes is held to stem from Genghis Khan's horsemen who swept down on Turkey in the eleventh century. By way of rations, they slung sacks of goat's milk from their saddles, but the violent jolting churned the milk into a substance resembling the clotted sheep or buffalo milk, *yoğurtlu*, still a staple part of the nation's diet. Thus it might be said that Turkish history is written across each plate.

Turkish dishes have evocative names, sounding as deliciously as they taste . . . Bread and Velvet – the Padishah's Pleasure – Turquoise Soup – Sweetheart's Lips – along with the celebrated *imam bayildi*, 'the imam who swooned' (no doubt because the egg-plant was cooked till almost too delicious, causing unwise indulgence). *Moussaka*, another egg-plant and meat casserole, is found with variations all over the Middle East, in countries much influenced by Turkish cuisine. Aubergine or egg-plant (*patlican* to Turks) is the back-bone of many differently prepared dishes. One called *karnıyarık* (or split belly) sounds less inviting than most, but Turkey has many anatomic references in the kitchen – 'ladies' navels', little round cakelets, 'ladies' thighs', *kadın budu köftesi*, very smooth, plump rissoles, being two examples of this seductive imagery. *Ekmek kadife*, or Bread and Velvet, is another supremely voluptuous concoction, where contrasting textures are the secret of the seemingly simple dish. In Turkey, velvet was once synonymous with all that was most beautiful, most desirable and treasured: thus the old-fashioned term of endearment, 'My satin! My velvet!' The dish of that name is merely a number of small chunks of coarse-textured bread, served with a large bowl of the thickest, richest clotted cream, the kind called *kaimak*, made from buffalo milk. That's all. There are no concessions to sugar, or even rose-petal jam as we find in so many Turkish puddings. Food such as this belongs to a patriarchal and pastoral past, where a fundamental sureness of taste discovered that the grainy texture of the bread beside the suave cream would add up to uncomplicated perfection. Likewise, we may suppose, faraway Swiss peasants were similarly discovering the delights of their melted cheese and bread fondues.

I first encountered *ekmek kadife* at a wedding feast held in the garden of a small restaurant at Bouna Batchi, on a hillside of the Bithynian Mount Olympus above Bursa. It had been one of Pierre Loti's favourite retreats, and indeed was far more retreated than the famous one at Eyoub, generally associated with him. As I was then re-reading *Aziyade*, a famous book by this curious Turcophile character, I was following his shadow from place to place. Under a dense green bower, the wedding feast was in solemn progress. The Turks are quiet in joy or grief, and always hospitable. I was pressed to take a place at the long table, and supplied with a brightly painted tin plate, and wooden spoon – just the sort of things I collect to use at home. '*Küçük!*' (little), '*küçük çok az*' (very little) I begged as they piled my plate with bread and cream, and cream again . . . To stem the tide of Turkish hospitality I have found this phrase, among the few I possess, one of the most useful. Later, a majestic village dignitary offered to share his *tchibouk* or water-pipe with me, and to its sociable glou-glou sound we puffed away, conversing through the medium of his grandson, a rather flash boy just returned from a course of business management in Minnesota. Over there, he said, they ate Jumbo Sundaes – such sundaes . . . but words failed him, and he made a sweeping gesture which, while indicating mythical dimensions for the sundaes, also contrived to dismiss *ekmek kadife* as old-fashioned, local stuff, which is precisely why it is so desirable.

FROM *From Wilder Shores* by Lesley Blanch

A thirteenth-century Turkish scribe, who compiled a cookery book, was at pains to give religious sanction to his passion when he wrote:

Whereas the delights of this world are of six kinds, to wit Food, and Drink, and Clothes, and Amorous Dalliance, and Scent, and Music: it appears that the most excellent and most important of these is Food since it is the mainstay of the body and the substance of life, and cannot be dispensed with without injury to health. Nor is it forbidden by the Faith to devote one's attention to refinements and luxury in the matter of Food, since it is written in the Koran: 'Say; who hath forbidden God's goodly raiment and the pleasant viands which He hath provided for his servants?'

Also it is recorded of the Prophet (Peace and Blessings upon him) that when one of his companions prepared a dish for him with all the refinements known to that age, and invited him to partake thereof, he accepted such invitations.

And a wise man has said: 'In four things all virtues are united and all delights made perfect: strong faith, pure acts, pleasant food and joyous drink', whereby he indicated that there is no harm in enjoying food and giving thought to it.

Or as the Turcoman nomads would have, in their traditional blessing of the importance of food, 'The soul enters by the throat.'

Irfan Orga, a Turkish writer who was forced to spend half his life as an exile in London, due to a politically unacceptable love affair, describes the breadth and sophistication of Turkish cuisine. Clearly, the terrible food of 1950s Britain helped make him even more passionate, and nostalgic, for the wonderful food of his homeland.

The craze for vitaminising food, for balancing meals so that the greatest dietetic value may be extracted, is lost on the Turks; for centuries they have served well-balanced meals quite by accident. Experts on vegetable dishes for generations, it must be remembered that the Turks, an Oriental people, were familiar with the cultivation of vegetables long before Pizarro swept down on Peru and brought back knowledge of the potato – they unknowingly vitaminised themselves by simply serving their vegetables in the liquor in which they were cooked.

Turks have always eaten better than any other people in the eastern Mediterranean and quite early in Ottoman times they spread their cooking throughout the region as, later, the French were to spread their cooking throughout Europe. This is not to say that French influence has not penetrated as far as Turkey; it has indeed, but mostly to Istanbul or Ankara and none of these dishes are sacred to the Turks – they have no great weight of tradition attached to them, no stories with which to regale guests, no nostalgic memories of the great days. An agricultural people, dour, un-emotional and with little sense of humour, conservative by nature rather than circumstances, the Turks have, since the eleventh century, been very much to the forefront in the affairs of the Middle East.

The eleventh and twelfth centuries were, undoubtedly, periods of great activity during which the Sultans, the Royal master-builders, the descendants of Alp Arslan, rivalled in the very heart of Asia Minor all the richness and artistry of the age of Pericles. The works of the great Seljuk Turks tell not only of local riches but of a time of prosperity during which the people had not only the leisure to produce their works of art but the encouragement as well. Food, naturally, took pride of place; where there is wealth the quality of food increases, and the great banquets of the early Turks produced many of the dishes we are still familiar with today. The whole roasted lamb or the young sucking calf stuffed with rice and exotic herbs, whilst never diminishing in appeal, gave way to more specialised dishes. The lamb and the calf were dissected and grilled chops (cooked over charcoal), kidneys ravished with butter and cream, kebabs wrapped in paper and cooked in pine kernels were discovered to have their appeal too. Rich in dress and ornamentation, succinct in speech imbued with the knowledge of architecture – acquired undoubtedly in their migrations across Asia and half the face of the world – the early Turks liked their foods well spiced and highly seasoned. The spice trade originated with the Phoenicians; cane sugar was brought in by the Venetians in the eleventh century – the Turks, acquisitive, sampled everything.

Even today the Anatolian peasant lives somewhat better than his European counterpart. Turkey is still an agricultural country despite the reputation of her soldiers, and many of the regional dishes –

Circassian Chicken, which comes to us from the mountainous Duzce, or Ankara Scoblianka, a product of the Tartars of old Ankara – come to us unchanged by time and are served in the hotels and restaurants (*lokanta*) of the big cities. Erzurum and Kars are regions rich in meat. Istanbul and the Black Sea coast give us fish unknown in any other part of the world. It might almost be said that life in Turkey revolves around food. Hours of long and patient effort are spent in the kitchens and in summer all meals are served in the open. Even in the shabbiest districts of old Istanbul each small house has its own veranda and its fig tree and perhaps an ancient vine or two and honeysuckle (most delicately named by the Turks '*hanim elli*' – lady's hand) smothering the wire fences between the houses. Roughly hewn wooden tables are covered with fine linen cloths, relics of a great grandmother perhaps or made for the trousseau when the present middle-aged housewife was a newly betrothed girl of ten. Cloths, napkins, cushion covers are all heavily embroidered in exquisite patterns; rich Sparta carpets cover the floors even though there may scarcely be a stick of furniture to stand on them. It is a land of carpets and prayer rugs and no Turkish family would ever be put to the shame of being without one or the other. Table arrangements differ from the European. Knives are used only for meat, all other dishes are eaten with a fork or spoon. Meat and vegetables are quite distinct dishes, each with its own honour, and are served as separate courses.

In this book it will be seen that some vegetable dishes are served cold. In Turkey this always applies to any vegetable which has been cooked in olive oil. Meats, kebabs, chops, steaks, are regarded as being best when eaten alone and even *pilav*, king of dishes, is handled separately. Very rarely, excepting in some of the French-inspired cooking, does *pilav* accompany the meat on the same plate.

Marketing is done daily and in the mornings, thus ensuring a continuously fresh supply of all perishable commodities. The markets are in the open and prices highly competitive – in a land of fruit, fruit is naturally very cheap. It is a hot country too (and therefore not immune to the dangers of cholera or dysentery) and being Muslim in character, the people are most fastidious about cleanliness. All fruit is washed before being eaten – even a bare-footed street urchin, hungry as a wolf more than likely, will not eat the piece of melon or peach that he has picked up beside a fruit seller's stall until he has first washed it in the fountains of the local mosque. The fish markets are colourful, noisy with the cries of the vendors and gay with the rigging and the bright sails of the little fishing smacks. The fishermen wear gaily-striped aprons and murderous knives attached to a broad leather belt in the middle. The markets stretch along the shores of the Golden Horn, where the mosques of the city reflect their sad nostalgic shadows and the sky in spring and summer is vivid cerulean. Here is a riot of colour and harmony – worth any visitor's attention if he doesn't mind getting his feet wet. The fish, freshly caught, lie in silver state, their scales a glistening iridescence, bright yellow lemons and emerald green parsley arranged symmetrically around them. Some of the fish look mysterious – blue and rose enamelled – too exotic to be subjected to dissection in the kitchen. The swordfish (*killiç*) sherry brown, the mullet (*barbunya*) glitteringly orange silver, the kalkan with its unexpected lime green bones and exquisite white flesh, the mackerel (*uskumru*) like a pearl in its bed of vines leaves, tufts of curly endive decorating it with artistry, give intellectual nourishment as well as, later perhaps, physical.

Freshly killed meats come to the cities two and three times in a week and to render them less tough, the Turks pound them thin with a heavy mallet then steep them in onion juice for a day or two until the meat has tenderised.

Pastrycook shops dominate city, village and town – next to the local coffee shops, where old men sit mulling over the day's news, they are the most popular innovations of Turkish community life. It is almost agonising to choose where to buy one's *baklava* or *lokma*, each little shop seems to have a more mouth-watering display than the next. These shops are famous throughout the land, often being handed down from father to son for generations and the secrets of sweet making guarded jealously. Bayram days (religious festivals) have their own traditional sweets – of which *baklava* is the king. But Turkish Delight (*lokum*) and *kadıngobegi* (*lady's navel*) are close seconds. *Lokma* is exclusively the going-to-school-for-the-first-time sweet; in the old days, perhaps, it was hoped to induce a sweet temper in the Imam who was the teacher. Imams were reputed men of notoriously short tempers and incredible meanness – witness the delightful name of *Imam Bayildi* – literally, the Imam fainted – called thus because the original Imam for whom the dish was created is said to have fainted at the expense of the olive oil used in the making. *Helva* has less happy associations, being used on the fortieth day after a member of the family's death when, according to Muslim belief, the chin of the deceased drops. This, it is believed, causes great pain, so in order to lessen the pain special family prayers are said on that day and *helva* eaten in the name of the dead person. In the houses of the wealthy great pots of *helva* are made and distributed amongst the poor. In this way it is hoped more prayers will be said and the dead will have nothing to complain about.

FROM *Turkish Cooking* by Irfan Orga

American travel writer Tom Brosnahan first visited Turkey in 1967 as one of President Kennedy's Peace Corps Volunteers, before deciding to compile a guidebook. The result, *Turkey on $5 a Day*, became the country's most popular guide of its day. Here a cocktail of Turkey's climate, history, hospitality and food led Brosnahan to feel 'as free and careless as I would ever be in my life':

I made it back to the Aegean coast at Kuşadasi, and used that as my base for day-trips to the many other archaeological sites in the region. On my third day in Kuşadasi I was finishing up. I hitched a ride as far as the great theatre at Miletus, walked around the site, took my notes, then looked for a ride south. There was nothing, so I headed out on foot. I had on a T-shirt, shorts and sneakers. My only impediment was a small Pan Am flight bag which contained an alternate set of underwear, a few toiletries, a bottle of sunblock, a spare notebook and a pen. I didn't even need a change of clothes. When I washed out my T-shirt and shorts the hot, dry Aegean summer air would render them as dry as a Balkan cabinet meeting in under 20 minutes.

I walked south from the huge theatre of Miletus toward the colossal temple of Didyma. The sun was bright, the country road bordered by a riot of wildflower color and framed by fields of ripening grain. Birds chirped and flitted among the branches in the fruit orchards near the road. I had work to do and discoveries to make, but I could do the work and make the discoveries on my own schedule, in my own way. This was the direct opposite of office work! I was ignorant of it at the time, but years later it became clear to me that at that time, on that day, walking along that road, with a minimum of possessions, attachments or worries, I was as free and careless as I would ever be in my life.

At the end of the day I was back in Kuşadasi, tired but satisfied. I washed up and went out for dinner, intent on treating myself to fish and wine as a reward for a few days' hard work well done. Though it would end up costing me three dollars more than I could really afford I decided on the Toros Canli Balik ('Taurus Live Fish') Restaurant right on the water by the ferry dock. My rationalization for blowing my budget was that I had to try out the Canli Balik in order to properly describe it to my readers.

The maitre d', a short, moustachioed, balding man who was also the restaurant's owner, showed me to a waterfront table and summoned a waiter. We discussed the available courses and I decided on *sigara böreği* (cylindrical pastry fritters stuffed with white cheese), a mixed salad, a small one-person fish, and a half-bottle of white wine. The waiter went away briefly, put in the order at the kitchen, and returned with my wine.

The evening air was warm and light, the sound of the sea water restful as it lapped the shore. I took a sip of wine. Every table at the Toros was furnished with a miniature basil bush planted in a white-washed olive oil can. You brushed your fingers among the leaves, lifted your fingertips to your nose, and took in the scent of the spice. I took another sip of wine, sniffed the fragrant basil, and enjoyed the feeling of relaxation seeping into muscles and flesh tired from the day's exertions.

The waiter returned with my appetizer and salad, and I eased into them, bite by leisurely bite. The evening was too perfect to rush.

After a respectable time and the credible consumption of the plates before me, the waiter brought my fish. He was about to set it down on my table when the maitre d' came running over, his face contorted in alarm.

'What are you doing?' the maitre d' asked the waiter, his eyes huge with apprehension, his eyebrows rammed up to his hairline.

'I–I–I'm serving the gentleman his fish,' the waiter replied, confused.

'Like that??' the maitre d' asked, his voice shrill.

All three of us looked at the fish. It was your standard ten-inch fish, silvery, nicely grilled and set in the middle of a white oval plate. A wedge of lemon and a sprig of parsley had been added for color. It looked good. I wanted to eat it.

'No, no, no, no, no!' the exasperated maitre d' cried. 'Come with me!' he said and dragged the waiter, still holding the fish, off toward the kitchen.

A few minutes later they were back, moving slowly in solemn, self-satisfied procession. The fish was on the same plate, but otherwise it had been utterly transformed. A half-dozen thin slices of lemon were artfully arranged like scales along its back. Around its sides were green and black olives, radishes carved into roses, a peacock-fan of arugula leaves, and a veritable banzai forest of parsley. At the far end by the tail was half a lemon wrapped in cheesecloth so that when I squeezed lemon juice onto my fish no pesky seeds would fall.

'Almost ready', the maitre d' said. He was holding a small square of paper, a glass of amber liquid and a box of matches. He took the paper, rolled it into a tube, dipped it into the liquid (which proved to be brandy), stuck it into the fish's mouth, struck a match and lit the tube. The fish-cigar burned gently with a cool blue brandy glow.

'Now,' the maitre d' said to the waiter, breaking into a wide grin, 'now you may serve the gentleman his fish.'

FROM *Turkey on $5 a Day* by Tom Brosnahan

THE HAMAM

Every Turkish town still has its public *hamam*, which is a key element in the Islamic emphasis on cleanliness and hygiene. For while washing of the hands, feet and face before a fountain was considered adequate before the five daily prayers, a visit to the *hamam* cleansed the whole body to be ready for the Friday prayers. Muslims are also enjoined to wash themselves after sex. Many foreign travellers visit *hamams*, and most visitors enjoy the experience, which is touched by the frisson of a new and possibly intimidating experience, with its own rituals and traditions. This is illustrated by Joe Pierce in his *Life in a Turkish Village*, where Mahmud, the son of a peasant family, is taken to the *hamam*:

> One hot August morning Mahmud's father told him that they were going to the city to the *hamam* (Turkish bath) and bathe so that they would be clean and ready to present their sacrifices to Allah on the following morning, which was the *Kurban* (sacrifice) *Bayram*. This holiday, along with others on the Moslem calendar, moves back ten days annually so that over a period of years it can occur at different seasons, and this year it was coming in the late summer.
>
> The trips to the bath were very exciting for Mahmud, as for most Turkish boys, because it combined an outing with his father, a trip to the city, and a picnic of sorts. When he had been younger, he had gone occasionally to the women's *hamam* with his mother, but he had been allowed to go with his father to the men's *hamam* for the past few years. This was just one further sign that he was growing up.
>
> While Mahmud stood talking with his father about the coming excursion, his mother came out of the house carrying a large basket piled with food that she had prepared for them to eat at the *hamam*. They would spend most of day there and would be very hungry long before they were ready to return to the village that evening.
>
> The basket contained five sheets of flat round *pide* (village bread), some fresh green grapes, white cheese, black olives, two cold eggplants stuffed with rice and oozing olive oil, and a small package of helva (a type of candy made of flour, sugar, and oil that comes in a

variety of forms and is fairly common throughout the Middle East). In addition, the basket held the following items: two copper bowls (*tas*), some soap, two small glove-like washcloths of heavy canvas, and some Turkish towels. These were the tools with which they would remove the accumulation of dirt from their bodies.

As they neared the city limits, they saw many others from different villages converging on the town. Some men and women brought produce to the city to sell, some came to shop in the markets, and many were, as Mahmud and his father, headed for the *hamam*. Movement into the city was always increased just before a Bayram. The city dwellers needed lambs to sacrifice and so they were willing to pay a higher price than usual for them. They also needed food for the meals celebrating the occasion, and the peasants required manufactured goods, such as material for new clothes from the stores in the city.

Near the outer edge of the town was a very old building that had been there for centuries. It was hexagonal in shape and topped by a cluster of domes, perforated with a design of holes, which was intended to let light in and steam out at the same time. An accumulation of vegetation and debris had covered about one-third of the structure so that it appeared to be growing right out of the earth. Beneath the floor there were a series of coal fires that heated the water as it ran through tiles after having bubbled up out of a nearby spring. This heated water was then piped up to the main bathing area and allowed to run freely into several large stone sinks without drain pipes. The water simply ran over the edges of the basins, onto the floor, and out of the building.

Mahmud and his father were met at the door by an old man wearing only a pair of black trousers and wooden, thong-like shoes. He welcomed them, took their money, and led them along a narrow marble-lined hallway to a row of small wooden stalls wherein they could undress, hang their things on pegs that protruded from the walls, and leave their food and other belongings there while they were in the bath itself.

Undressing quickly, Mahmud and his father walked out of the little room, down another short marble-lined hallway that was damp with moisture but very clean, and out into a large open space bounded by six walls and covered by a cluster of domes. The larger of these was supported by six smaller ones, resting on the top of each wall. Below each of these small domes, with one exception, was a marble bowl without a drain. Into these spilled two constant streams of water that came from pipes protruding from the walls just above them, and the excess water overflowed around the edges and fell to the floor where it disappeared into drains. On both sides of these were marble benches on which the bathers could sit. The air was filled with steam that swirled around just below the small circular holes in the ceiling as cold air tried to get in and warm steam out at the same time.

Passing several men already engaged in bathing, Mahmud and his father went over to an unoccupied basin and seated themselves on either side of it. Once in a comfortable position, Mahmud caught a little of the cold water in his *tas*, mixed some of the hot water with it, and poured the mixture over his body. Sitting silently as his father talked to him about things of interest to grown-ups but unintelligible to children, he poured one *tas* after another of water over himself, each one a little warmer than the last. This was accomplished by putting less cold and more hot water into the bowl each time: so that the mixture was as hot as he could stand. The warmth relaxed him completely, except for the hand that poured the water, and he watched the steam swirl about in the air currents from the holes in the roof or listened to the talk, as suited his mood at the moment, because his father's remarks rarely required an answer anyway.

With each succeeding bowl his body grew redder and hotter until he was finally pouring the liquid directly from the hot pipe onto his body with no discomfort. Mahmud continued this operation until even the hot water seemed cool. Then his father, apparently also having finished with this phase, rose and started to walk toward two stone tables in a small alcove off the main room. A great deal of time had been passed in the preceding activity. It was past lunch time and he and his father were both very red and hot when they reached two tables where an attendant appeared to be rubbing the dirt off one man by sheer force. Mahmud's father climbed up on the empty table that was unattended for the moment and waited for someone to come. Mahmud relaxed for a few minutes while the available attendant finished with the man he was working on, and then he climbed up and waited to be washed. Actually, washed was perhaps the wrong term for what happened. Perhaps scrubbed would be a better word for it, because the attendant grabbed his arm, took the *kese* (the canvas washcloth) that Mahmud carried in his *tas*, and began to rub the boy vigorously with it. As the rough canvas was pressed hard against the skin, large blackish beads of dirt began to form and fall off on the floor, as the attendant kept mumbling half to himself, '*çok pis, çok pis*' (very dirty).

Occasionally the attendant would throw a bowl of water over his victim to remove an accumulation of dirt so that he could continue. Mahmud felt as if the man were taking part of his skin off, which he may have been, despite his comments about the dirt. When the first arm was clean, Mahmud's assailant grabbed the other one, flipped him over as if he were a dead fish and began to work on it. He and his father were both scrubbed all over, except on the face, the genitals, and the bottoms of their feet.

When the man appeared to be satisfied that he had scraped as much dirt off as was possible, he took the soap that Mahmud's father had been carefully protecting and sudsed the boy into a blob of froth before dousing him with warm water to wash away the soap as well as any specks of dirt that might still remain on his body after the rubbing operation. The water, soap, and all ran onto the marble paved floor and into the only drains in the room. When he was completely clean, including a thorough washing of his hair, Mahmud climbed off the table and waited for the man to finish with his father. By this time they were both exhausted and extremely hungry, so they walked very slowly toward the cubicle in which they had left their lunch basket. Once inside the small room they fell limply on the seat and just sat there for a few minutes. Then, with a great effort, Mahmud's father managed to open the basket and draw out some food for them to eat.

Along the sides of the dressing area were two boards covered with Turkish towels on which they could rest. They ate very slowly, but managed to consume all that the basket contained and wished that there had been more in it. They then lay down to rest and spent the better part of the afternoon lying down. However, sometime before the sun touched the horizon, they had regained enough strength to get up and start homeward, despite the fact that the walk seemed long in their half-exhausted state. Mahmud concluded that bathing was an experience that he would not want to repeat too often, but now he was clean enough for the Bayram that would come the next day.

FROM *Life in a Turkish Village* by Joe Pierce

It has to be said that the public *hamam* is not for everyone, and one individual who did *not* enjoy her experience was Nancy Phelan, a witty Australian writer travelling around south-west Turkey in the 1960s. Here she recalls her memories of a visit:

A swarm of taxi-men gathered round me, shouting the names of hotels, but I waved them back while I looked in my little book from the Turkish Press, Broadcasting and Tourist Department. With a weary kind of obstinacy I announced I would go to the X Palas Hotel. If it was a palace it must have a bath, I thought vaguely, and that was all I cared about.

X Palas was very hard to find but eventually the taxi turned into a large garden and stopped at a rambling building with a splendid view. I was too tired to question anything and after an impossible discussion with a proprietor who spoke only Turkish, a room was secured and the driver paid off.

The one thing I really understood in the proprietor's discourse was the word *banyo*, which he used frequently, but when I set out to look for the bathroom I could not find it . . . I wandered about the house and gardens until rescued by a plump French-speaking Turk who was sipping tea in the rose-garden.

Side by side we pattered through the dark and echoing halls, for the bathroom was a long way from everywhere . . . and I began to wonder how I should find this bathroom again. We descended a staircase, crossed a lower room and approached a second staircase made of stone. A curious smell was rising from below and for a second I wondered if it were a joke, even an ambush; then I realized what it was.

'Banyo à la Turque?' I asked. My companion nodded.

'Oui madame. Banyo à la Turque. Beaucoup de vapeur.'

He led me down the stairs, into the humid earthy smell and handed me over to a businesslike woman in a white overall, with wooden clogs on her feet and a towel round her head. Shutting the door, she demonstrated briskly that I was to remove my clothes. When this was done she handed me a pair of wooden pattens and directed me to a marble enclosure where water ran from silver taps into a marble bowl. Thrusting the soap into my hands she told me to wash myself, pointing to a little silver basin with which I was to bale the water from the marble bowl over my body.

It was a curious atmosphere, a combination of steam-laundry and catacomb. Steam was everywhere, and the damp, shut-in smell, slightly sour and repellent. We were under the ground where neither light nor fresh air ever entered. I was not sure that I really liked it but there was little I could do without my clothes, and the heavy door shut on me like a prison.

When the bathwoman returned she gave a cry of contempt at my slowness and snatched the soap from my hands. She set to work on me with a kind of dish-cloth, turning on all the taps till the water cascaded from the marble basin upon the floor, sloshing about to get a good lather, then applying it vigorously to my body as though to remove the outer skin. When all the lather had been washed off she led me, skating through the soapsuds in my pattens, to a chamber of tombs, where in long rows separated by a central aisle were marble sarcophagi, each without a lid, each with a curve cut from one end on which the neck might rest. Hot water from silver taps was running into the coffins, the surplus cascading into a marble gutter. Through the steamy air I was aware of a muted light and looking up at the domed ceiling I saw the daylight filtering in through small octagonal blisters of thick glass, those symmetrical bubbles like bottle-ends stuck in the roofs of Turkish baths.

I was led to a coffin and pushed down under the hot water until only my face emerged. An involuntary movement to escape from the sudden heat brought a shrill rebuke and I was thrust back with a firm hand. Emphasizing that I must not move, that I must stay boiling, the bathwoman tested the water with her hand, looked at a thermometer and clattered away to other victims.

Apart from the light and the heat it was not unlike being buried alive; there was the same restriction of movement and sense of suffocation that might be expected in such circumstances. I could hear a body being massaged in an adjoining room and someone had taken my place at the running tap in the ante-room, but I was alone as I lay in my coffin, sweating and stupefied, listening to the ceaseless splash of the water running along the central aisle. When at last the bathwoman came to release me I feared to touch my scarlet skin lest it peel off.

FROM *Welcome the Wayfarer* by Nancy Phelan

CHAPTER THREE

Turtles, Lions and Lilies: the Flora and Fauna of the South Aegean Coast

As in other parts of the Mediterranean coast, the waters of the Aegean are much less abundant than they were one hundred years ago, and very much less abundant than they were two thousand years ago. In the days of Aristotle, whales were a common sight and dolphins and porpoises were so numerous that fishermen would nick their tails so that they could tell them apart.

Sadly, there are no longer any whales in the Aegean, but there are still some dolphins. If you are lucky you may catch sight of the pod whose territory seems to be the Gulf of Kos, but who stray north and south – for I have seen them play around the ferry from Datça to Bodrum. I have been told that they may be one of only two schools of dolphins now surviving in the eastern Mediterranean. Flying fish are quite a common sight, and if you scuba dive you will see small fish around the rocks, and occasionally an octopus especially if you search around the windward, more oxygenated, shores.

TURTLES

A sea-creature that you are now very unlikely to see is a turtle. These were seriously over-fished as late as the 1960s. Fortunately since then, the turtle has become a protected species in Turkey. A landmark victory for environmentalists was the official recognition, in the late 1980s, of İstuzu Beach near Dalyan as a nature reserve. The beach is an important nesting ground for the loggerhead turtle (*Carretta carretta*), but very nearly became the site for an 1,800-room hotel. The battle to save this beautiful place was led by June Haimoff, an English lady then in her sixties, who was living in a beach hut on

İstuzu at the time. Here, in the book she wrote describing her struggle to save the beach from development, she describes her first sight of a turtle:

Next day early, after my morning swim in the calm sea (it was always calm in the mornings and rough in the afternoons), I walked further than usual and saw several turtle tracks. Some seemed to loop back into the sea, some were much bigger loops that also returned to the sea, and these larger loops had a disturbed area of sand at some point. I wondered whether that could be where a nest was? I decided that that night I would make a determined effort to see a turtle nesting . . . but I would do it alone. Somehow I had a feeling that it was something to be undertaken discreetly, something private.

That night I waited . . . [until everyone was safely inside their huts] . . . before setting off across the now cold sand to the sea.

It was eerie alone there on that vast expanse of beach but, looking back, I did not feel apprehensive for I could see a few dim lights from the huts, the familiar silhouette of my own hut and those near to mine.

I had gone about a half a mile along the shore when I spotted a dark shape ahead of me. A turtle? My heart skipped some beats. The object was lying half in, half out of the surf. I approached stealthily, hardly able to breathe from excitement. Was I about to see my first Logger-head? I crouched low and proceeded, somewhat like a commando, not wanting to alarm her. Then I saw I was mistaken – this was no turtle, but a large chunk of reeds broken from the river bank and washed up here. What a disappointment . . . well what else but to go to bed? I started back towards the hut when, suddenly to the right, I saw it. How could I have missed it before? A dark hump about thirty feet in from the sea. I lay on my stomach and slithered towards it with bated breath, hoping that my presence wouldn't ruin everything.

She was half dug into the sand and was about the size of a coffee table. She was facing away from the sea and away from me – a good thing as she could not see me approaching. Slowly I crawled nearer until I could almost have touched her. It was pretty uncomfortable lying on my stomach on the cold sand. Her flippers made a slight rustle as she cleared the sand making her nest and she seemed to sigh, expelling air through her nostrils. Then there was a creaking sound as she shifted her weight. The hole she had made appeared to have a sort of tunnel astern and I soon knew what this was for, for there was a kind of 'plop' and an egg fell from her directly into the tunnel. It was followed by another and then another, some coming in quick spurts, others after a pause. More sighs, heavings, shiftings and plop . . . plop . . . the eggs looked exactly like ping-pong balls. They were coated with a slimy liquid like egg white.

I watched, stunned and moved by this incredible scene I was privileged to witness, until, slower and slower the eggs came and at last there were no more. Altogether I had counted about a hundred. I was ready to cry, but not with sadness, rather with joy for this lonely, primeval creature come to repeat the life process just as her forebears had done through the millennia.

She rested a while then used her flippers to sweep sand over the nest, carefully camouflaging the area. Then she heaved herself upright and turned towards the sea. She looked even bigger when standing. I watched in awe as she lumbered to the water. At last I could stand for she had her back to me and so I followed her to the water's edge just in time to see the glint of water on her shell as she disappeared beneath the surf.

The encounter with the turtle was a watershed for me. From then on I began to identify with them and to seek knowledge about them. I wrote to various animal protection societies and eventually learned that 'my' turtles were the rare Loggerheads, or *Caretta caretta*, the second largest species of the existing seven within the worldwide turtle population. They are one of earth's oldest surviving species, said by scientists to have lived over a hundred million years ago. By comparison, homo sapiens is a newcomer with his fifteen million.

During the rest of the summer I read what I could about my new friends and I learned that they mature in 15 to 30 years; have a possible life expectancy of a 100 years and an average weight when fully grown of 120 kilos. I learned that the eggs hatch in approximately sixty days and that hatching and nesting only occur at night and between the months of May and September. Their diet consists of small crustaceans, sea grasses and jellyfish. Logger-heads in fact perform a useful service by acting as marine vacuum cleaners, gobbling up the feared plagues of jellyfish which are the scourge of many bathing beaches.

On the beach I now regularly plotted the tracks of nesting females and their hatchlings. These latter were tiny tank-like spoors often to be seen on the sand in the early morning. To my horror I found one day a dried-up dead one. This, I learned, was the fate of any hatchling which failed to reach the sea before sun-up when it would dry out and die or fall prey to seagulls or ghost crabs lying in wait for them. Local fishermen filled in my sketchy portrait of my new friends. In fact, they did not have much time for them and said, '*pis kaplumba*' (dirty turtles), because turtles can damage fishing nets.

An intriguing tale came from [my friend] Ahmet who claimed to have known many a turtle. According to him, the males preceded the annual arrivals of the females by some days and lay in wait at a reef not far off the beach, like bridegrooms waiting at the altar. The mating then took place in the shallows off the beach or in the river near the beach. Ahmet's explicit hand-signs and sounds made up for lack of verbal communication though, at that point, I could have wished for the help of a veil to hide my blushes and my mirth.

Other information, which reached me by mail via the village post office, was precise and chilling – many countries of the Medi-terranean were no longer visited by the *Caretta caretta*. Italy had reported but one nesting female and that in 1984. Greece's record was bad too – on the island of Zakynthos the turtle population was suffering because of destruction of nesting beaches on behalf of tourism. In an English newspaper brought to the beach by a friend, I read of conflict on the beautiful island of Zakynthos between developers and conservationists. Reading it, I trembled. Dalyan was so exceptionally beautiful, how could it remain 'undeveloped'? Would the present trickle of tourists turn into a flood? I'd heard rumours of a hotel to be built on our beach. How would that affect our turtles? Looking at the untouched expanse of sand and the few dilapidated huts it was hard to imagine it trodden by thousands of feet; peppered with sunbeds and parasols; neon-lit and pulsating to disco rhythms. Surely we were far removed from all that ... or was I guilty of wishful thinking?

FROM *Kaptan June and the Turtles* by June Haimoff

Partly as a result of June Haimoff's efforts İstuzu Beach, Patara Beach and other beaches where turtles are known to nest were declared protected areas in 1995. The Mediterranean's current population of loggerhead turtles is small but thought to be stable.

MONK SEALS

The chances of seeing a turtle, though small, are considerably greater than of seeing this coast's rarest marine mammal, the monk seal *Monachus monachus*, which is listed by UNESCO as being among the rarest marine mammals on earth, with a surviving population of perhaps only two to three hundred, about half of which are thought to be in an area around the Dodecanese Islands and Turkish Aegean. But in truth no-one has any very precise estimate of what current numbers are. The monk seal remains an obscure, largely unknown inhabitant of the Mediterranean. Intensely shy, it breeds in caves and remote bays – places that are now few and far between and in fact particularly prone to human disturbance. It is a large animal – typically 2.4 metres long and needs something like three kilogrammes of fish, molluscs or octopus per day, which must be difficult to find when Mediterranean fish stocks are so low. Unfortunately its pupping season, from May to November, coincides with the tourist season. It is probably very sensitive to sea pollution.

So all in all there seems to be very little grounds for any kind of optimism about this poor animal's future. Its chances of extinction within the next few decades seem depressingly high, although a reserve has been established for some years now at Foça, north of Izmir.

Adult males are black with a white belly patch; adult females are generally brown or grey with a lighter belly coloration. Other irregular light patches are not unusual, mainly on the throats of males and on the backs of females. If you do see a monk seal, on land or at sea, it is important to leave it alone. Contact with humans seems to do the monk seal no good at all.

FISH

From the point of view of snorkelling the wonderful thing about the Turkish Aegean is its astonishing clarity. This is because the water is low in phyphotoplankton. And although this means the sea is wonderfully clear, there is one major drawback – that phyphotoplankton are the first link in the marine food chain, and without it the sea can support only a limited amount of life. Which means that on your first dive the waters can seem empty of life. Though once you learn how and where to look, there are many interesting species which inhabit crevices, holes and the spaces under rocks. Lifting stones and scraping the sandy bottom can be rewarding.

First of all there is marine plant life. The humblest of the living things in this sea are the algaes (of which phyphotoplankton is one). They like rocky shores and the very clear waters around the Turkish coast allow plants to thrive at depth due to the availability of light, essential for photosynthesis to occur in plants. They are generally green, brown or red in colour and they often have a flat or feathery appearance.

In sandy or muddy areas and between rocky outcrops, there is eel grass, a flowering marine plant related to seaweed and terrestrial plants. The flowers are inconspicuous in the leaf bases. Unlike algae it has a complex root system which is important in the stabilisation of sediment and another reason for the exceptional clarity of the water around this part of the Turkish coast.

There are usually some bivalves about, or their old shells. The most distinctive is the Mediterranean fan mussel. It stands upright in sandy and gravelly areas and is usually attached to sunken stones or rock, often covered with a growth of weeds and other plants. They feed by filtration, syphoning water continuously between their partially open valves. If disturbed they quickly close, then reopen slowly when they sense no danger. You can usually find examples of burrowing bivalves by sifting through the top surface of sandy bottoms. Live specimens should, after examination, be returned to their natural habitat under the sand.

The most exciting of the cephalods is the common octopus. Despite being remorselessly fished for the table, there are quite a lot of them about, but they are very difficult to see. They adapt their colour to their surroundings and they hide in crevices and among stones. The entrance to their lair is usually camouflaged with an arrangement of stones and shells, neatly piled up. Despite their affinity for rocky areas they can be found in sandy areas where they burrow into the sand forming a funnel-shaped lair lined and reinforced with rocks and the shells of their unfortunate victims. They rarely grow to more than fifty centimetres in length.

It is exciting to see an octopus on a night dive with a torch. In the torchlight you can see sometimes pick them out as they roam over the rocks in search of prey. During the early part of the season, around May and June, the female octopus builds a specially prepared nest in a hole in the rocks in which to lay her eggs. Although these nurseries are easy to find, it is best to leave the mothers undisturbed.

Jellyfish were once rare in Turkey, but seem to be seen more and more often. The common jellyfish is the most likely to be encountered in Turkish waters; it is transparent with a blue-white tint, saucer-shaped and can grow up to twenty-five centimetres in diameter. It is recognisable by four distinctive purple-coloured, horseshoe-shaped, reproductive organs visible when viewed from above.

Much more dangerous is the smaller jellyfish. Still extremely rare in these waters, it reaches a maximum diameter of ten centimetres, with four arms around its mouth and eight slender trailing tentacles. It is transparent with a yellow-red tint; if disturbed at night it becomes luminescent. Its stings can be severe and painful.

Crustaceans – crabs, crawfish, lobsters, prawns and shrimps – seem to be very thin on the ground, or more accurately, in the sea. The one you are most likely to see is the hermit crab. These are carnivorous scavengers of the sea bottom. At the first sign of danger they withdraw quickly into their shell covering the entrance with one or both of their comparatively large claws.

You will see plenty of echinoderms – brittlestars, featherstars, starfish, sea cucumbers and sea urchins. Turn over any rock, not forgetting to replace it of course, and you will inevitably find a brittle-star or two, even several different species together. There are a wide variety to be found here, but the most common is the brittlestar, which has a disc two centimetres in diameter and is often pentagonal in shape. Its upper surface has many minute spinelets. Featherstars can be found clinging to rocks either singly or more often in groups. Their arms radiate from a very small green or brown-coloured body. They are very fragile.

The absence of pollution provides the perfect habitat for sea urchins. They appear at first sight to be sedentary but they can move relatively quickly on short spines located on the underside of the body. The black sea urchin seems to be attached to every rock near the shore. They are usually between five and seven centimetres in diameter when mature and the sharp spines are up to three centimetres in length. They are not poisonous, but if the spines enter the skin the tip breaks off and the wound then becomes infected.

There are not many fish to be seen on a daylight dive, and most of these are quite small but they all have their enchantments.

Blennies have bulging eyes, a long dorsal fin and a habit of sitting on the bottom propped up on their pelvic fins, often with their tail fin curving to one side. They rarely exceed five centimetres in length, and can be found in small holes in the rocks with just the tip of their head showing. Their bulging eyes tend to follow you around as you swim by.

The cardinal fish looks like its domesticated 'cousin' the goldfish, because of its bright red-orange colouring. In almost every cavern, cave entrance and dark place you will find them in moderate shoals. They are primarily nocturnal and have large eyes with two cross bands. Their maximum size is fifteen centimetres, although they are rarely seen exceeding ten centimetres here, usually in shallow areas.

There are plenty of damsel fish. As juveniles they are vivid blue fry. As they progress towards adulthood they become dark brown and sometimes almost black. Their dorsal fin has two sections and they have a distinctive forked tail. Small shoals can sometimes be observed hovering almost motionless in mid-water for no apparent reason. They rarely exceed eight centimetres in length.

Garfish are pretty rare, but are one of the easiest fish to identify, with long jaws and a long slender body. They are often seen swimming in small shoals near the surface from about August.

There's a good chance of seeing a parrot fish or two (they are often seen in pairs). The males are grey and females brown and yellow. They can be up to twenty centimetres in length. The front teeth of parrot fishes are fused into a tough beak which is used to bite the surface of rocks or, if available, the tips of growing coral. Large grinding teeth chew the rocks or coral, food is extracted and the residue is excreted. The crunching sounds made by grazing parrot fish are clearly audible underwater.

The picarel can be seen in Turkey in large shoals around reefs and rocky areas. Nearer to shore in shallow areas smaller shoals often follow divers having learned that the odd titbit might be forthcoming. At some of the more popular dive sites they will follow divers for the entire dive. Adults grow to twenty centimetres in length and the body is ovoid in shape with a rectangular shaped spot on the side. They have a long dorsal fin and a short anal fin, both with sharp spines.

If you see a bigger fish it is likely to be either a red mullet (which the Turks particularly enjoy eating) or a wrasse. The red mullet's distinctive features are two long sensory barbels on the lower jaw which they use to furrow in sandy bottoms in the search for food. They have the ability to change colour depending on the time of day or if stressed, and so often don't look very red. The wrasse has a yellow streak running from the snout towards the tail.

There are some small, rather fragile coral communities to be found around the Turkish Aegean, usually in infrequently dived areas and places protected by overhanging rocks or in crevices. Some very colourful, soft corals can be found in cave entrances and caverns. Hard and soft corals are rare here and delicate and great care should be taken not to cause damage.

LAND ANIMALS

The land animal that you are most likely to encounter on a walk is the tortoise, confusingly known as the 'Greek tortoise' or as the 'spur-thighed tortoise' (*Testudo graeca*). This survives in great numbers all along the coast of the Turkish Aegean, and on the islands. Their abundance was described back in the 1840s by Lieutenant Thomas Spratt:

> Among Lycian reptiles the tortoise (*Testudo graeca* and *marginata*) is the most conspicuous and abundant. The number of these animals straying about the plains, and browsing on the fresh herbage in spring, astonishes the traveler. In April they commence love-making. Before we were aware of the cause, we were often surprised, when wandering among ruins and waste places, at hearing a noise as if some invisible geologist was busily occupied close by trimming his specimens. A search in the direction of the noise discovered the hammer in the shape of a gentleman tortoise, who, not being gifted with vocal powers, endeavoured to express the warmth of his affection to his lady by rattling his shell against her side. The ardour of the tortoise is celebrated by Aelian. In ditches and stagnant waters, the fresh-water tortoise (*Emys caspica*) is equally plentiful. In fine weather long rows of them may be seen sunning themselves on the banks; whence, on being alarmed, they would waddle, and plunge with it rapidity into the water, apparently always following a leader, who made the first plunge from one end of the row.
>
> FROM *Travels in Lycia* by T. Spratt and E. Forbes

During the twentieth century, the spur-thighed tortoise was one of the most popular tortoises in the European pet trade. Countless individuals were collected from the wild and some regional populations were much reduced. Turkey banned the export of wild tortoises in 1992 and their numbers seem to have recovered. But why should the slow, vulnerable tortoise have survived so well, when almost every other animal – bird, land mammal, reptile or fish – has been decimated? The usual explanation is that Turks are reluctant to kill tortoises, because they believe it is unlucky to do so. But it may also be, if you are inclined to a more cynical way of thinking, that humans have found no very profitable use for the tortoise, and although the tortoise is sometimes a nuisance it is certainly not a threat. We are therefore prepared to leave it be.

The subspecies of the *Testudo graeca* which you are mostly likely to encounter is the *Testudo graeca ibera*, which is about the size and shape of a pineapple. The shell is slightly elongated with slight flares around the rear legs. They vary in colour from light yellow-green to a dark gray-black. This species is quite common in western Turkey and appears in various subspecies throughout the Aegean and Mediterranean such as *Testudo marginata*, which is larger and greyer.

What is really charming about the tortoises is their apparent indifference to man. They do not scuttle away, but continue to munch away at the wildflowers and the buttercups, which seem to be their particular favourites. They will hiss at you if you pick them up. But otherwise they will ignore you.

During a short walk in May 2006 I discovered six individual tortoises. They ranged from a breeding pair, to a female digging a hillside nest, to a tiny youngster foraging near the pebbly beach. This was last year's hatchling experiencing his first spring. He was barely four centimetres across. A female can lay three clutches of eggs over a summer, generally about fifteen eggs per clutch. She digs a hole with her back feet, which she refills, covers over and stamps down once the eggs are laid.

LIONS

Persian, Greek and Roman tombs in south-west Turkey sometimes feature lions, which did indeed roam the mountains of the coast in this period, and there were one or two recorded beasts still at large in the mid-nineteenth century, but sadly no more. In remoter parts of the coast there are thought to be bears as well as large numbers of wild pig. Here Charles Fellows describes both animals in a wild part of western Lycia, near Sidyma, in the 1840s:

> The present state of this district is extremely wild; only three or four huts are amidst these ruins on the mountain, and their

occupants have always their gun slung over their shoulder, even within the limits of their own cultivated fields. On inquiry as to why this custom prevailed, we were told that the country was full of wild animals, and of the fiercest kind. I was extremely cautious and particular in my inquiries as to their nature, and have no doubt of the truth of the account which I heard from many of the people of the surrounding district, and each unknown to the other. In this village alone, four or five lions, called Aslan by the Turks, and other animals called Caplan (the leopard) are killed every year. The man who first told me, had himself taken the skins to the Aga, to present to different Pashas, and these presentations had been rewarded by sums of one to two hundred piastres, which he had himself received. The lions, he said, are timid unless surprised or attacked, and I could not hear that they did much injury to the flocks. Wolves – and, if I understand rightly, the hyaena also – are found here; and the latter are described as gnashing their teeth together . . . Bears are certainly found here in great numbers. I observe the most costly buildings in this district are the apiaries, which are formed of a square of high walls, open at the top only; within this the hives are placed, and a ladder is used, if entry is required, a precaution which is essential to keep away the bears from the honey . . . Snakes are also abundant in this district, but they are most numerous in the lower valleys. An island opposite to Macry, at the foot of the Cragus range, is wholly given up to them; and the ruins of an earlier village, called Macry-vecchia, probably of a late Roman age, are shown as the remains of a· town deserted on account of the number of snakes. The people object even to approach the island, and I doubt not that their fears greatly exaggerate the number and size of these animals. My servant saw one, which he considered small, among the ruins of Cadyanda; it measured six feet, and was as thick as his arm.

FROM *A Journal written during an excursion in Asia Minor*
by Charles Fellows

Magnificent wild deer and goats inhabitant the highest mountain ranges of Caria and Lycia. Inevitably, sportsmen have long prized them as trophies. Frederick Selous was a famous big game hunter, explorer and bird-egg collector who spent much of his life in Africa. Here he describes his efforts to shoot a wild goat in the Lycian mountains, using *yürük* (nomad) shepherds as guides. Selous first visited Turkey in 1894 'to try to obtain some precise information as to the habitat of the large long-faced red deer (*Cervus maral*) and the magnificently horned wild goats (*Capra aegagarus*)'. But even then finding trophy goats was clearly not easy:

The descent of the mountain was easy enough; and before very long we had got down to the neighbourhood where we had first seen the goats lying, and the old Turk gave me to understand that if we reached a certain buttress of rocks we should command a view of the spot where we had last seen them.

Before reaching these solid rocks, however, we had to cross one hundred yards or so of loose stones; and to accomplish this noise-lessly was an absolute impossibility, as they lay all loosely heaped together at a steep angle on the mountain-side in such a way that the displacement of one moved several others and was bound to make some slight noise even if it did not send a small avalanche down to the valley below. Across this treacherous piece of ground my guide and I moved cautiously with bare feet; at least his feet were bare and mine only covered with socks. It seemed that it took an age to cross it, but at last we reached the solid mass of rocks that had been our goal, and, climbing hastily to the top, eagerly scanned the ground beyond, and almost immediately saw the wild goats of which we were in search. Fortune so far had befriended us, as, although the slight noise we had made in crossing the loose stones had disturbed them, they had not been able to quite locate the sound, and were approaching us instead of retreating. Had we not disturbed them, I do not think we should ever have seen them at all amongst the bushes where they had been lying, until they had made us out, and crept away without offering a chance of a shot.

As it was, they were at first about three hundred yards below us, but as they were climbing upwards every step brought them nearer to us. They advanced very slowly, and with great caution, until at last they were within two hundred yards of where I stood. Nearer than this they were not likely to approach, so, putting up the two hundred yards' sight, I prepared for a shot. The two rams appeared about the same size, and their broad curving horns looked very fine. Soon one of them stood in full view on a rock, and offered a capital shot. Standing as I was, he was too far off for me to feel at all sure of hitting him, but Allah was with me on this day, and as I fired I had the satisfaction of seeing him fall headlong off the rock, and disappear in a small crevasse. I very nearly got a shot at the second ram, as he jumped from rock to rock, but he was a little too quick for me, and got out of sight before I could manage to slip another cartridge into my single-barreled rifle. Barefooted as I was, it did not take me long to get down to where my prize lay. The old Turk pronounced it to be a five-year-old ram; and, such as it was, I was very pleased to have secured it, for, although its horns had not attained to the magnificent proportions sometimes seen in old rams of his species, he still carried a very pretty head, his horns being quite symmetrical, and measuring just twenty-four inches over the curve. He was still in his summer coat of red brown, with a short black beard, but with the broad shoulder-stripe, which becomes so conspicuous later on in the season, almost entirely wanting. His legs were short and strong, and well suited to carry their owner's heavy though symmetrical form up and down the mountain-sides on which he had passed his life. He was in excellent condition, and his flesh proved surprisingly good, quite equal, it seemed to me, to the best of mutton, and without any trace of goaty flavour about it. I would much rather, however, have had a good stinking old ram with a real big head. It did not take us long to cut him up; but it was already late when we started for camp, which we did not reach till after dark.

On the morning of the following day we were unable to make sail for Fineka, as the wind proved unfavourable, so I skinned and preserved my goat's head, and then had everything carried down and packed in the boat, all ready for a start as soon as the wind changed. But all day long it blew steadily from the same direction, until I began to fear that we should miss our steamer. The Greek boatmen, however, declared that there would be a change at sunset, and they were right, as the wind dropped altogether about that time, leaving us still stuck for the want of any wind at all. A little before midnight, however, a breeze sprang up from the east, and we at once got underway, and reached Fineka about one o'clock on the following day.

That same night our steamer arrived from Adalia, when we at once went on board, and were soon on our way to the famous island of Rhodes, which we reached on the afternoon of September 30. Here we were put in quarantine for eighteen hours, and so did not arrive at Smyrna until late on the afternoon of October 3, thus bringing to a close my first journey in a (to me) new and most interesting country, where if I had not had much sport, I had spent a pleasant time in quest of it, and gained experience which may be useful to me at some future time.

FROM *Sport & Travel, East & West* by Frederick C. Selous

BEARS

Brown bears are believed to still inhabit some of the remoter parts of south-west Turkey, for instance the Datça peninsula and the Marmaris National Park. But I can find no evidence of any sighting for some years and I suspect a certain amount of optimism in the habitat maps. If there are any bears in this part of Turkey they are Syrian brown bears (*Ursus arctos syriacus*), the smallest sub-species of the brown bear.

Until the 1980s dancing bears were still a reasonably common sight in Turkey. In 1996 the very last of them were confiscated from their owners and housed in a bear sanctuary near Bursa.

In June 1937 there was an extraordinary incident involving a bear shot by hunters on Uludağ, a mountain south of Bursa (this is not within the area of the Turkish coast covered by this book, but it is too interesting a story to leave out). For after killing the bear, the hunters realised that it was accompanied by a human female of about nine years old, and that she had almost certainly been raised by the bear since a baby.

The hunter, Ali Osman, told the story to the correspondent of *The American Weekly*:

'It was the most exciting event in my life,' Ali Osman told me. 'Accompanied by another hunter, named Bahri, I climbed up the Ulu Dağ to shoot one of the bears inhabiting this mountain. For a long time we wandered about in vain and the sun had already sunk below the horizon when I suddenly sighted an enormous she-bear at a distance of only a few yards. I leveled the gun and fired. The bear reared up and then dropped. I drew nearer to the carcass, and when I reached it I heard my friend Bahri set up a cry to chill one's marrow. I turned around and saw him throwing away his gun and rushing off headlong. I turned again in the opposite direction and – I swear the thing I saw made my hair stand on end, made the blood curdle in my veins, and made my heart stand still.

'Growling and spitting, a naked wood spirit leaped forward from the thicket and rushed towards me. It was standing upright, but stooped in walking. Its hair, long and beautiful, flew in the wind. And its eyes, Effendi, its eyes! They seemed to me to be burning and to shine like two searchlights.

'I could not even form an idea as to what to do, when it reached me and threw itself with a howl of rage upon me. It attacked me with teeth and nails and tried to bite through my throat. Finally I succeeded in forcing the creature down. Only now I saw that the "wood spirit" was nothing but a little girl endowed with abnormal strength.

'When my friend Bahri saw that I had survived the struggle, he timidly approached and, after I had set him right concerning the girl, he summoned up courage and we were able to bind the child with our belts.

'Not far from the place where we killed the bear we saw its lair and we found there conclusive proof that a human being had shared the lodging of the beast over a period of years.

'After having visited the bear's lair we returned to the place where we had left our captive. She was exhausted and she followed us with bound arms without offering any resistance. The very next day we brought her to Istanbul, and then to the hospital of Bakirkey where she has been living up to now.'

'Some questions are yet to be answered,' I said, when Ali Osman finished his tale. 'Who is the girl? Who are her parents? How many years did she spend in the forest reared by the she-bear?'

'I am sorry but I cannot answer your questions,' answered Ali Osman. 'We informed the local authorities about our capture and they made extensive inquiries about the origin of the girl. But as far as I know they learned that the probable parents of the girl have been dead for a long time and that no other relatives of hers are living. Perhaps you may learn some details about the origins of this girl at the village of Mussalilar. If you like, Bey, I shall accompany you to this village.'

I accepted with thanks, and at six in the morning of the following day Sedad Ataman, Ali Osman and myself started with a car to the village. One hour and a half with the car we followed a beautiful road; then we had to travel on foot one hour more, until we reached the village.

The peasants received us hospitably; a carpet was brought and unfolded in the shadow of a tree. Turkish coffee was offered to everybody.

After the peasants learned about our errand they called for the eighty-year-old *hodja* – a 'teacher' of the village, who knew everybody and everything.

'Uludağ is great and its mysteries are numerous,' said the *hodja* when we asked him to tell us all he knew about the bear-child.

'Our village,' he continued, 'has been at war with bears throughout the memory of man. Night after night they come, steal everything they can, devastate our gardens and fields.

'But only once has it ever happened that a child was kidnapped by a bear. It was eight years ago, when a woman came to our village bringing with her a three-months-old child and asked us to procure her work and bread. Hands are always needed at our village and so it came about that Fatma and her daughter Esma remained with us. One day Fatma went to the forest to gather some brushwood. She took her daughter with her and left her on the ground not far from the place where she herself was working.

'Half an hour had passed when she suddenly heard a cry, and turning round she saw to her horror an enormous she-bear clutching the child's long clothes in the teeth and trotting off with it toward the forest. Fatma tried in vain to reach the bear. When the beast saw that it was followed by the woman it doubled its speed and disappeared in the thicket. A hunter heard the screams of Fatma and rushed hither. They searched long hours, but in vain.

'Fatma said always that the sight of Uludağ reminded her of the horrible thing. One day she said good-bye to us and left our village. Nobody knows whence she came – nobody knows where she went.

'You wish to know whether the child recently found by hunters may be the little Esma lost eight years ago? I think it possible but it will be never ascertained with certainty. Numerous are the mysteries of Uludağ, but it never lets anybody into its secrets.'

George Maranz in *The American Weekly*

BIRDS

As in many other places, an expanding human population and intensive agricultural activities have largely destroyed the natural habitat for birds. Fifty years ago the silted-up deltas of the Maeander, the Dalyan and other rivers were a haven for resident and migrating birds. Freya Stark describes enormous numbers of wintering birds on the Maeander delta in 1953. But since then drainage schemes have turned these marshes into vast, irrigated cotton fields or orange groves, heavily fertilised and regularly sprayed with pesticides.

However, there has been one remarkable survival – the beautiful, brackish lake of Köyceğiz, just west of Dalaman airport. This remains magically untouched, despite being between the sea and the coastal highway.

Köyceğiz is very big, around 3,000 hectares, and still supports a huge population of migrant and resident birds – ducks, cormorants, pygmy cormorants, pochards, storks and other birds. The white-tailed eagle is presumed to breed in the surroundings, whilst white-breasted kingfisher and pied kingfisher still breed but in small and declining numbers.

Twitchers' blogs report an amazing variety of birds, even in summer – red-backed shrikes, wryneck, whinchats, European rollers, reed warblers, sedge warblers, barn swallows, sand martins, crag martins, blue rock thrush, western rock nuthatch, chiffchaffs; also little egret, white stork and corn buntings, and many others.

On a boat at sea you will see very few birds – the occasional rather sinister-looking cormorant on a headland, perhaps, or a gull. If you step on to land it is a different story. In my garden there are owls, turtle doves and woodpeckers. And on the occasional magical evening the sky over the bay has filled with swallows or house-martins, apparently pausing during migration to feed on insects. In the mountains eagles soar on the thermals.

A number of important bird species migrate through the region, primarily the pygmy cormorant, the Dalmatian pelican, the white-headed duck and the lesser kestrel. All of these have a European threat status of vulnerable except the white-headed duck, whose conservation status is endangered, according to Birdlife International.

FLORA

Botanists have long been fascinated by Turkey and despite serious erosion (each year Turkey is thought to lose some 500 million tonnes of soil through erosion, enough to cover the whole of Cyprus to a depth of ten centimetres) the south-west coast of Anatolia remains very rich botanically. The area west of Marmaris – the Hisarönü peninsula and the Datça peninsula – has a wonderful variety of plants from the south Aegean Islands, from Crete and from Anatolia, a remarkable mix found nowhere else in the Mediterranean.

Particularly rare and interesting are sub-species of Cretan plants such as the aristolochias and arums. The latter are smelly and poisonous, and pollinate by tricking flies into believing that they contain decaying meat. Here Andy Byfield, an English botanist who has spent many years working in Turkey, describes his own expedition in the area in the mid-1990s in search of arums:

> It was a particular treat for me to see the little-recorded *Arum creticum* and other Cretans growing abundantly in their Turkish haunts in the earliest spring days of last year. For the arum, a botanical friend and I traveled to the most south-westerly point of

all, the Hisarönü peninsula – a narrow finger of land that stretches out from Bozburun and Talica, crowned at its extremity by the Roman fort of Loryma.

This remote part of the coast cannot be reached by car, so we hired a fishing boat from the tiny village of Söğüt to drop us at the fort. It was up to us to walk the fifteen kilometres or so back to civilisation. Unlike the forest-covered hills further east, this promontory is, at best, clothed with scrub, while much is glaring, naked limestone rock, affording little protection from the astonishing heat of the March sun, and with all too few sources of fresh water. But what the area lacks in comforts for the rambler, it makes up in scenery of quite exceptional beauty. *Arum creticum* was at its best and grew abundantly here, on secluded rocky outcrops and as a path-side weed, and was just one of many beautiful plants we saw.

The arums found in the coastal slopes and foothills of Turkey are remarkable plants – supremely adapted to their environment and among the most highly specialised examples on earth in terms of floral structure. While so many of Turkey's other plants are decreasing in range through the destruction of their natural habitats, the arums continue to thrive. Many are found in some of Turkey's most beautiful landscapes, where they usually appear in the scruffiest of microhabitats. They are perfectly at home in field margins and in dusty pasture grazed to death by the ubiquitous goat and sheep; they even thrive in farmyards and unkempt gardens.

Part of the secret of their success lies in their sap, which is at best unpalatable, and at worst highly poisonous. This I can personally vouch for, having once nibbled a flower stem. The sap from all parts of the plant is full of needle-sharp calcium oxalate crystals, which bury themselves in the softest parts of the mouth before slowly dissolving. The result is an excruciating physical and chemical sensation, and even the most hardened of grazing goats try the tempting lush foliage only once. All parts of the plant are poisonous. Iraqis are reported to eat tubers of *Eminium spiculatum* (a close cousin of the arum, also found in south-east Turkey), but only after double-boiling them to denature the toxins. What became of the first brave soul to eat these tubers, who presumably would have boiled them only once?

Arums require only the services of flies to effect pollination at the time of flowering. The flies are not pollen or nectar feeders, but instead seek carrion on which to lay their eggs. In a remarkable example of botanical deception the flies are lured to the flower by a realistic odour of rotten meat, often combined with the plant's blotchy, and in some cases reddish, meaty appearance. The greasy inner surface of the flower provides an inadequate foothold, and the flies lose their grip and slip into a bulbous, prison-like chamber at the base of the bloom, wherein lie the true flowers – tiny males and females in two adjacent rows. After a few days' imprisonment the bloom withers, allowing the flies to escape and carry their coating of pollen to the female flowers of the next plant. During this process the female flies are often fooled into laying their eggs. But life for the hatching maggots is short: their vegetative prison provides no sustenance and they soon perish.

Remarkable as the floral structure of these plants is, another group of totally unrelated Turkish plants has developed much the same process of pollination. These are 'Dutchman's pipes' (*Aristolochia*), whose tubular flowers have all the appearance of a bizarre creation from the hands of a meerschaum-carver. While most have strongly curved pipe-like flowers, others have vertical flowers that look more like the mammalian fallopian tube. One tradition among medieval herbalists was to treat the ills of particular parts of the body with the plant that most resembled them (irrespective of any other medicinal benefits or side-effects). These aristolochias were accordingly called 'birthworts', and used to cure a range of birthing ailments. Their flowers, like those of the arums, are often mottled, in shades of brown and yellow-green. But it is their foul smell that often draws one's attention first.

Both the arum and the herbaceous aristolochia occur in a greater diversity in Turkey than in any other country. Arums are spread widely across the country, although the distribution of individual species is often restricted. *Biarum davisii* and *Arum creticum* are among the most localised and you need to make a special effort to locate them, basing yourself either in Marmaris or in the smaller villages further west.

FROM *Cornucopia* 1996

In 1788 Dr John Sibthorp, the thirty-year-old professor of Botany at Oxford, accompanied by his brilliant Austrian illustrator Ferdinand Bauer, made several stops in the Turkish Aegean, gathering material that would later be used in the *Flora Graeca*, published between 1810 and 1830 and generally thought to be the first systematic survey of eastern Mediterranean plants.

In March 1778, after surviving a storm near Samos, their ship the *Bethlehem* stopped for a few days in Karabağlar Bay, near Bodrum. Here Sibthorp listed 172 plants collected, some of which he regarded as new to science, and enjoyed the spring weather.

> The temperature of the air was delicious . . . our eyes were ravished with the sight of a number of fine plants in flower or on the eve of unfolding their petals. The list of these will shew better than a meteorological journal the difference which exists between the climate of Caria and that of the Troad though the distance is only 3 degrees of latitude.

A few days later he stopped at Porto Cavaliere (now Osmaniye, south of Marmaris).

> The roughness of the ground & of the thickets permitted us not to stray far from the beach . . . nevertheless we were sufficiently amused and occupied by the abundance & diversity of fine plants which grew within our reach & which were now mostly in flower. The Luxuriance of vegetation was even greater here than at Kara-baglar and exceeded any thing that we had before seen, the Conservatories of Kew contain not a richer display of vegetable beauty . . . Cap'n Imrie who was by far the most agile of our party after much labour & difficulty reached the summit of the nearest mountain & brought back with him a new and elegant species of *Fritillaria*.

On his return journey from Cyprus in May Sibthorp and Bauer

stopped near Finike in Lycia. Botanising along the foot of the
mountains on May 23rd, the party penetrated five miles inland:

> as far as several scattered hamlets whose inhabitants leading a
> pastoral life had mostly retired into the mountains to milk their
> goats and make their cheese. Here the pomegranate glowing with
> its scarlet flowers ornamented the hedges while the *Vitis* . . . over-
> hung the river and perfumed the air with the most fragrant odour.
> Orange & Lemon trees crowded in a wild luxuriance around
> the habitations of these untutored peasants and in vain solicited
> their art to prune and improve them. Fatigued with our walk &
> oppressed by the heat of the day we sought little repose under the
> shade of a spreading Plane tree on the margin of the clear & silent
> Lymirus and in front of a Caramanian cottage . . . We returned
> highly satisfied with our walk and richly laden with curious plants.

A few days later they stopped again at Porto Cavaliere. Sibthorp
was astonished at how quickly the Aegean summer obliterates all
evidence of spring:

> What had appeared nine weeks before as a beautiful garden enameld
> with some of the most curious plants of the East . . . now presented
> a dry and weathered scene of desolation and furnished me only with
> the opportunity of collecting some seeds from the skeletons of those
> plants which I had before gathered in flower.

FROM 'The Travel Journals of Dr John Sibthorp'
quoted in *The Magnificent Flora Graeca* by Stephen Harris

One of the great figures of Turkish botany in the second half of
the twentieth century was Dr P. H. Davis, who published *The Flora
of Turkey* in ten volumes between 1950 and 1970. Even for the
botanically ignorant, this description of his expedition and discoveries
in the mountains of eastern Lycia (made in August 1948) is exciting,
and conveys the sheer diversity of the flora in these mountains:

> From Antalya I had intended to travel eastwards in the Taurus as
> far as Ermenek. But the Lycian Taurus south-west of Antalya, with
> its fabulous maze of limestone gorges, looked so inviting that I

decided to change my plans in favour of Tahtalı Dağ which had never been botanically explored. One should always, I think, be prepared to change one's plans in an unfamiliar country, if an area is seen that looks particularly fruitful; like a witch-doctor, one soon learns to smell out the likeliest hunting-grounds.

The peak of Tahtalı Dağ – 'Mountain of Planks' and ancient Solyma – stands rather isolated from the main range of the Lycian Taurus, and rises in a steep calcareous pyramid of nearly 7,800 feet above the coastal hamlet of Kemer. To that little cluster of cottages we hired a gay Antalyan boatman to take us across the bay, a crossing, on so placid a morning, of three and a half hours by motorboat. There are no roads on the precipitous Lycian coast. In the afternoon, with an adequate bevy of guides, mules and small boys, we straggled out across a narrow coastal plain and soon reached the entrance to the gorge at the foot of Tahtalı Dağ and known, in its narrowest part, as Kesme Boğaz. It was a very lovely place, and we decided to camp beneath the planes that flanked the ice-green river. There we could bathe in the pools, and potter about collecting. But Kesme Boğaz was much too thrilling to potter in. I moved in jerks, in a series of small runs.

Cupressus sempervirens var. horizontalis was abundant on the slopes of the gorge, growing with *Pinus brutia*; but it also clung to the precipices above – the only tree that could – as it does on the cliffs of Crete and Cyprus. A new species of *Origanum Sect. Amaracus*, related to the Greek *O. scabrum*, occurred locally, and a single bush of an undescribed shrubby *Phlomis* was found, resembling the purple-flowered *P. elliptica* from South Persia. In the narrowest part of the chasm, where the river cuts a passage through limestone precipices rising for 2,000 feet on either side, I felt I should burst a blood vessel at the sight of an extraordinary new *Globularia*. This was the dominant plant on the vertical rocks, and formed a shrub up to 3 feet across and about half as much in height, the stems clad in bright green leaves, and bearing unusually spicate inflorescences of lilac-blue. An *Inula* occurred too, very woody, with broad white leaves bigger than one usually finds in *I. heterolepis*; but the flowers were over. It was very satisfactory to find that wonderful Heath, *Pentapera sicula* (*var. libanotica?*) hanging down the shadier parts of the limestone cliffs in 3-foot bushes of yew-green. This archaic monotypic genus grows only in the rocks of Sicily, Cyrenaica, Cyprus, Lebanon and South-West Anatolia. The large pentamerous bells are pink in the Oriental variety – at least in Cyprus – but in the Sicilian plant (which flowers more readily in cultivation) they are white.

Leaving the gorge we climbed up through the luxuriant pine forest towards the hamlet of Kuzdere at 3,300 feet; thickets of *Laurus nobilis* filled the ravines, with *Myrtus, Cotinus*, and *Styrax* – all probably relict types. Seeing a cliff looming through the pines, I ran towards it and found it hung with the most curious new *Echinops*: the leaves, often a foot and a half long, woolly-white and scarcely lobed, were like those of *Onopordon insigne*, and grew at the ends of long curved perennial trunks; it reminded me of *Centaurea Clementei* in the Rif. The heads were white-flowered but impossible to reach, even with my 10-foot bamboo ending in a small saw; the plant flowered only where the cliffs overhung. By throwing many stones one battered head was at last dislodged. Exorbitant bribes to the guide failed to secure any more, though he came very near to breaking his neck.

We shared our lunch with a peasant at Kuzdere, sitting beneath a cultivated tree of *Celtis australis*, and then passed on our way up the steep slopes towards Çukur Yayla. No more cypresses grew above the village, but *Cedrus libani subsp. stenocoma* replaced *Pinus brutia* at 3,500 feet. The black pine occurred only as a few isolated trees; this species and the cedar appear to be mutually exclusive. A little below 5,000 feet (a fruitful altitude) we came to a good spring where the mountains enclosed a large rocky hollow. It was a rich collecting ground, one of the most satisfactory discoveries being a new poppy in the Pilosa section. The leaves were clad in a dense mat of appressed rather tawny silk – which even extended to the ripe pods – reminding one of *Meconopsis superba*. The flowers were orange like those of *P. Heldreichii*. The very pretty blue *Echinops Ritro*, with a bountiful supply of small blue baubles, was in flower beside two undescribed Labiates: a charming ballota with very grey leaves and woolly-crested white hoods, and a new *Origanum Majorana*. Sturdy bushes of *Dorystaechas hastata* were plentiful; this monotypic genus related to *Salvia* is apparently confined to this corner of Turkey and is evidently an old type. The shrubby *Phlomis Bourgaei* was found in the vicinity, growing with *P. grandiflora* which we had already seen on Baba Dağ. Indeed, the two mountains have more in common with each other than either has with Girdev Dağ in the central *massif*, probably due to their maritime situation.

At dusk, met by the usual pack of ferocious dogs, we came to the Çukur Yayla at 5,300 feet. I do not believe I have ever tumbled out of bed at dawn with greater anticipation (or justification) than I did the following day (August 16), knowing that such a promising unexplored peak was at hand. Passing *Digitalis ferruginea* and *D. cariensis* we were soon out of the Cedar forest and on to the steep west shoulder of Tahtalı Dağ. A tremendous scree on the north slope was full of interesting plants for the presses; it needed a couple of hefty fellows to carry them. A form of the intensely aromatic *Calamintha origamfolia* lay on the stones, and, on moving scree, an extraordinary dwarf *Peucedanum* was found, probably *P. pisidicum*, with simple glaucous leaves; it is closely related to a Cretan species, and with that plant holds a very isolated position in this unwieldy genus. Higher up were the colossal jade globes of the undescribed *Echinops* found earlier on Baba Dağ, besides more homely species of *Acantholimon* and *Astragalus*. The remains of a dwarf fritillary, harried by the wind, chattered dryly among the stones.

And so he goes on, discovering a *Salvia* here and a *Rosa glutinosa* there. The following day he almost loses his life and all his pressings in a storm at sea:

We sailed from Kemer at night. An hour or so after leaving the shore a storm suddenly bore down upon us from the Lycian Taurus, as it can do so treacherously in Crete on the island's south coast. The little boat was badly tossed about and we came in under the cliffs for shelter. There was a sudden grinding lurch, throwing us to the bottom of the boat. The stern had struck a hidden rock. We tried to free it, but it was a difficult task. The skipper and his mate were in and out of the sea, heaving and pushing, while every now and then a particularly large wave nearly succeeded in overturning the boat. It was not a pleasant thing to happen at midnight, with no conceivable chance of being rescued. We were told to remove our clothes and be ready to swim for it. Have you ever taken off a pair of climbing boots in a rough sea at midnight? It is not very easy, but they came off in the end, and we clung hopefully to the mast in underclothes of varied type: a forest officer, Kunil and I, and three soldiers who could not swim. We awaited the worst. The fanged coast was quite uninhabited. The situation was so dangerous that it was frightening only in a coldly numbing way. It seemed to be happening to someone else, and I was mainly concerned, I believe, that someone in Europe, beyond those breakers flogging the cliffs that a few days before had seemed so inviting (and do today!), should know of the flora of Tahtalı Dağ. Only four or five people would care, but it seemed desperately important at the time. Resisting the attempts of the captain to throw the presses and 'less valuable' luggage overboard, I pushed and heaved our baggage into the bows. Whether due to this, or to the renewed exertions of the skipper, or to the audible prayers of the huddled soldiers, the boat came free. There were awkward moments before the engine decided to start, then off we dashed for the open sea (the storm having abated a little) and rolled, rather leakily, back to Antalya. By changing the presses continuously for the next two days not a specimen was any the worse for the adventure. We swore we would never go in a motorboat again. And yet, three days later, we sailed in an elegant motorboat eastwards to Alanya, reclining on sacks of grain.

FROM 'A Journey in South-West Anatolia'
by P. H. Davis in *Journal of the RHS*, April 1949

There are several endemic *taxa* on the Turkish Aegean coast. The most famous is oriental sweet gum tree (*Liquidambar orientalis*). It is endemic to this area and has a highly restricted distribution. The trees are cut for firewood and the resin is collected to produce a fixative in the perfume industry. In 1949, *Liquidambar orientalis* forests covered over 3,000 hectares, but there are now only 1,215 ha remaining. Its main stronghold is around Köyceğiz, where at least fifty per cent of all the planet's *Liquidambar orientalis* occurs. The Datça palm (*Phoenix theophrastii*) is another highly localised endemic species in this ecoregion. It is mainly restricted to deep, isolated coastal valleys of the Datça peninsula, where it grows in two valleys: Hurmalıbük Valley, facing south, which has the larger population and Eksere Valley, facing north. Although this species has a very restricted range and a small population, it is considered less endangered than *Liquidambar orientalis*. Finally, *Quercus aucheri* is the other endemic tree species whose occurrence is restricted to south-western Anatolia. In Datça it can be found on Emecik Mountain and Kocada, and in Köyceğiz it forms good communities around Çandır and Yangı villages. The tree that grows everywhere on this coast is the beautiful olive, some of them very old indeed. Thomas Pakenham, in his book *Remarkable Trees of the World*, admires the olive tree for its ability to re-shoot. He describes a very old olive tree growing amongst the tombs at Kekova, in Lycia.

> The olive tree makes a perfect match with the tombs, giving the necropolis a cheerful sense of immortality. No other tree can combine the sense of resurgent life – of sprays of silver-green foliage heavy with fruit – and happy senility. The trunks of olive trees, bowed under the weight of 600 or 700 years, become gradually perforated like a colander. Then they die or are blown down or are cut down by an invading army – only to leap up, young trees again, from their ancient roots. If only we could imitate the olive.
>
> FROM *Remarkable Trees of the World* by Thomas Pakenham

MOSQUITOES

The Turquoise Coast was once famous for its mosquitoes. So unbearably prolific was this insect in some places that much of the local population would desert the coast from May to September, and drive their animals to the pastures on the high plateau. However, insecticide was used against mosquitoes to deadly effect in the 1940s,

and with ever less deadly effect ever since. Here George Bean
describes the mosquitoes of Caunus:

> Caunus at present time is some two miles from the sea, but the
> intervening area is not firm ground but rather an expanse of reeds
> holding together a little soil. There can be no doubt that all this area
> was in antiquity sea, but it is likely that similar marshy area existed
> near the city and afforded a rich breeding ground for mosquitoes.
> When the present writer first visited Dalyan in 1946 the room in
> which he slept was singing with mosquitoes, and the least flaw in the
> mosquito net meant a sleepless night; in 1948 the Turks began a
> serious campaign to exterminate malaria, and that year not a single
> mosquito was in evidence. Such perfection has naturally not been
> maintained and the insects have to some extent found their way
> back, but the visitor need no longer be deterred by this menace.
>
> FROM *Turkey Beyond the Maeander*
> by George E. Bean

The operations to remove the ruins of Xanthus in 1842 were
plagued by mosquitoes:

> A great part of those who had been members of the shore party
> were disabled with fever. The officers and men were beginning to
> suffer much from the mosquitoes, which at sunset rose in myriads
> out of the adjoining morass. It was impossible to escape from these
> merciless tormentors, and the countenances of many of the party
> bore witness to their tortures.
>
> FROM *Travels in Lycia* by T. Spratt and E. Forbes

CHAPTER FOUR

An Ancient Coast

The Ancient World is evident everywhere on this coast, both on the shore and beneath the waves. It is useful to remember that, until very recently, transporting goods and people by sea was much cheaper, and usually much faster, than by land. The sea was a vast highway, not a tranquil backwater, with ships of all sizes making all sorts of journeys – from city to city, but also from one end of the Mediterranean to the other. Amazing discoveries in underwater archaeology made over the last few decades mean that we know much more about this world than we once did. So that between the physical remains recovered by the archaeologists and the surviving textual descriptions a suprisingly vivid picture emerges.

ANCIENT MARINERS AND THEIR SHIPS

What kind of ship did Odysseus sail? Vast amounts have been written on this subject. There are passages of Homer's *Odyssey* and *Iliad* that provide tantalising clues. When Odysseus was shipwrecked on the island of Ogygie where he remained for seven years as captive of the Nymph, he was given logs and tools for building himself a boat. He adzed the logs into planks and then: 'Bored them all and fitted them to each other, then he hammered it with pegs and joints . . . then he worked away setting up decks by fastening them to close-set frames.'

It seems certain that his boat was quite small – perhaps ten metres long, square-rigged, and with a crew of perhaps twenty, with ten oars to each side. It would have been open-decked, shallow-drafted and keel-less. There would have been a shiftable mast, steering would have been with a paddle, attached to the stern with leather straps. Common epithets attached to ships in the Homeric poems are 'swift', 'well-balanced', 'hollow', and 'black' (which suggests they would have been tarred as a protection against the sea and sun).

However, Odysseus's ship is also described as 'blue', which suggests that her topsides were painted indigo, one of the earliest natural colours used by Mediterranean peoples. It is possible she had an oculus or 'eye' painted on her bow, a custom that survives to this day and derives from the ancient Egyptian eye of Ra, the Sun God.

Ancient mariners had no charts or compasses, so kept close to the shore, navigating by familiar landmarks. They did not venture out in a storm. At night they would pull up their boat in a bay and sleep on shore.

The slow progress and regular stops of Homeric mariners seem surprisingly similar to the journey of the modern-day *gulet*, with the major difference that when there was no wind the 'engine' for Ulysses would have been his oarsmen.

There is a passage in Apollonius's *Voyage of Argo* that describes the Argo's launch and departure in search of the Golden Fleece. Here Jason, who has been nominated captain by his shipmates, launches the *Argo*:

'If you do indeed entrust me with this honourable charge, let nothing further keep us back – there have been enough delays already . . . let us drag the ship down into the water. Then you must get all the tackle on board and cast lots for your places on the rowing-benches. Also, we must build an altar on the beach for Apollo, the god of embarkation, who promised me through his oracles that he would be my counsellor and guide in our sea-faring if I offered him a sacrifice as I set forth on my mission for the king.'

He was the first to turn to the business in hand. The rest leapt to their feet and followed his example, piling their clothes on a smooth ledge of rock which in the past had been scoured by winter seas but now stood high and dry. First of all, at a word from Argus, they strengthened the ship by girding her with stout rope, which they drew taut on either side so that her planks should not spring from their bolts but stand any pounding that the seas might give them. Next they quickly hollowed out a runway wide enough to take her beam extending it into the sea as far as the prow would reach when they launched her, and as the trench advanced, digging deeper and deeper below the level of her stem. Then they laid smooth rollers on the bottom. This done, they tipped her down on to the first rollers, on top of which she was to glide along. Next, high up on both sides of the ship, they swung the oars inboard and fastened each handle to its thole-pin so that a foot and a half projected.

They themselves took their stance on either side, one behind the other, breasting the oars and pressing with their hands. And now Tiphys leapt on board to tell the young men when to push. He gave the order with a mighty shout and they put their backs into it at once. At the first heave they shifted her from where she lay; then strained forward with their feet to keep her on the move. And move she did. Between the two files of hustling, shouting men, Pelian Argo ran swiftly down. The rollers, chafed by the sturdy keel, groaned and reacted to the weight by putting up a pall of smoke. Thus she slid into the sea, and would have run still farther, had they not stood by and checked her with hawsers.

They fitted the oars to the tholes, and got the mast, the well-made sail, and the stores on board. Then, after satisfying themselves that all was shipshape, they cast lots for the benches, which held two oarsmen each. But the midships seat they gave to Heracles, selecting as his mate Ancaeus, the man from Tegea, and leaving this bench to the pair for their sole use, with no formalities and no recourse to chance. Also they all agreed that Tiphys should be the helmsman of their gallant ship.

Next, piling up shingle on the beach, they made a seaside altar for Apollo as god of shores and embarkation, and on the top they quickly laid down some dry logs of olive-wood . . .

FROM *The Voyage of Argo* by Apollonius of Rhodes

The writer Tim Severin built his own *Argo*. He became so interested in the Homeric journeys that in 1985 he attempted Odysseus's voyage from Troy to Ithaca, aboard a 54-foot reconstruction of a Bronze Age ship. He had used the same ship the previous year to make the 'Jason

Voyage', from Greece to Soviet Georgia, to find the Golden Fleece among the Svan people of the Caucasus mountains.

He used, as Odysseus would have done, a mixture of sail and oar-power, and made progress at an average of four knots. But he was constantly aware of the danger:

> We must never forget that Bronze Age sailing was a high-risk business, and the galleys proceeded very cautiously. They stayed near the coast and dashed from anchorage to anchorage or used the Aegean's myriad islands as stepping stones. Space on these heavily manned vessels was so limited that it was awkward to sleep. With barely room to lie down on their narrow benches, the crews needed to come ashore to get proper rest as well as to prepare their meals, for it seems that they did not like to cook aboard, perhaps because of the risk of fire or the limited space to prepare a cooked meal for so many men. The ships were victualled with leather sacks of grain to be pounded into flour and baked for bread, and well-stoppered jars of wine and water which were blended together before they were drunk. At every landing place the crews foraged enthusiastically and it was an unlucky shepherd or cowherd whose flocks or cattle were near the beach when the sailors landed. They stole whatever they could, butchered and ate the best animals on the spot, and carried off as many of the remainder as they could truss up and stow beneath the oar benches.
>
> FROM *The Ulysses Voyage* by Tim Severin

ROMAN SHIPS

The Romans had a fleet of giant transport ships able to take grain from Alexandria to Rome, perhaps 180 feet in length, and designed to carry 1,200 or 1,300 tons of grain. These were to the Roman World what oil supertankers are to ours. Lucian, in the first century AD, saw one of the Alexandrian grain fleet in Athens harbour (it had probably been blown off course) and describes it:

> What a size the ship was! 180 feet in length, the ship's carpenter told me, the beam more than a quarter of that, and 44 feet from the deck to the lowest point in the hold. And the height of the mast, and

what a yard it carried, and forestay held it up! And the way the stern rose up in a gradual curve ending in a gilded goose-head, matched at the other end by the forward, more flattened, sweep of the prow with its figures of Isis, the goddess the ship was named after, on each side! Everything was incredible: the rest of the decoration, the paintings, the red topsail, even more, the anchors with their capstans and winches, and the cabins aft. The crew was like an army. They told me she carried enough grain to feed every mouth in Athens for a year. And it all depends for its safety on one little old man who turns those great steering oars with a tiller that's no more than a stick. They pointed him out to me; woolly-haired little fellow, half-bald. Heron was his name, I think.

FROM *The Ship, or the Wishes*
a Dialogue by Lucian of Samosata

It is an interesting thought that the *Isis*, if she could carry more than a thousand tons of grain, was a good deal larger than any merchant-man sailing between Europe and America before 1820.

Isis would have carried several hundred passengers as well as cargo. The Apostles Paul and Luke, after their arrest in Caesaria were taken to Rome, with several other prisoners and under the charge of a centurion. The second 'leg' of their journey, from Myra (in Lycia) was aboard a grain freighter bound for Rome. 'And we were in all in the ship two hundred, three score and sixteen souls', writes Luke. The ship was wrecked in a storm off Malta, but all the passengers survived.

CARGOES

The period from 900–500 BC was a time of colonisation as Greeks and Phoenicians settled all over Asia Minor to the Black Sea, Sicily, Spain, Southern Italy and North Africa. These small states constantly exchanged goods. The most common cargo seems to have been grain – which was moved from places like the Black Sea and Egypt where there was a surplus, to small city states where there was a shortage. Wine, olive oil, dried fish and a fish paste called garum are also typical of a merchant cargo from this time. Knidos exported large quantities of wine, and cargoes could be very large – sometimes thousands of amphorae. Some ships had permanent fitted clay containers that could hold up to 4,000 litres.

This is a ship's manifest of cargo arriving in Alexandria, c.250 BC. The ship had been loaded in a Syrian port and carried 'gourmet' food, presumably for a very rich and discerning Egyptian.

table wine	15 jars
dessert wine	6 jars
olive oil	138 jars
dried figs	15 jars
honey	9 jars
wild boar meat	4 baskets
Black Sea nuts	2 containers
pomegranate seeds	2 jars
venison	2 crocks
goat's meat	1 crock
rough sponges	1 basket
soft sponges	1 basket
pure wool	22 lb in a box

FROM *The Ancient Mariners* by Lionel Casson

ROMAN TOURISTS

The Roman tourist travelled in a united world with a universal language. In this respect, at least, travel must have been rather easier than in the modern world (as you will soon discover if you try to sail from Turkish to Greek waters, something that involves much paperwork and large fees, despite quite good relations between the two governments).

If we could suddenly whisk ourselves back to the heyday of Pax Romana, who might we find travelling on this coast? The answer is an amazing variety of people, because travel by sea was cheaper and more comfortable than by land. There would have been a great variety of boats of all sizes, and we would meet Romans travelling for all sorts of different reasons.

Romans often travelled to make pilgrimages or for their health (the two were often combined). There was also medical merit in the sea journey itself. Aulus Celsus, a Roman medical authority of the first century AD, wrote 'in the case of tuberculosis, if the patient has the strength, a long sea voyage is called for . . . for this purpose, the voyage from Italy to Alexandria is perfect'.

Romans in poor health travelled to the sanctuaries of Asclepius. There was one of great importance at Kos, which was home to Hippocrates and his school of medicine. There was another in Pergamum, established by Galen. These were the Swiss clinics of their day, attracting well-heeled *malades-imaginaires* in search of a cure.

The procedure in these places was not unlike at pilgrimage places today. The patient entered the sanctuary, took a ritual bath to purify himself, entered Asclepius's temple, prayed, spread a pallet, and lay down on it to spend the night there.

This is a testimonial by a grateful Greek who, some time in the first or second century AD, visited the establishment which Asclepius shared with the Egyptian healing god Imhotep at Memphis:

It was night, when every living creature was asleep except those in pain; the moment when the divinity used to manifest itself in its more active state. I was burning with fever and convulsed with loss of breath and coughing because of the pain in my side. My head was heavy from my suffering and I was dropping off half-conscious into sleep. My mother . . . was sitting without enjoying even a brief moment of sleep, distraught at my torment. Suddenly she spied . . . a divine apparition, someone of more than human height, clothed in shining garments and holding in his left hand a book; he merely eyed me two or three times from head to foot and then disappeared. When she had recovered herself, she still all atremble, tried to wake me. Finding me drenched in sweat but with my fever completely gone, she knelt down in worship to the divine manifestation . . . When I spoke with her, she wanted to tell me about the god's unique ability, but I, anticipating her, told her all myself. For everything she had witnessed with her own eyes had appeared to me in my dreams. After these pains in my side had ceased, and the god had given me one more healing treatment, I propose his benefactions to all.

FROM Travel in the Ancient World by Lionel Casson

For Romans the Southern Aegean was renowned for its many 'sights' of great cultural interest. Cicero, writing in 70 BC, lists some half-dozen 'must-see' works of art. They include Praxiteles's statue of Aphrodite in Knidos and a painting of Aphrodite in Kos by Apelles (who was considered the greatest painter of the Ancient World). A half-century after Cicero wrote this, Augustus bought the painting and had it transported to Rome and installed in a temple dedicated to Caesar. Of Pliny's Seven Wonders of the Ancient World, three are in the South Aegean – the Colossus of Rhodes, the Temple of Diana at Ephesus, and the Mausoleum at Halicarnassus.

Praxiteles' statue of Aphrodite at Knidos set a standard by which all other sculpture was judged and was as famous and admired in the ancient world as the David by Michelangelo is in ours. Large sums were offered for the sculpture but the Knidians refused to sell it.

Aphrodite was visited and described by Lucian, a normally scathing satirist of the first century AD. Usually quick to mock, Lucian appears humbled by the masterpiece:

We then determined to enter the port of Knidos, in order to see the place and from an anxiety to visit the temple of Venus celebrated for its statue, the exquisite production of the skill of Praxiteles.

We gained the shore in almost perfect stillness, as if the goddess herself was guiding our path, under the influence of her own bright and unruffled serenity. Whilst the crew were occupied in the usual preparations I made the circuit of the town, having one of my agreeable companions on either arm . . . When we had visited the portico of Sostratus and had seen everything else that was interesting, we proceeded to the temple of Venus; Charicles and myself with eager curiosity, while Callicratides, who has a kind of aversion to the sight of women would rather have paid a visit to the Cupid of Thespiae.

In approaching the Sacred Inclosure we were fanned by the most delicious breezes, for within no polished pavement spreads its barren surface. As suited to a sanctuary of Venus, it abounds with productive trees extending their luxurious foliage to the sky and canopying the air around. Chiefly the blooming myrtle, fertile from earliest growth and covered with fruit, graces its mistress; nor do any of the other beautiful plants suffer from the decay of age, but are ever vigorous and putting forth new shoots.

Having satisfied ourselves with admiring these beauties of nature, we entered the temple. In the centre stands the goddess, in Parian marble – a most beautiful and splendid work. A half-suppressed smile is on her mouth. No drapery conceals her beauty, nor is any part hidden except that which is covered unconsciously, as it were, by the left hand. Such has been the consummate skill of the artist that the rigid and repulsive marble perfectly represents the delicate formation of every limb. Charicles, as if bereft of his senses, cried aloud 'Happy amongst the gods he that was enchained for thee', and springing forward with neck outstretched as far as possible, he repeatedly kissed the statue. Callicratides stood by in humble and silent admiration.

The temple has an entrance at either end so that the whole statue may be admired and examined. The second door is particularly intended for seeing the back of the statue. We were at once struck with the beauty of the figure. We could not refrain from repeated exclamations of admiration, and particularly on the harmony of the back, the wonderful fitting of the flesh to the bones, without too great plumpness, and the exquisite proportion of the thigh and the leg, extending in a straight line to the foot.

FROM *The Loves*, a dialogue by Lucian of Samosata

The statue remained at Knidos until the fifth century AD when, together with other classical treasures from these parts, it was removed to Constantinople by the Emperor Theodosius. There it was destroyed in a fire, which also consumed the imperial library of a hundred and twenty thousand books, including a unique copy of the *Iliad* and the *Odyssey*, written in letters of gold on the intestines of a serpent a hundred and twenty feet in length.

TEMPLES

Pilgrimages to the great sanctuaries were an important element within the animate bustle of the ancient trade routes. The two most famous temples on this coast were the Temple of Apollo at Didyma, and the Temple of the Fish at Sura. Here Pliny describes the Temple of the Fish at Sura:

> At Myra in Lycia at the fountain of Apollo whom they call Surius, the fish are summoned three times on the pipe. They come to give their augury. If they tear the pieces of meat thrown to them, this is good for the client, if they wave it away with their tails, this is bad.
>
> FROM *Historia Naturalis* by Pliny

A second description of the same shrine by the writer Polycharmus has also survived:

> When they come to the sea, where is the grove of Apollo by the shore, on which is the whirlpool and the sand, the clients present themselves holding two wooden spits, on each of which are ten pieces of roast meat. The priest takes his seat in silence by the grove, while the client throws the spits into the whirlpool and watches what happens. After the spits are thrown in the pool fills with sea water, and a multitude of fish appear as if by magic and of a size to cause alarm. The prophet announces the species of the fish and the client accordingly receives his answer from the priest. Among smaller fish there appear sometimes whales and sawfish and many strange and unknown kinds.
>
> FROM *A History of Lycia* by Polycharmus

Two thousand years later George Bean picks his scholarly way through these two variant descriptions:

> These accounts are at variance in one respect only, namely whether it was the species of the fish or their behaviour which determined the favourability of the oracle. We may also distrust the whales and sawfish, though of course sharks are not unknown on the Turkish coasts. But in all other respects it is interesting,

indeed fascinating, to observe how exactly the present conditions illustrate the ancient accounts. The 'harbour' is the marshy inlet, which was undoubtedly sea in antiquity; the fountain of Apollo is still there, a fine abundant spring which issues from the foot of the hill a few paces from the temple and quickly forms a good stream which flows through the marsh to the present sea-coast a mile or so distant. Just in front of the temple a number of springs well up in the stream, that is in the sea in antiquity, giving a swirling effect to the surface of the water; this agrees exactly with the local inhabitants' account of the 'whirlpool', and explains the curious expression 'a well of sea-water'. Even the mysterious filling of the pool could be managed easily enough by the priest by means of some apparatus to control the fountain of Apollo. There are not now, so far as the present writer could see, any actual structural remains that could be associated with the oracle, but they would hardly be expected to survive.

FROM Lycian Turkey by George E. Bean

Interestingly, both the temple of Apollo at Didyma and the Temple of the Fish at Sura are close to the coast and their visitors came mainly by boat. This is a modern description of a visit to the Temple of the Fish at Sura:

Untouched by coachloads of tourists that disgorge on the jetty, the ruins of the Temple of the Fish Oracle of Apollo, most famous of the Lycian oracles, sit serenely in a nearby valley. It is a pre-cipitous scramble to reach them. The holy site was later built on by the Byzantines, who left a ruined church in silent remem-brance. The sacred spring still bubbles healthily in a corner of the valley, flowing on through antique masonry to wind past what were once the steps of the temple, now marked by fallen columns half-buried in mud. Here the priests would toss sizzling kebabs into the water, making pronouncements according to the order in which different species of fish rose to take the meat. I had no meat to offer, but tried a packet of sesame biscuits, whose label claimed they were 'good for skin and sex'. But not, alas, for oracles: my offering sank without a fish rising or even moving among the gently swaying reeds. As I waited a frog croaked, a butterfly fluttered by and a pair of dragonflies made love. What would the priests have made of that?

FROM 'Aegean Odyssey' by Barnaby Rogerson in *Cornucopia*

The grandest and richest shrine on this coast was the Temple of Apollo Branchidae at Didyma, in the territory of the great classical city of Miletus. Next to Delphi, Didyma was the most renowned temple of the Hellenic world, and the third-largest edifice in the Ancient Greek World. Now it is a particularly beautiful and evocative ruin that stands dramatically in the middle of a village built mainly from stones from the temple complex. This is a description of a visit in 1764, by the antiquarian Richard Chandler:

In descending from the mountain toward the gulf, I had remarked in the sea something white on the farther side; and going afterwards to examine it, found the remains of a circular pier belonging to the port, which was called Panormus. The stones, which are marble, and about six feet in diameter, extend from near the shore; where are traces of buildings, probably houses, overrun with thickets of myrtle, mastic, and evergreens . . .

The temple of Apollo was . . . two miles and a half, from the shore . . . It is approached by a gentle ascent, and seen afar off; the land toward the sea lying flat and level. The memory of the pleasure which this spot afforded me will not be soon or easily erased. The columns yet entire are so exquisitely fine, the marble mass so vast and noble, that it is impossible perhaps to conceive greater beauty and majesty of ruin. At evening, a large flock of goats, returning to the fold, their bells tinkling, spread over the heap, climbing to browse on the shrubs and trees growing between the huge stones. The whole mass was illuminated by the declining sun with a variety of rich tints, and cast a very strong shade. The sea, at a distance was smooth and shining, bordered by a mountainous coast, with rocky islands. The picture was as delicious as striking. A view of part of the heap, with plates of the architecture of this glorious edifice, has

been engraved and published, with its history, at the expense of the
society of Dilettanti.

We found among the ruins, which are extensive, a plain stone
cistern, covered, except an end, with soil; many marble coffins,
unopened, or with the lids broken; and one, in which was a thigh
bone; all sunk deep in earth; with five statues, near each other, in a
row, almost buried. In the stubble of some Turkey wheat were a
number of bee-hives, each a long hollow trunk of wood headed like
a barrel, piled in a heap. An Armenian, who was with me, on our
putting up a hare, to my surprise slunk away. This animal, as I was
afterwards informed, is held in abomination by that people, and the
seeing it accounted an ill omen.

The temple of Apollo Didymaeus seeming likely to detain us
some time, we regretted the entire solitude of the spot, which
obliged us to fix our quarters at Ura. Our Armenian cook, who
tarried there with our baggage, sent us provisions ready dressed,
and we dined under a shady tree by the ruins. Our horses were tied,
and feeding by us. Our camel-leader testified his benevolence and
regard, by frequent tenders of his short pipe, and of coffee, which
he made unceasingly, sitting cross-legged by a small fire. The crows
settled in large companies round about, and the partridge called in
the stubble.

At our return in the evening to Ura, we found two fires, with
our kettles boiling, in the open air, amid the huts and thickets. A
mat was spread for us on the ground by one of them. The Turks of
Ura, about fourteen in number, some with long beards, sitting
cross-legged, helped to complete the grotesque circle. We were
lighted by the moon, then full, and shining in a blue cloudless sky.
The Turks smoked, talked, and drank coffee with great gravity,
composure, and deliberation. One entertained us with playing on
the Turkish guitar and with uncouth singing. The thin-voiced
women, curious to see us, glided as ghosts across the glades, in
white, with their faces muffled. The assemblage and the scene was
uncommonly wild, and as solemn as savage . . .

We retired after supper to one of the huts, which was near the
fire, and, like the rest, resembled a soldier's tent, being made with

poles inclining, as the two sides of a triangle, and thatched with straw. It was barely a covering for three persons lying on the ground. The furniture was a jar of salted olives . . .

FROM *Travels in Asia Minor 1764–5*
by Richard Chandler, edited by Edith Clay

This is a more recent description (1988) of the same temple by Brian Sewell, who visits with his friend Petter, but without Ayhan, his driver.

The Temple of Apollo was across the road. Petter & I went to it alone, for Ayhan had found some minor problem with the car that he thought required urgent cure, and it was a relief to wander in so strange and haunting a building without his intrusive presence . . .

In scale and grandeur it gives a clear impression of a Wonder of the World, for it is vast, and though all but three of its columns fell in the great earthquake of 1493, their tall stumps are still in position, and the walls of the *cella* still stand as they originally were, unroofed. One of the huge standing columns is unfinished in the sense that it is unfluted apart from a neat collar of fluting extending halfway down the topmost drum below the capital – evidence yet again that columns were sometimes fluted after the erection of buildings. The visitor must climb steps to the entrance, make his or her way through the remains of the thirty-two columns that supported the porch – a strange experience in itself for the stumps are not cleanly broken but like snapped tree trunks, and their bases are set so close as to obstruct passage, exclusive rather than welcoming – and then he must descend arched passages into the deep interior, which even in high summer seems unaccountably cool; here there still is a sacred spring, and there was once a grove or avenue of small trees leading to the shrine of Apollo, a tempietto within the temple, with the enchanting appeal of an enclosed garden – perhaps the first *hortus conclusus* that medieval northerners found so necessary in their imagery.

It was known as the fountain oracle of Apollo before the Ionians came, and the first temple (of which there is no trace) was approached by a sacred way from the nearby harbour of Panormus, flanked with enthroned portrait figures from the mid-sixth century BC, some of which stayed in position for 2,400 years before they were removed to the British Museum by Sir Charles Newton in 1858, who, having robbed the site, then abandoned it to confusion. One of these is inscribed 'Chares, son of Kleisis, Ruler of Teichioussa' (another dependency of Miletus, a few kilometres to the south-east); another, less appealing, is signed 'Eudemos made me'; all were presumably members of the Branchidae, a noble Carian family descended from Branchos, whose name is occasionally used for Didyma.

FROM *South from Ephesus* by Brian Sewell

The greatest and grandest city on the coast of Asia Minor was Ephesus, which was famous throughout the Roman Empire for its wealth and splendour. The Temple of Artemis, known as the Artemision, was the largest building of the Hellenic World, and one of the Seven Wonders. It was built over 120 years, and seems to have completely overawed its ancient visitors. It was described by Antipater of Sidon, who compiled a list of the Seven Wonders:

I have set eyes on the wall of lofty Babylon on which is a road for chariots, and the statue of Zeus by the Alpheus, and the hanging gardens, and the colossus of the Sun, and the huge labour of the high pyramids, and the vast tomb of Mausolus; but when I saw the house of Artemis that mounted to the clouds, those other marvels lost their brilliancy, and I said, 'Lo, apart from Olympus, the Sun never looked on aught (anything) so grand.'

FROM *Greek Anthology* by Antipater of Sidon

But the Artemision has completely disappeared. In her travel book *Ionia: A Quest* (1954), Freya Stark searches for the ghost of the Temple of Artemis amongst the ruins of Ephesus:

Few places can minister like the site of the temple in Ephesus to the triumph of Time. The process of building, ever richer and more magnificent, went on through centuries, till the stream of religion changed its bed, and offerings which had raised the second temple in the age of Alexander (or the third or fourth as the case may be), failed after the looting of the Goths six hundred years later. Yet for eight or nine hundred years the riches of the faithful were brought to a shrine where an ancient goddess and her priestesses had become transformed into the Grecian Artemis with Amazons; and the final ruin, when it came, was less due to foreign barbarians than to Christian zeal, to the collector's fervour, and to Justinian, who transported what marble he could to Constantinople.

What is now left of one of the richest of sanctuaries is sunk in a swampy hollow: and indeed nothing is left except an ideal shape floating with known dimensions in the mind and anchored to a single block of existing masonry, the moulded base of the podium, by which alone the two latest floor levels of the temple can be defined. The whole of the altar, filled, one may say, with the works of Praxiteles; the pillars given by Croesus; the one hundred and forty-seven pillars, some with figure-sculptured bases, the gifts of kings; all must be attached in the mind's eye to this poor piece to reconstruct what was once one of the Seven Wonders.

The tourist agency will tell you that it is not worth visiting; nor is it, if the tangible alone is to count in this world. But if we treat history as a friend, and ease its bets with love and knowledge, the imagination can supply much of truth; as in a palimpsest, the ghost of the temple of Artemis stands in the swamp. Sad hillocks of archaeological mud surround it, where fig trees grow on the bare ground and a man is ploughing the earth of lives long past. A wandering cow rubs herself and flicks her ropy tail against the single stone, passive now with its meaning and purpose forgotten, yellow and delicate as an old woman's hand that lies idle among shapeless draperies of age. Every other vestige the restlessness of man has carried away, or the swamp has eaten.

FROM *Ionia: A Quest* by Freya Stark

This is another description of Ephesus, by Patrick Kinross:

Ephesus, like Miletus, is cut off from the sea this time by the Little Meander. Thus, unlike Smyrna, much of it survives in ruin. From an amphitheatre of rough blue hills, its bay lay spread like an arena beneath us, its waters stained at the river's mouth by a tell-tale crescent of mud, its roadstead filled with a half-moon of land, where camels grazed on soft pink mosses. Here is no landlocked trough, like the harbour of Smyrna, but a broader, windswept gulf, swayed by the varying moods of the Aegean. In a north wind it sulks, in a west wind it rages, in an east wind it scintillates, lucid and clear, the walls of Colophon moving sharply into focus beyond it.

Where the camels now graze a fair wind brought St Paul, sailing in a galley from Corinth, up the channel and into the harbour of Ephesus. The quay where he landed, the baths where travellers washed off the grime of the journey, now peter out into a marshy wilderness. But the street up which he walked, from the harbour to the city, survives, twelve yards broad and paved with marble, revealing traces of a colonnade, of statues, of porticoes, befitting a triumphal avenue. It culminates in the theatre, hewn from one of the twin hills which mark the site of the city, a place designed on a sumptuous scale, no longer for the intimate Greek drama but for the lavish Roman spectacle. Its audiences – at least in the upper rows – had much to distract them from the scene, since the centre of Ephesus, compact for all its grandeur, lay, as its ruins still lie, visibly spread beneath them.

There, at the foot of long and crowded avenues, was the harbour, crowded with shipping. Here, at the head of it, is the gymnasium with its spacious courtyards, where they could watch the youth of the city at its sports. To the left another marble street, hardly less wide than the first, with vaulted drains beneath it, leads to the agora, the bazaar where the merchants traded in an opulent Roman setting, beneath a wealth of imperial inscriptions. Adjoining it stands the public library, a retreat well suited, by contrast, to the affairs of the mind. Its calm harmonious reading-room, once paved with mosaic and adorned by statues of Wisdom, Virtue, Fortune and Knowledge, gives on to a marble courtyard. Its shelves are let into the walls, by a practical municipality, in such a way as to protect the books from damp, and raised on a surrounding marble ledge to protect them against dirt and damage. Between them is a niche for the statue of Celsus, the Roman senator and Governor-General of Asia whose heirs built the library in his honour; marble panels on the walls were inscribed with his biography in Latin and Greek; and his body lies in a marble sarcophagus, adorned with garlands, beneath the library – a resting place becoming to any scholar or patron of literature. To the right of the theatre, quarried out of the hillside, a stadium, as big as a pair of football fields, looks out over the plain where the city's leading industry once stood: the Temple of Artemis, that Diana of the Ephesians whom St Paul was to challenge and eventually defeat.

FROM *Europa Minor* by Patrick Kinross

The Chimaera – an unquenchable flame that the ancients took to be the work of the gods – is mentioned by Homer and other authors of the ancient world, but it was always assumed that this was a myth. But in the early nineteenth century it was rediscovered by Captain Francis Beaufort, when surveying the coast of eastern Lycia. It fact it still burns today. This is Captain Beaufort's account of the discovery:

We had seen from the ship the preceding night a small but steady light among the hills; on mentioning the circumstance to the inhabitants we learnt that it was a Xanar, or volcanic flame, and they offered to supply us horses and guides to examine it.

We rode about 2 hours through a fertile plain, partly cultivated, and then winding up a rocky and thickly wooded glen, we arrived at the place. In the corner of a ruined building the wall is undermined so as to leave an aperture of about 3 feet diameter, and shaped like the mouth of a man – from this the flame issues, giving out an intense heat, yet producing no soot on the wall.

The phenomenon appears to have existed here for many ages, as unquestionably this is the place to which Pliny alludes in the following passage: 'Mt Chaimaera, near Phaselis, emits an unceasing flame, that burns day and night'. We did not, however, find the adjacent mountains of Hephaestia quite so inflammable as he describes them.

FROM *Karamania* by Captain Francis Beaufort

Dr Edward Clarke, a few years later, on board a Turkish warship, sees the Chimaera:

Stupendous mountains, as the shadows increased, appeared close to the ship, towering above our top-masts; the higher parts being covered with snow, or partly concealed by thick clouds; the air around us becoming every instant more sultry and stagnant. Presently the whole atmosphere was illuminated. The mountains seemed to vomit fire. A pale but vivid lightning darted innumerable flashes over every object, even among the masts and rigging. Never surely was such a scene elsewhere exhibited! The old Greek pilots crossed themselves; but comforted us with the assurance that this appearance of the kindling elements was common upon this coast; and that it denoted favourable weather. We heard little thunder; but streams of living light ran continually from the summits of the mountains towards the sea, and, seeming to separate before they reached the water, filled the air with coruscations. Since, reflecting upon this circumstance as characterizing the coast, it seems to explain a fabulous notion which the Ancients entertained of the Chimaera disgorging flames upon the Lycian territory, alluded to by Ovid in the wandering of Biblis.

FROM *Travels in Various Countries of Europe, Asia and Africa*
by Dr Edward D. Clarke

This is a more recent description of the Chimaera, by George Bean:

Olympus is noted for its high-quality saffron, for Bishop Methodius, its only distinguished citizen, and above all for the perennial fire which burns on the mountain close by.

This remarkable phenomenon lies some 800 or 900 feet up in the hills a few miles to the north-west of Olympus. On foot it is reckoned an hour and a half each way, but with a vehicle capable of travelling over sand and loose shingle it is possible to drive to the foot of the mountain, from where it is a short half-hour's climb to the spot. The path is a good one, and in several places remains of the ancient paved way are to be seen. The fire, called by the Turks *Yanar*, has been burning continuously since classical antiquity at least, and no doubt since long before then, though it changes its appearance from time to time.

As a whole the hillside is thickly wooded, but at one point is an open space almost bare of vegetation, some 50 yards wide and long, strewn with white and grey stones. Towards the bottom of this the fire is burning in a deep hole 2 or 3 feet in width; at night it is visible from far out to sea, but by day it is much less spectacular. The flame hardly rises above the mouth of the hole; its volume is about that of a small bonfire. This is very much the same that Beaufort saw in 1811, but other reports vary considerably. Spratt in 1842 says that in addition to the large flame there were smaller jets issuing from crevices in the sides of a crater-like cavity 5 or 6 feet deep . . . At present there is only one minor place where a gas emerges, just above the main fire on the south side; it burns only when a match is applied.

There are numerous ancient notices of the *Yanar*, and all agree that the flame cannot be quenched with water, but only by throwing earth or rubbish on it – though, of course, it will break out again. How many and how large vents there were in antiquity is uncertain; today the minor fire is easily extinguished by a small quantity of either soil or of water, and can even be blown out, and the main flame, too, will succumb to a glass of water, though it re-ignites itself in ten or fifteen seconds.

FROM *Turkey's Southern Shore* by George E. Bean

CHAPTER FIVE

Travellers in the Nineteenth Century

Descriptions by early travellers within the Ottoman Empire tend to be focused on the great trading cities of the Levant, especially the port of Beirut in the Lebanon, Aleppo in Syria and Smyrna (modern Izmir) in the centre of the Aegean. Even those travellers who had no interest in business were forced to follow the existing trade routes which connected these cities together. Smyrna was the hub that lay at the heart of all these maritime routes, so that the first travellers within the Ottoman Turkey inevitably spent time in this port-city. As it was often their first sight of Asia, it usually made a big impression. It was a beautiful city, mainly built in wood, with separate quarters for the Levantines, Armenians, Jews and Turks.

A visitor to Smyrna in the early nineteenth century was Thomas Hope, a wealthy son of an Anglo-Dutch banking dynasty, whose Eastern travels were amongst the most successful and ambitious of his day. His visit to Smyrna inspired his novel *Anastasius*, where Hope created a fictional Greek anti-hero who betrays and schemes his way around Turkey. Here Hope's villainous narrator portrays, with some distaste, mercantile Smyrna, before providing a vivid portrait of a regional Aga:

Had my fancy for trade continued in full force, Smyrna was the place in which to gratify that taste to the utmost of my faculties. In that trucking, trafficking city, people's ideas run upon nothing but merchandise: their discourse only varies between the exchanges and the markets: their heads are full of figs and raisins, and their whole hearts wrapped up in cotton and broad-cloths: they suppose man created for nothing but to buy and sell; and whoever makes not these occupations the sole business of his life, seems to them to neglect the end of his existence. I verily believe that they marry for no other purpose but to keep up the race of merchants and bankers.

But that unbounded indulgence in the luxuries of commerce was rather calculated to give a man of my variable appetite a surfeit of its sweets. Full two months had now elapsed since I first launched into the commercial line, a circumstance sufficient in itself to diminish my enthusiasm for its charms; and in the course of those two months a single fortunate speculation had rendered me independent of its drudgery. I therefore slackened in my ardour, began to lose the good opinion of the Smyrniotes, and, reciprocating their abated regard, resolved again to return to Stambool; there to become, if possible, a pasha for my money. The plan, indeed, might not be quite consistent with my recent solemn renunciation of all ambitious schemes, when yet fresh from seeing their dismal end in Valachia; but, when was I consistent? or when was not the wish to rise the ruling passion of my soul?

My last mercantile transaction at Smyrna consisted in buying of Isaac-bey a pair of pistols, made for use in England, and rendered ornamental in Turkey. They were destined for Hadjee Bollad-Ogloo, chief of the mighty house of Kara-Osman, lords paramount of a great part of Anadoly. I had long purposed visiting this venerable old aga (for notwithstanding his real power, his nominal rank rose no higher), at Magnesia his residence; and now, in my way to the capital, put the often abandoned scheme in execution.

When presented to the chief, in his thriving residence, 'Accept these arms,' said I, 'as the homage of a grateful traveller, who has found them useless amid the security which you have established in your wide domain.'

Hadjee-Bollad received my offering, not with the contemptuous indifference of a Constantinopolitan upstart, afraid lest the smallest symptom of admiration should be construed into an acknowledgement of inferiority; but with the courteousness of one, whose ancestors for many generations back had stood high in public estimation, as well as himself. He praised the beauty of the present, and appeared anxious to make an immediate trial of its excellence. 'Age,' said he, 'has somewhat impaired my strength; but between this sort of weapon and my hand there has subsisted so long an acquaintance, that they often still seem to understand each other, almost without my participation.'

He then, from his very seat, took aim across the wooden trellis of the window at a magpie, chattering on the top of a cypress tree in the court. To this bird had been given the name Tchapan-Ogloo. It was that of another great territorial proprietor in Anadoly, the rival of the house of Kara-Osman in wealth, in power, and in extent of domain. He fired, exclaiming, 'Fall, Tchapan-Ogloo!' and brought down the bird.

'I do not know,' continued he, in great glee at this achievement, 'whether you think your present thrown away, but I am quite sure that the one here suing for your acceptance cannot be better bestowed.' This was a handsome horse, richly caparisoned, which Hadjee-Bollad desired of me to keep, 'in remembrance,' he said, 'of the patriarch of Magnesia'.

Impatient to justify his compliment, I vaulted into the saddle, wrested a spear out of the hands of an attendant, and at full gallop hurled it deep into the trunk of the tree on which had sat the magpie.

'Well done!' cried the Aga. 'Your race, I perceive, has resembled my own: with this difference, that you are just starting in the career, and that I am near its end. You may tell them so at Stambool; but lest their joy at hearing it be too extravagant, tell them too that the old stock leaves a few offsets like yourself!'

I had intended to continue my journey the same evening: but, without pressing me to stay, the lord of Magnesia seemed to have contemplated my going away again so soon as a thing so totally impossible, that I felt not resolution sufficient to take leave. I had not even the opportunity of representing the prolongation of my visit as a deviation from my original plan. To the Aga's hospitable disposition, it would have appeared like owning a nefarious design.

Seeing me in admiration of the activity and bustle which prevailed throughout his residence; of the piles of cotton, the strings of camels, the goods loading and unloading, and the guides coming and going on every side: 'This,' said the Aga, 'is only our peace establishment; but we are equally well equipped for war. At a day's notice we can bring into the field twenty thousand sturdy horsemen, as well mounted as armed for the defence of the empire or for our own!'

'And with so much wealth,' cried I, 'and so much power, you have been able to avoid thus long the sultan's dangerous honours?'

'It has cost us little,' hastily rejoined Hadjee. 'We have paid greater sums to keep our heads out of the noose than others do to thrust their necks into it: but simple agas we came into the world, and simple agas we are determined, God granting, to go out of it. Independence, and the right of leaving our vast domain, inherited from a long line of ancestors, to a long line of descendents, would be ill exchanged for the empty name of the vizier, with servitude as the certain, and confiscation of the paternal estate as the probable result.'

At this moment a steward advanced to inform Hadjee, that a troop of Albanians, fled from the oppression of some Roumiliote pasha, were just come to crave his protection, and to beg some employment, or some waste land.

'Tell them,' replied the Aga, 'they shall have both.' Then turning to me: 'in granting such requests,' he added, 'the giver is the gainer.' I praised him for his liberality.

'Praise me for my sense,' answered he, 'in having discovered that my income bears more fruit in my tenants' hands than in my own coffers. You complimented me on the security of my roads. It was obtained, not by watching my subjects, but by giving them work. When people toil in mind and in body to improve their own property, they have not leisure to covet that of others.'

For three days my ears feasted on Hadjee's wisdom, and my palate on his good fare: the dawn of the fourth ushered in the preparations for my departure. 'I suppose,' said my kind host, 'that you only quit my residence for that of the younger branches of my family, at Bergamo and at Yayakeui.' Without pledging myself to perform this more extensive circuit, I begged permission on my return from Stambool again to visit the chief himself. 'Then do not tarry long,' answered Hadjee: 'I myself have a journey to perform, in which, old as I am, I may safely engage to outrun you, in spite of all your activity.' On this we took leave. I mounted my new horse, and departed.

But though my person sped onward, my mind, as if wholly detached from its case of flesh and blood, continued stationary with Hadjee. It seemed riveted to the happy spot where the old aga exercised his mild dominion; and all the way to Constantinople, my thoughts still dwelt at Magnesia. There was in its to me novel scene in what tranquil enjoyment of life's present sweets, first truly witnessed under Hadjee's friendly roof, an inexpressible charm. It left insipid, it almost converted into positive pain in the comparison, the pitiful half-tasted pleasures, snatched from fleeting time by the wretched victim to ambitious schemes: schemes of which the labour is certain, the accomplishment doubtful, and the very success productive only of fruits too often insipid or bitter.

It was true, indeed, that many possessed not the means thus to saunter at leisure, like Hadjee-aga, along paths strewed with roses. The greater number of mortals must first clear their way through tracks bristling with thorns and briars: they must toil to support life, ere they could afford leisure for its enjoyment. I myself had experienced that condition: I myself had been obliged to labour of no avail to obtain it; and only an event wholly unlooked-for amid all my schemes had at last given me that independence, so long pursued in vain.

But I finally possessed it: and I might now purchase every luxury of life, calculated to content the man exempt from ambition's maddening thirst: I might now command every species of tangible gratification, save only that which consists in the power of diffusing very extensive misery. Pleasant dwellings, a plenteous board, a handsome retinue of servants, a well-assorted harem, and whatever else was of a nature directly to delight the sense, were things now within my easy reach; and the only circumstance still wanting to set them off to the greatest advantage, was the power of inflicting a certain quantity of starvation and torture, wherever the too bright sunshine of the picture might require the relief of deeper shadows; the right to maintain a certain number of humble instruments and witnesses of my pleasures, who should tremble at my frown, and turn pale when I spoke.

Here, also from *Anastasius*, Hope conjures an insight into eighteenth-century fashion as modelled by the engaging character Aly:

As my former connexions with the arsenal gave me a certain predilection for whatever belonged to the navy, I speedily formed an acquaintance with one of the tchawooshes of the captain-pasha, who, like myself, was only a passenger. Aly was his name, and Crete his country. This latter circumstance added much, in my eyes, to the merit of his society. The Turks of Candia, by their constant inter-marriages with Greek women, to whom they permit every latitude of worship, become divested of much of their Mohammedan asperity, and Aly, himself half a Greek, was not entitled to any great prejudice against me for being only half a Turk. In the refinements of his toilet, however, Aly tchawoosh might be considered as a finished Osman-lee. Nothing could exceed the exquisite taste of his apparel. His turban attracted the eye less even by its costliness of texture than by its elegance of form. A band of green and gold tissue, diagonally crossing the forehead, was made with studious ease completely to conceal one ear, and as completely to display one other. From its fringed extremity always hung suspended, like a tassel, a rose or a carnation, which, while it kept caressing the wearer's broad and muscular throat, sent up its fragrance to his disdainful nostril. An hour every day was the shortest time allotted to the culture of his adored mustachios, and to the various rites which these idols of his vain-glorious heart demanded such as changing their hue from a bright flaxen to a jetty black, perfuming them with rose and amber, smoothing their straggling hairs, and giving their taper ends a smart and graceful curve. Another hour was spent in refreshing the scarlet dye of his lips, and tinting the dark shade of his eyelids, as well as in practicing the most fascinating smile and the archest leer which the terzhana could display. His dress of the finest broad-cloth and velvet, made after the most dashing Barbary cut, was covered all over with gold embroidery, so thickly embossed as to appear almost massive. His chest, uncovered down to the girdle, and his arms bared up to the shoulder, displayed all the bright polish of his skin. His capote was draped so as with infinite grace to break the too formal symmetry of his costume. In short, his handjar with its gilt handle, his watch with its concealed miniature, his tobacco-pouch of knitted gold, his pipe mounted in opaque amber, and his pistols with diamond-cut hilt, were all in the style of the most consummate petit maître; and if, in spite of all his pains, my friend Aly was not without exception the handsomest man in the Othoman empire, none could deny his being one of the best dressed. His air and manner harmonised with his attire. A confident look, an insolent and sneering tone, and an indolent yet swaggering gait, bespoke him to be, what indeed it was his utmost ambition to appear, a thorough rake. Noisy, drunken, quarrelsome, and expert alike in the exercise of the bow (the weapon of the country), and in that of the handjar, he possessed every one of the accomplishments of those heroes chiefly met with on the quays of Constantinople, whom a modest woman avoids, and to whom a respectable man always gives way.

FROM *Anastasius* by Thomas Hope

The Rev. Francis Arundell, in *A Visit to the Seven Churches of Asia*, describes Ephesus in 1828. Arundell was the resident British chaplain in Smyrna, and this reads very like a sermon. The anti-Islamic sentiments are not untypical of visitors to the Christian sites of Asia Minor in the nineteenth century:

What would have been the astonishment and grief of the beloved Apostles and Timothy if they could have foreseen that a time would come when there would be in Ephesus neither angel, nor church, nor city! When the great city would become 'heaps, a desolation, a dry land, and a wilderness, a land wherein no man dwelleth, neither doth any son of man pause there long!' Once it held an idolatrous temple celebrated in magnificence as one of the wonders of the world, and the mountains of Corissus and Prion re-echoed the shouts of 10,000 tongues, 'great is Diana of the Ephesians'. Once it had Christian temples almost rivalling the pagan in splendour, where many tongues moved by the Holy

Ghost made public avowal 'Great is Lord Jesus'. Once it had a bishop, the angel of the church, Timothy, the beloved disciple of St John, and tradition reports that it was honoured with the last days of both these great men and of the mother of our Lord. Some centuries passed on and altars of Jesus were again thrown down to make way for the delusions of Mahomet; the cross is removed from the nave of the church and crescent glitters in its stead, while within the keble is a substitute for the altar. A few years more and all may be silence.

Even the sea has retired from the scene of desolation and a pestilential morass, covered with mud and rushes, has succeeded to the waters which brought up the ships laden with merchandise from every country.

FROM *A Visit to the Seven Churches of Asia*
by Rev. Francis Arundell

Beyond Smyrna travel was uncomfortable and occasionally dangerous. Roads were bad, but accommodation was available at a network of 'khans'. We can get a very good idea of what it was like to travel in Turkey in the mid-nineteenth century from the journals of Charles Fellows, an enterprising gentleman-scholar who travelled extensively in Lycia and other parts of south-west Turkey between 1838 and 1842. Conditions for the tourist were still uncomfortable, but not dangerous:

Hoping that some of my friends may be induced to visit this interesting country, I shall give a few hints as to the machinery of travelling, which may be found of use to them. A tent is the first requisite, the old cities and places of the greatest interest being frequently distant from the modern towns or khans; and a good tent makes the traveller quite independent of the state of health of the town, which I found a very important advantage. It is desirable that the tent should be of a waterproof material. I found great use in an oil-cloth hammock, which was occasionally slung from pole to pole, but always of service to spread under my mattress when the ground was wet. A carpet may be procured in the country, but a mattress must be taken; also a canteen, containing the usual requisites for cooking and for making tea, and a lantern. Arrowroot is the most portable and convenient material for the traveller's store; it may be prepared in five minutes, and a basin of this will stay the appetite until the dinner can be prepared, which, what with pitching the tent, lighting the fire (often with green-wood), and the process of cooking, must be frequently delayed an hour or two after the traveller halts. Rice is necessary, and tea a great treasure.

I have always found the convenience of carrying a gimblet among my travelling stores; it is a substitute for nail, hook, and hammer: inserted into the wall it forms a peg by which my clothes are frequently kept from the dirty or damp floor, or to which I can hang my glass, watch, or thermometer. The traveller will of course be prepared with every requisite for the tailor, and will take a few simple medicines.

The most acceptable presents to the inhabitants are not such as are of the greatest intrinsic value, but articles of use which it is difficult for them to procure. The traveller will do well to supply himself with copper caps for the people in authority who have had percussion guns given to them, but which are rendered useless from the want of these, and also gunpowder for the peasantry: by all classes a sheet of writing-paper is much valued; leads for patent pencil-cases are very acceptable; and a common box-compass will furnish much pleasure, occasionally directing the Mahometan to the point for his prayers. I have been often asked in a delicate manner by the Greeks if I possessed a picture of our queen or reigning sovereign; a common print of this kind would be highly prized.

The traveller sleeping in a room without glazed windows, in a tent, or on the floor, will find the bed which I will attempt to describe a great treasure. For the plan of this bed I was many years ago indebted to my friend Mr Godfrey Levinge, and have ever since by its use been rendered independent of all the insect world. The gnats, flies, beetles, etc., never agreeable even if harmless, are constantly attracted by the light of the candles or the warmth of the mattress; and this simple contrivance I have found the only plan for preventing their intrusion. Thus insuring an undisturbed night, I have cared little for their attacks by day. The whole apparatus may be compressed into a hat-case. A pair of calico' sheets (No. 1.), six feet long, sewed together at the bottom and on both sides, are continued with muslin of the same form and size sewed to them at their open end (no. 2), and this muslin is drawn tightly together at the end with a tape; within this knot are three or four loose tapes, about 18 inches long, with nooses at their ends, through which, from within, a cane is threaded so as to form a circle, extending the muslin as a canopy, which in this form is suspended.

FROM 'Remarks for the Guidance of Travellers'
in *Journal written during an excursion in Asia Minor*
by C. Fellows

Unlike so many of his contemporaries, Fellows is refreshingly unprejudiced about the local population or their religion. In his preface he is candid about his prejudices on arrival:

It will be gathered from my Journal that at the time of my arrival in the country I was strongly biased in favour of the Greeks, and equally prejudiced against the Turks; and it will be seen in the course of the narrative how this unfavourable idea of the Turkish character was gradually removed by a personal intimacy with the people, generally in situations where they were remote from every restraint but those which their religion imposes.

One of the most widely-read books of the mid-nineteenth century about travel in Ottoman Turkey was William Kinglake's *Eothen* of 1845. Here he describes Smyrna:

Smyrna, or *Giaour Izmir*, 'Infidel Smyrna', as the Mussulmans call it, is the main point of commercial contact betwixt Europe and Asia; you are there surrounded by the people and the confused customs of many and various nations; you see the fussy European adopting the East, and calming his restlessness with the long Turkish 'pipe of tranquility'; you see Jews offering services, and receiving blows: on one side you have a fellow whose dress and beard would give you a good idea of the true oriental, if it were not for the gobemouche expression of countenance with which he is swallowing an article in a French newspaper; and there, just by, is a genuine Osmanlee, smoking away with all the majesty of a Sultan; but before you have time to admire sufficiently his tranquil dignity and his soft Asiatic repose, the poor old fellow is ruthlessly run down by an English midshipman, who has set sail on a Smyrna hack. Such are the incongruities of the 'infidel city' at ordinary times; but when I was there our friend Carrigaholt had imported himself, and his oddities, as an accession to the other and inferior wonders of Smyrna.

Every day after breakfast this lover of the Good and the Beautiful held a levee: in his ante-room there would not only be the sellers of pipes and slippers and shawls and suchlike oriental merchandise – not only embroiderers and cunning workmen patently striving to realize his visions of Albanian dresses – not only the servants offering for places, and the slave dealer tendering his sable ware, but there would be the Greek master waiting to teach his pupil the grammar of the soft Ionian tongue in which he was to delight the wife of his imagination, and the music master who was to teach him some sweet replies to the anticipated tones of the fancied guitar; and then, above all, and proudly eminent with undisputed preference of entrée, and fraught with the mysterious tidings on which the realization of the whole dream might depend, was the mysterious watch-maker.

FROM *Eothen* by William Kinglake

Before the invention of the steam engine a journey to Smyrna, via Gibraltar, took at least a month, and if the weather was bad or the wind failed to blow, it could take much longer and was very dangerous. But by 1840 there were railway lines linking the great cities of Europe and the first steamboats were coming down the Danube. Using a combination of both it was possible to reach Smyrna in only ten days from London, a change that must have seemed simply astonishing at the time.

Murray's first *Handbook for Travellers in Turkey*, published in 1854, gives an impression of how fast the world was changing.

The main routes from England to Turkey direct are:
I. From London to Constantinople, by Vienna, the Danube, and the Black Sea (in about 10 days).

From London to Vienna, by Ostend, Cologne, Dresden, and Prague in about 72 hours. Vienna to Constantinople, by the Danube and Black Sea, in about 7 days. A quick steamer leaves Vienna every Friday at 9 a.m. reaching Galatz on the following Tuesday afternoon. Here passengers are trans-shipped into a larger steamer, and reach Constantinople on the following Thursday. To reach Constantinople by this route or the next (II) need not cost more than £20 first class. Second-class fare is about one-third less.

A variation of this route would be to leave the steamer at Semlin, and then ride to Constantinople from Belgrade.

II. From London to Constantinople, by Vienna and Trieste (in about 12 days).

London to Trieste, by Ostend and Vienna in about 5 days. Trieste to Constantinople in about 7 days, by the Austrian Lloyd's Steamers, which start every Thursday at 4 p.m., stopping at Corfu, Syra, Smyrna, the Dardanelles, &c.

III. From Southampton to Constantinople, by Gibraltar and Malta (in about 15 days).

The Peninsular and Oriental Company's Steamers sail from Southampton for Smyrna and Constantinople on the 27th of every month. Fare, first-class, £30; second-class, £19. Also on the 4th and 20th of every month for Malta, whence there are French steamers to Athens, Smyrna, and Constantinople, on the 5th, 15th, and 25th of every month.

It will be seen that, of the above Routes, I and II are both cheaper and more expeditious than III. All heavy luggage should be sent by the Mediterranean steamers, to meet the traveller at Smyrna or Constantinople. Full information may be obtained at the Peninsular and Oriental Company's offices, 122, Leadenhall Street.

FROM Murray's *Handbook for Travellers in Turkey*

A revised edition of Murray's *Handbook* came out in 1873, nineteen years later. By this time the Danube route from London to Constantinople took only five days, and was considerably more comfortable.

The age of steam also brought a new kind of luxury tourist. In 1888 Edith Wharton, the wealthy American writer, chartered the steam yacht *Vanadis*. After cruising in the Aegean she briefly stopped in Smyrna, before proceeding to Rhodes. She describes the bazaar in Smyrna:

> There are trains of loaded camels, the donkeys with necklaces of large blue beads to protect them from the evil eye, the stalls hung with silks from Aleppo, the open spaces planted with blossoming acacias, the latticed fountains, the mosques with their fore-courts and minarets for the bazaars are a city in themselves, with khans, mosques, cafés, squares and fountains. Then there are the picturesque people: the Turkish women in brightly striped garments like dominoes, with yellow shoes, and black veils over their faces; the Jewesses wearing long, loose robes of silk, with little caps embroidered in gold on their plaited hair, the gorgeous canvasses of the foreign consulates, in embroidered dresses, with sashes full of jewelled pistols and *yataghans*, the old Turks in flowing robes and white turbans, the lemonade-sellers in bright yellow coats, the negresses in gaudy colours, the gypsies, the Greek priests, all forming a medley of different types which I have never seen equalled anywhere.
>
> Nothing, in fact, can be more curious than the mixture of Orientalism and European civilization which meets one at every turn in Smyrna. I could not get used to seeing the tramways blocked by trains of loaded camels, the *voitures-de-place* filled with veiled Turkish women, and the savage-looking Turks and Albanians with weapons in their belts, side by side with fashionably-dressed Levantines and Europeans. In Frank Street one can buy Zola's last novel, a ready-made dress, or a *batterie de cuisine*, while in the bazaars close by are sold *narghilehs*, clogs from Bagdad, *rahat-loukoum*, and other Eastern products.

FROM *The Cruise of the Vanadis* by Edith Wharton

CHAPTER SIX

Twentieth-Century Travellers

Tourism was remarkably late in reaching this part of the Mediterranean. Until at least the mid-1980s the Turkish coast from
Antalaya to Kuşadasi remained a package-holiday-free zone, and a
paradise for any reasonably adventurous independent traveller. Long
after Ibiza and the Algarve and the Costa Smeralda were covered
in concrete, the south-west coast of Asia Minor remained more or
less untouched. Twenty years after the invention of the jumbo jet,
Marmaris was still an orange grove, Bodrum was still a fishing village,
Datça did not exist and Kalkan was still a crumbling, semi-abandoned
Greek village on an inaccessible part of the coast of Lycia.

With hindsight we can see that a combination of extremely
fortunate circumstances conspired to make the Turquoise Coast a
difficult place to 'develop' in the 1960s and 1970s. Firstly, the roads
and other infrastructure of tourism remained in a poor condition
until very late. Secondly, south-west Turkey was fortunate to have
had very few airports. Dalaman opened to civilian traffic only in
1982. Bodrum Milas airport opened in 1999. Package operators
turned to other, more easily developed areas, such as Pamphylia, to
the east of Antalya.

H. V. Morton, the prolific and much-read travel writer of the first
half of the last century, published *In the Steps of St Paul* in 1936. He
laments the lack of a 'good motoring road'. It was many decades
before that road was constructed. The bus journey from Antalya to
Marmaris in the 1960s took two days (according to Michael Pereira,
author of *Mountains and Shore*). A road from Marmaris to Datça was
opened in 1956, but the bus journey, according to George Bean, took
eight hours, and food was hard to come by on arrival. The thirty
kilometres from Datça on to Knidos remained a bumpy dirt track

until the 1990s. The coast road of Lycia, connecting Kalkan and Kaş, was completed only in 1988.

It took many decades for this coast to recover from almost ten years of war (from 1914 to 1923) and the shock of the Exchange of Populations in 1924 (see chapter seven), when under the terms of the Treaty of Lausanne the Greek population moved to Symi, Rhodes, Crete and other islands. In some areas, like the Datça peninsula, this caused the loss of perhaps one third to one half of the population and near-paralysis of the local economy.

Irfan Orga, a Turkish writer resident in London, returned to Izmir in the mid-1950s:

The Aegean Sea sparkled and, from the shore, windows winked in the sun. Izmir came closer, a toy city of white houses and new concrete wharves. The boat heaved gently, creaking. The glare from the noonday sun was intense, burning my eyes even behind dark glasses.

There was a smell of salt in the air, and something tangyer, lemon trees perhaps. The seagulls swooped, cruel-beaked, low over the water. A gannet cruised on long wings, dazzlingly white where the sun caught the downy underbelly. It fell suddenly, like an arrowhead, sending up a tall shower of spray as it plunged into the sea after fish.

In the foreground the peak of Kadife Kale rose mistily, heat hazed, the shifting shadows violet coloured, and tenuous as spun sugar. Farther back the undulating curves of Manisa Dağ were like pale watered silk, their peaks growing less and less substantial as they climbed to the brazen sky.

Passengers began to crowd the rails, their suitcases, wicker baskets and other belongings dumped beside them, so that to step back was to be in danger of breaking one's leg.

It was hot. We all complained of the heat, resenting its invisible presence. We mopped our steaming faces, loosened our too civilised ties, discarded our jackets, and commiserated with each other's discomfort.

We sailed close inshore, the wake widening out behind us like quicksilver broken into little drops by the eddying waves. Sickened by the smell of sweat mixed with stale perfume, I took my small case and went under the captain's bridge where it was shadier but just as hot. With the aid of binoculars I watched the city coming closer. On the beach a few people lay about in swimming suits. There was a casino with a bright striped awning. Shifting my gaze I saw the hangars of the old seaplanes, and felt a surge of nostalgia for my youth that was gone. I had once spent two feverish years there. I looked at Güzelyalı, where the villas and summer residences of the rich stood in large gardens, and the sea washed their lower windows, so close were they built to the shore. On the opposite side was Karşıyaka, my destination. In Karşıyaka the houses stood well away from the sea, yet in summer the spray flung itself against the windows, and in winter metal fastenings became brown with salt.

The boat was nearly in and I put away my binoculars, leaning over the rails as we turned before docking, the water foaming madly under the propellers. The harbour was full of fishing. Greek, American, Swedish and British flags hung limply in the heat, and on shore lorries were unloaded by sweating men in their vests.

A group of people had assembled to watch us dock.

Greetings were called, handkerchiefs waved and I searched for my brother, Mehmet, catching sight of him at last seated on a crate of dried fruit. His eyes caught mine, and we waved laconically. His first words after I had disembarked were:

'My God, haven't you got fat!' to which I agreed sadly, noting his own slender elegance.

His young son, Kaya, was waiting for us in the car which was parked in the main street. In the back of the car lolled an enormous Afghan hound who bared his teeth when he saw me but fawned over Mehmet. I said very firmly that I would sit in the front and pushed Kaya into the back with the dog, who made a great fuss of him, but growled every time he caught my eye.

Driving out to Karşıyaka my first impression of changed Izmir was of light and too much open space. The main boulevard was too wide for the numerous small shops. There were public gardens everywhere, the bright flowers drooping wretchedly and only the lush palms revelling in the almost tropical heat. We passed a statue of Kemal Atatürk – something that was to become an inevitable part of one's wanderings across the country, as familiar as a land-mark. His memorial in Izmir showed him stern of face, implacable, his hands pointing seawards. Certainly the new wide, white Izmir would have been after his own heart. A vast building, nearing completion, was, so Mehmet told me, a hotel which would house two hundred and fifty people. It was to be all chrome and plush, luscious introduction to the Aegean for rich Americans.

The heat was intense. The glare burned the eyes, and the sea glittered like a gigantic sunburst of diamonds. The leaves of the city trees hung like green rags, weighed down by the intolerable burden of the heat. Mehmet opened all the windows, remarking:

'In about an hour's time it will be a little better. At one o'clock inbat will come' – looking at me anxiously to see if after ten years I still remembered inbat, that westerly sea wind which is the breath of life to the people of Izmir.

We ran along the kordon and the sea seemed to shine like a vast mirror, reflecting light whitely, bleaching the pastel tinted houses.

I think, that first morning, I was struck by the brightness of everything, by the cleanliness, the elegant little villas and the purple bougainvillea that flung itself luxuriantly across garden walls, in public gardens, and the facades of old houses. The scene was un-Turkish. It had wit and gaiety. It was hot and Mediterranean. Furthermore, there was an absence of mosques. There was an air of sun-washed expectancy, and a flaunting lewdness that was enchanting and wholly Levantine. Reconstruction and demolition seemed to be going on in about equal proportions. Marble-faced blocks of flats stood eyeless, facing the sea. A new port was under construction, which would benefit the export trade. Here and there, villas stood raw and new in weedy gardens. In one street a whole row of old houses were being pulled down.

FROM *The Caravan Moves On* by Irfan Orga

By far the most famous figure associated with the Aegean coast, and in particular with Bodrum, is the bohemian intellectual Cevat Şakir Kabaağaçlı (1890–1973) who under the nom-de-plume 'the Fisherman of Halicarnassus' wrote some dozen volumes of fiction (much of it set in Bodrum) and an autobiography called *The Blue Exile*. He is generally credited for bringing the formerly sleepy fishing and sponge-diving town of Bodrum, as well as the entire shoreline of the Turkish Aegean, to the attention of Turkish high society and for generally putting Bodrum 'on the map'.

He was an erudite, colourful personality with a highly inquisitive mind. Thirty-five years after his death he is still revered in Bodrum, and indeed all over Turkey. He has even appeared on Turkish postage stamps, an honour rarely awarded to writers in any country.

His background was anything but bohemian. He came from a well-off, upper-crust Ottoman background, and his father was ambassador to Athens. In 1914 Kabaağaçlı was convicted of manslaughter for killing his father and sentenced to fourteen years in jail. He was paroled in 1921, after serving half the sentence. But in 1925 he was prosecuted for seditious writing and exiled for three years to Bodrum.

Bodrum at the time was remote and its peninsula almost unconnected by road with the rest of Turkey. His journey from Istanbul took more than two weeks. The last stretch of the route from Milas was passable only on foot and by mule. On a curve of the road, he first glimpsed the sea, which 'cracked upon the horizon without warning like a vast blue thundering infinity'. The sea dominated the town, where it 'infiltrated through alleys and courtyards with a shimmering transparent light'. It 'sparkled to an incomprehensible depth full of yearning and beauty and terror'. The air was 'dry and bright as if lit by an inner light'. The town was 'modest and dazzling white with straight lines that cut the sky's blue with knife-like precision'.

The exile fell in love with Bodrum and elected to remain there for most of the rest of his life. He became the town's grand old man, introduced new fishing techniques, planted trees (the palms lining the quay were planted by him) and above all told tales of an ancient Aegean. Two generations of Bodrum's youth grew up under his spell. He felt that the people of Bodrum represented the distilled wisdom of countless civilizations.

Apart from being concerned with the general welfare of the area, Kabaağaçlı took an interest in its monuments. He famously wrote to the British Museum requesting the return of the sculptures excavated from the site of the Mausoleum. He also invented the concept of the *Mavi Yolculuk*, or 'Blue Voyage'.

This is an extract from his autobiography *The Blue Exile* (*Mavi Sürgün*). In his autobiography Kabaağaçlı's describes his first impressions of Bodrum when he arrived there in 1925:

I immediately rented a small peasant house, a one-room, white-washed stone structure, where I was allowed to live as long as I stayed within the village limits and reported daily to the gendarme, who represented the only state authority there. That first evening I spent in Bodrum I was alone for the first time in weeks without the guards who had escorted me on the endless, tedious journey from Ankara. When I opened my door, I saw the sunset over the sea and the scarlet rays of the dying sun falling on the shores and the islands. Against the sky stood the old Crusader fortress in the bay, black and sharply silhouetted, The whitewashed houses on the shore had turned pink and the sea a dark violet, I could hear the rustling of the vine leaves and the murmur of the sea. The seaweed strewn on the shore was like silver filigree. I went out on the little beach in front of the house and plunged my hands into the sand and the sea, letting first one and then the other stream through my fingers. As if in a religious ecstasy, I fell on my knees and felt my spirit rising out of my inanimate body like a million twittering birds. As in a flash of lightning I saw the sea for what it was – the same sea that, in my early childhood, I had seen at Phaleron near Athens when my father had been ambassador to Greece. I had come home to the sea.

I rushed into the village and bought a bucket and a rope and began hauling water out of the well in the little courtyard. I splashed water everywhere over the cobbles of the courtyard, and when I had done this several times I returned to the beach and hauled out buckets full of sea water, which I then threw about in the same manner on the sand and then up further and further on the shore, until I was totally exhausted.

FROM *The Blue Exile* (*Mavi Sürgün*) by Cevat Şakir Kabaağaçlı

An essential companion for any exploration of this coast are the books of the archaeologist and classical scholar George E. Bean, who described the archaeological sites of south-west Turkey in four pioneering volumes published in the early 1970s and reflecting a lifetime of exploration and study. Here Barnaby Rogerson pays tribute to him:

[George Bean's] labour was to identify, record and tease out the ancient history of Turkey's Aegean shore. This he achieved, not for fame or fortune, but out of love for his work. His influence is incalculable, for aside from identifying literally hundreds of new inscriptions and sites, he acted as an unwitting catalyst for con-servation. His quiet dignity, humanity and learning impressed thousands of Turkish villagers with the importance of these monuments to their own past. Ruins that had been used as occasional quarries were treated with a wholly new respect after they had received the attention of the courteous British professor who spoke such beautiful Turkish.

George Bean's series of archaeological guide books, *Aegean Turkey*, *Turkey beyond the Maeander*, *Turkey's Southern Shore* and *Lycian Turkey*, form an extraordinary 850-page compendium of learning. The guides bridge the yawning gulf between the unreadable pedant and the gushing populist. They are lucid, neither talking down to, nor losing the reader in the mysteries of a technical vocabulary. Above all they are authoritative, not only about the history but also the spirit of the place.

The great chunk of south-western Turkey covered by Bean must be one of the richest archaeological regions in the world. In addition it is a sublime landscape, a veritable Arcadia (or perhaps a Lycia) of forests, rough goat-grazed scrubland, limestone crags and well-watered valleys. To all those educated by centuries of European landscape painting and the ruin-hunting prose of John Betjeman and Rose Macaulay, this region of Turkey is a form of paradise. For many thousands of tourists, travellers, students and holiday-makers, Bean has been the guide to all this enchantment. His books have appeared in numerous editions, have been translated into dozens of languages, as well as pirated, pillaged and quarried by later writers.

As a Classics teacher at St Paul's in the 1930s, he organised summer holiday school trips to the classical sights of the Aegean. At first they were rather modest expeditions, but once he got the help of the Whittall family, a famous clan of English merchants in the Levant, they started exploring the Turkish coast around Izmir by boat. This was in the days when the local bus driver would get lost trying to find the way to Ephesus. In 1943 the British Council sent him off to work in Turkey, teaching English at Izmir. A few years later Bean was recruited by a Turkish friend to help set up a new archaeological department in Istanbul.

Bean's holidays, from 1943–71, were devoted to travelling around the villages of Turkey, discovering ancient remains, identifying cities and recording hundreds and hundreds of Greek inscriptions. In the competitive world of archaeology he was remarkable for his modesty and his willingness to share his discoveries and help others with information.

The work was physically demanding stuff, especially in postwar rural Turkey which had no maps, hotels, made-up roads or telephones. George Bean took a bus as far as it went and then he walked, if need be, for days. His impressive presence and fluent Turkish, spoken in a deep bass voice in an educated accent, made him unforgettable. The exquisite manners that he had maintained, even in the vicious environment of an English public school, at last found their true home in the land of the Turks. He never allowed himself to appear in a rush or stand on his dignity. Indeed at each village he would respectfully wait upon the village headman and take coffee. Only in conversation would these men gradually find out that they were in the company of an eminent professor, and only after talking about the affairs of the village, the crops, the condition of the herds and the roads would they learn the purpose of his visit. His patience was rewarded time and again as villagers rushed to assist the professor in his work. Doorsteps would be proudly dug up to reveal a buried inscription on the other side, while in the evening the local intellectuals as well as the herdsmen would be consulted about the location of carved stones in the hills. Bean would invariably be lodged as an honoured guest in the wooden house of the headman but being six foot six in height, he often found that conditions were too constricting for 'a full grown man'.

The villagers, although they certainly respected the professor, did not always understand his mission. They would beg to be given a translation. Usually this was nothing more exciting than 'so and so, son of so and so, is buried here and any transgressor of his tomb is to pay a fine to the town council'. Hoping to hear of the whereabouts of buried treasure the villagers were often a little disappointed. On many an occasion they would wait for a suitable opportunity for a private consultation and whisper, 'Tell us where to dig and we'll give you half the gold.'

Eventually his patient explanations were believed. His honesty only added further to the reputation of the man they called 'Bin Bey', also affectionately referred to as the little minaret of Cilicia or the two metre man. He knew nothing of corruption, not even the casual sweetener (usually no more than the price of a few coffees) which used to speed the way of bureaucracy. His second wife, Jane Bean, remembers that even after living in Istanbul for twenty years George remained blissfully ignorant of these traditions and found it impossible to book a marriage until he was advised that a ten lira note would help the process along.

If archaeology was still in its infancy, tourism hadn't even been thought of. Troy was a forbidden military zone, the only bed available at Antalya was in the Archaeological Institute and it was not until 1964 that they first made use of a car on any of their expeditions. It is extraordinary to think that only a generation ago there was only a single track out of Alanya, no forestry tracks and no road east of Anamur.

Few archaeologists could practice George Bean's saint-like patience as he sat for hours on a hard wooden chair waiting for the initial suspicion of the villagers to break into hospitality. Well did Bill Campbell write, 'George Bean was a deeply generous man, who loved and was loved by poor farmers, struggling day labourers who helped him to excavate, map and preserve, and by the faithful wardens of small museums – some of them merely guardians set to watch over remote and rarely visited sites. Visit any of these places and say you are a friend of 'Uzun boylu Professor Bean' and you have a village full of friends. In a period when Turkey's treasures were often endangered, and many lost abroad, George Bean stood forth as a scholar . . . determined to find, describe and keep that heritage . . . for the benefit of the noble and generous Turkish people to whom it has descended.'

No single man knew the countryside of south-western Turkey so well. At a dinner in London he was sitting next to the publisher, Ernest Benn, and talked about the irritating inaccuracies of the old *Blue Guide to Turkey*. By the end of the evening they had sketched out the idea for a new series of archaeological guides. To perfect the research for these guidebooks George Bean needed to criss-cross his old haunts, whilst he continued to hunt out new inscriptions. Many of these trips, especially in the 1960s, were undertaken with classicist and scholar Terence Mitford. Mitford shared Bean's enduring love for south-western Turkey's ruin-haunted hills, as well as his disdain for comfort while he travelled. He was intensely single-minded, self-willed and independent, loathing cities and the world's ever-growing obsession with speed and noise. Although he would later attend many a city-based academic conference he seldom, if ever, made use of a hotel. In Athens he would walk out into the countryside and sleep under an olive tree, in Cairo he slept in the sand dunes and at Oxford he would wrap himself in a copy of *The Times* newspaper and sleep in the Port Meadow. Although he had been trained in the use of every sort of mechanical device in wartime he refused to drive, a task his wife took over. He adored the wild places and could survive in any wilderness, either camping with his growing family (three sons and a daughter) or sleeping rough by himself. Mitford was far removed from the image of a modern hiker or camping holiday-maker. He had no need for backpack, walking stick or wallet let alone guidebook. He would forage for his subsistence, be it sea urchins, eels, nettle soup or rabbits, and once spent a contented month on the bank of the Euphrates without spending so much as a bean. As a conclusive mark of their friendship, they published a book together, *Journeys into Rough Cilicia*, which covered their joint explorations in June and July 1961, June and October 1962 and June 1963.

They would die, Bean in 1977 and Mitford 1978, as they had lived, working to the last. Mitford's study on Roman Cilicia and Roman Cyprus and Bean's guide to Lycia were all published posthumously. Books, articles and memorial lectures remain to perpetuate their names though their style of modesty, energy, commitment and absolute integrity is increasingly rare.

FROM *Cornucopia* by Barnaby Rogerson

This description of a ramble through the archaeological site of Caunus in the 1950s conveys all the pleasure of exploring ruins. And although all Turkish archaeological sites are more crowded than they were in the 1950s, it is still not unusual to find yourself alone and, like Freya Stark, captivated by the past:

We went on up the hill, following the wall to a gate; its monolithic posts and lintel faced the empty bend that held the harbour. The river sprawled beyond to its estuary, as if written in light with a careless pen. In the lap of the wide landscape, small as pebbles, lay a handful of cultivated fields. In the swamp, a few cows were browsing. A heron flew by. It was as if man and his histories were not so much forgotten as absorbed into the activity of nature, spinning her world and its sunshine through the restful afternoon. As we descended, after an hour or so, we still heard the tortoise battering his road towards the female heart, and went to watch him: and a touching thing happened: for as she moved away, and he with his wrinkled neck pursued her, he mewed with a high and eloquent note of longing. They disappeared together, and the sound of hitting stopped on the hill.

Brambles, the prickly holly-oak and spiky thickets of acacia grew thick as we reached the ruins where the city streets once led. A Roman bath with brick outlines to its arches fed a tree on its high wall; near it stood a small temple, with four fluted engaged columns and a door between them. All here was hard to reach because of growing trees, and barriers of thorns laid to keep the cattle in small enclosures. We struggled, scratched and bruised, and lost ourselves and each other, and finally emerged over the blocks of a fallen scene into a grey stone theatre, roughened and mossed over by time. Between the seats and through the gangways, twisted olive shoots had pushed their way till their roots had grown hard and colourless as the stone, and their leaves threw a small life of moving shadows on the places of the spectators who once walked up in white gowns and holiday sandals from the streets and the harbours below. Surrounded like the sleeping princess with thorns and thickets, the scarce-visited theatre of Caunus held its gaiety, as if the pleasantness that has once been could live for ever. Its seats, which the wind has scoured and the lichens have patched with colour, show row upon row the curve which the workers in stone once fashioned, to accommodate the legs of the spectators, and lighten and beautify the whole. And though every trapping that belongs to man has vanished, and the trees and the weather are alone there, a difference exists between the theatre and the surrounding loneliness, a comfort of civilization, though all that ever made it has gone.

FROM *The Lycian Shore* by Freya Stark

Here John Freely, a well-known writer on Turkish subjects, articulates the strange feelings of melancholy that can so often mingle with happier thoughts when visiting ruined cities:

Miletus always evokes a feeling of desolation which somehow goes beyond the inevitable sadness that one feels when wandering among ancient ruins, and the feeling is accentuated here because in its time this was the greatest city in the Greek world, though it is now utterly marooned in the midst of the alluvial delta that has left it four or five miles from the sea it once ruled. But something of the vanished grandeur of Miletus survives, particularly in the sombre magnificence of its ruined theatre which looks out over what was once one of the four harbours of an ancient city which Milesians proudly called the first settled in Ionia and the mother of many of the great cities in the Pontus and Egypt, and in various other parts of the world.

FROM *The Western Shores of Turkey* by John Freely

The American writer Carla Grissmann spent a year living with a Turkish village family. The willingness and warmth with which her neighbours welcomed and accepted her not only results in an unforgettable experience for the writer, but gives her portrait of Turkish life, *Dinner of Herbs*, an exceptional intimacy. In this passage she describes the part music and performance play in the social lives of her Turkish friends:

Veli had a small room in the back of the shop, with reed matting on the walls, a low bench and cushions along three sides and two big metal trays in the centre as tables. A door opened onto the back alley. Whoever was sitting nearest the door, without getting up, would lean over and open it a crack, lean out into the street until someone trotted into sight and then give out orders for cheese and bread, olives, cigarettes, raki, or whatever was needed at the time. Minutes later things would begin arriving, from the restaurant at the end of the alley or the shop next door or the market, and be briskly passed from the dark alley into the room.

There was always music. Veli sang and played the saz, the eight-string Turkish guitar. He had learned without lessons, the gift was innate. Lying back on the cushions I watched the blurred mosaic pattern of colour spreading over the darkened ceiling from an old lantern of cut glass. The slender metallic music filled the room.

'What was that song about?'

'It was about love.'

As Veli played, one of the men sat upright against the wall, his hands on his knees, his eyes staring ahead. He raised his head, began to sing, in long filigreed phrases, his body moving with the movement of his voice.

'That was also a song about love,' said Veli.

The room was full of smoke and men in dark shabby jackets, open shirts and heavy mud-caked shoes. The saz was passed to one of the older men, who strummed a soft, slow melody. Several voices followed the song. Someone leaned over and said, 'Do you know what this song is? What means ninni? It is the sweet words for the baby when it sleeps.'

I looked around the room and thought in disbelief, 'These men are singing a lullaby.'

They took me to the local theatre, a dusty room in the attic of an old wooden house, with everyone there like a big picnic. There were several short plays, all with the same young actors, stuffed with pillows or tottering on a cane with flour on their hair. They waved and chatted into the audience. One little boy sitting next to us was laughing so hard he kept falling out of his chair. Kâmuran translated punch-lines when he could: 'Your donkey is dead, too!' and, 'Well, your brass pot just had a baby pot in my house,' with everyone shrieking with laughter. Kâmuran was laughing so much himself each time he set the little boy back onto his chair that he had tears running down his face, and I did too in the end.

FROM *Dinner of Herbs* by Carla Grissmann

Nancy Phelan, an Australian writer who visited the Turquoise Coast in the early 1960s was surprised at the absence of charm, comforts or sophistication in the Turkish seaside towns at the time:

In the late afternoon we reached Finike, more tropical than Mediterranean, a dirty neglected little town without trees or flowers, with ugly boxlike houses on the water's edge. The valley behind it, where oranges, rice and cotton grow, is hot and airless, and though the setting of the town is beautiful, with a sweeping bay, and mountains reaching back into the sky, the hand of man has done nothing to show that he appreciates them. The harbour seems dead, with no bright caiques tied up or fishing nets out to dry; the best hotel is out of sight of the sea, facing the hot valley, and in the gazino by the water crude chairs and tables are lined up on a concrete slab by the pier, with a coal heap and petrol drums at hand.

The Turks don't seem to have the same touch with sea towns as Spaniards, Italians, Greeks and Provençals. Here, on this southern coast, no one has bothered at all to make the best of the exquisite settings. The locals look at the blue mountains behind, the silky bay before them and say, 'çok güzel', but they make no effort to enjoy them in aesthetic or even comfortable conditions. The things I missed most in Turkey were not the mod. cons. or comforts of travel but the little vine-hung places for sitting to enjoy the view, to drink a glass of something or eat a simple meal. I missed them bitterly and increasingly and I resented the Turks' complete lack of understanding of what a sea town should be like. Sometimes, at first glance, or from the distance, a town would appear to have the white simplicity I loved, but at close quarters it proved an illusion, a remnant of the Greeks who lived along this coast for hundreds of years, until the War of Turkish Independence. When Atatürk drove them away they left behind their square white houses on the sea, or climbing up the hill among the prickly pears, their Cyclades chimneys, their domed churches, now in ruins; and though they are surrounded with hot-looking Turkish additions, the Greek touch is still there for those who recognize it.

I am sure the Turks really love their beautiful country and would kill or die for it without hesitation, but in some ways their love resembles that of a man for his old mum or his faithful doormat wife; a constant unchanging fundamental emotion that never bothers about compliments, birthdays or other trifles that make life so pleasant. With the Turks it takes the form of complete neglect of appearance. Beautiful places lie covered with garbage and dirt, and new buildings are usually hideous and unsuitable, giving the impression that no one cares enough to co-ordinate them. People just run up any old thing anywhere they like, as they do in Australia, where the same lavishness of large-scale beauty is regarded in the same off-hand way, or taken as a challenge to man's ingenuity to spoil it.

Hussein, who was staying with friends, took me to the stifling little hotel, where we found the owner, fat and unshaved, watering the garden in nylon vest and underpants. He was not in the mood for visitors and had to be persuaded to let me in, but finally took me to a tiny room, clean but completely airless. The tariff on the back of the door said:

T.L. 3.50	Single bedroom	2.50	Three beds
3.00	Two beds	1.50	Bed on floor

I never saw him again. Next morning I paid my bill to a baffled little girl of seven, the only other occupant of the building.

Here she describes Fethiye, which had recently been hit by an earthquake:

> Hussein swept me off to the Palas Oteli and installed me in a hot, cleanish room which opened upon a verandah where a number of Turks were sleeping in striped pyjamas. He would come back, he said, when I had had a siesta, and show me round Fethiye and guide me to *çok güzel lokanta*.
>
> I slept immediately, drugged with heat, dirt, exhaustion and weakness brought on by hunger, and woke to find that Hussein had come to show me the sights.
>
> Outside, the heat was formidable. Lying at the far end of its Gulf, almost in an enclosed bay, Fethiye seemed to be cut off from any breeze that might have relieved the torrid atmosphere. For all its classical associations as the ancient Telmessus, and the charm of its modern inhabitants, it was not enticing, resembling one of those little towns in the Middle East through which victorious armies have swept. There was the familiar Turkish air of catastrophe, blitz or hurricane, with ruined buildings open to the sky and jagged walls leaning weakly up against each other in the heat, and rubble and masonry lying about in the dust. There was also the impression that the mains had been bombed and the water supply run loose in the streets; but this time the disaster had really happened. Fethiye is subject to earthquakes, and these ruins were the souvenirs of the last visitation. Like the boy who cried 'Wolf', when you come upon genuine earthquake scars in Turkey you find them hard to believe, so indistinguishable are they from the normal appearance of so many places.
>
> Hussein glowed with pride as he conducted me along the street, pointing out the more spectacular ruins as though they were architectural gems.
>
> 'One year,' he said over and over again. 'One year . . . plenty houses finish. Twenty people kaput.' He took a childlike pleasure in the fact that Fethiye had been so distinguished by nature. 'Plenty

earthquake,' he assured me. 'Plenty earthquake Fethiye. Plenty houses finish,' and he laid them all out flat with a smart gesture of his hand.

It was quite true, there were plenty houses finish. They lay where they had fallen, with doors and windows gaping. In one part of the town streets of little wooden boxes had been set up like a wartime settlement, and people were carrying on in these. They were so close together that you could barely squeeze between them, and rather surprisingly in the middle of a row was an upright Lycian tomb with a top like a fireman's helmet. The hillside behind the town was studded with doorways to other tombs, carved from the rock, as at Myra.

However, the town that Nancy Phelan dislikes the most is Marmaris, where she spends an intensely unhappy twenty-four hours during *Bayram*.

I could not wait to get to Marmaris. I was so sure that comfort and peace awaited me there that I hugged my heat and tiredness, the better to savour the joys of my marble hotel by the sea.

'Marmaris,' said one of the men, and the drunk stopped saying 'Madame, je suis – je suis', and changed to 'Marmaris, *çok güzel, çok güzel*'.

I peered eagerly out through the crack in the tarpaulin at the white houses scattered below in the valley; then suddenly we were among them, running along narrow cobbled streets. Incredulous, I saw the ramshackle buildings, the garbage in the streets, the squalid cafes, the familiar air of cyclone, earthquake or blitz. Where was Marmaris? The truck stopped and we all fell forward upon each other.

'*Tamam*,' said Mustafa, and he began to grope for my luggage. I still stared rather blankly, and the men, all waiting politely for me to get out, stared back. 'Marmaris?' I said.

'*Evet! Marmaris!*' they cried in a reassuring chorus.

It was too cruel. I said good-bye and climbed out after Mustafa who, with an encouraging smile, was waiting for me to follow him.

'Marmaris?' I said once more, faintly.

'*Evet. Marmaris, çok guzel.*'

Since he refused to leave me, I accompanied him wearily through the hot smelly streets, trying to keep my mind a blank, to expect and hope for nothing. We rounded the corner and came out on the quay.

'*Oteli*,' said Mustafa, jerking his head to the west, and I hurried after him.

'Where?'

'*Burada!*' (Here). He set down the bags and wiped his grimy forehead with a dirty handkerchief.

'Oh, no!' I said. 'No!' The cry was forced through my lips before I could stop it. His startled face pulled me up. 'But you said it was çok güzel,' I cried helplessly. 'Where is the çok güzel hotel?'

'*Oteli Ak Deniz*,' he said, as though that explained everything.

It was a bleak grey building on a corner, with a dreary fly-blown cafe underneath. I knew without crossing the threshold what I should find inside, I had been in too many others like it to have any illusions. There would be no baths, no cool white rooms, no breakfasts in the garden or dinners on the quay, watching the little boats. *Yok, yok, yok.* There would be impossible lavatories, no washing facilities, flies, dirt and an all-pervading smell of urine.

'*Tamam*,' I said at last. 'Come on.'

With its landlocked bay the little town slumbered, drugged by its nocturnal humidity. At the quay, fishing boats were reflected in the placid water, their crews, wrapped in old sails, asleep among the nets. On the hill behind the town are the ruins of a castle, and on the slopes, white houses and clumps of cactus, relics of the departed Greeks, which give a faint look of the Aegean islands . . .

. . . At this hour the muted light gave to the dreary little buildings more grace than they possessed, and across the dreaming bay, green misty headlands and blue hills were pleated into one another. People were up already, preparing for the holiday. Little children in their best clothes followed me about on my walk or embraced, dry-eyed, the sacrificial lambs, so tenderly petted during the last weeks, now meekly awaiting execution. The air smelt greasy and bloody; flies buzzed excitedly. From time to time bare-chested men would hurry out from sinister side streets with spattered hands and clothes, some carrying pathetic fleeces or pairs of horns, like trophies, or loops and coils of entrails.

As the morning wore on, the butchers became busier and busier. They walked about the streets with their knives dripping blood, and the coiled entrails appeared in a less orderly fashion, dropped into the gutters where dogs tore them apart and fought over them. The thought of all this innocent blood so quietly shed behind high walls, the timid, bewildered bleats of the animals hustled to their death was odious and unnerving.

Though barely seven o'clock, the holiday was in full swing.

Families were crowding into launches, to visit a mosque across the bay; the cafes were full of men busily getting drunk. I looked, without much hope, for a cleanish place where I might find breakfast.

I left them all at the quay and wandered away gloomily. A long insupportable day stretched ahead in this terrible little town, and after that a hot and horrible night. The hotel was too hot and smelly to be endured; I could not walk about the streets all day, even if there had been any attraction in them, and there were no shady tavernas or lokantas by the water where I could sit and read. The cafes were dark and noisy, full of men slapping down tric-trac dice and radios blaring out Turkish music or political meetings.

As the day wore on the smells of lavatories and slaughtered sheep mounted and mingled in the sickening heat with the noise, the flies and the increasing number of drunks lurching about. I spent a miserable afternoon on the quay, trying to read, on an upright chair, closely watched by a little boy who stood hugging a raw leg of lamb. *Kurban Bayram*, so far, had not impressed me as an aesthetic treat, and the colour, enchantment and gaiety described by Gerard de Nerval and others were all noticeably absent from Marmaris.

By evening the air was saturated with blood, and the silence which had fallen while people slept off their lunch was once more broken by distorted radios, the crackle of static and the slapping of dice. Only a few little groups strolled or sat on the quay. Life in Turkish sea towns takes place in the back streets rather than by the water.

Wearily, in the breathless night, I made my way to the Ak Deniz
and once more stepping over the exhausted butchers on the landing
I fell upon my bed and passed into a stupefied slumber.

FROM *Welcome the Wayfarer* by Nancy Phelan

SEA JOURNEYS

Journeys by sea remained much more comfortable and convenient
than journeys by land until the 1970s. Freya Stark, the famous British
travel writer, toured the coast from Izmir to Antalya aboard *Elfin*, a
small *gulet* owned by David Balfour, the British Consul in Izmir. She
describes a coastline substantially unchanged from the days when
Capt. Beaufort had published Karamania. Here is a selection of letters
written from *Elfin* to her publisher, Jock Murray.

Knidos, 4 October 1952
DEAREST JOCK – It is almost unutterable luck to have hit upon a full
moon to anchor at Knidos. Think of all the pictures you have seen,
those careful drawings by mid-nineteenth-century young clergy-
men and squires, travelling in the footprints of the Classics or the
Apostles, and you see this harbour on the most lovely of peninsulas,
a gaunt ridge of a submerged range, backbone of rock trees and
thorny sea cliffs, the first village a two and a half hours' walk away in
the first arable pocket, and here a lighthouse like a small white
church high up, a little imamzade and two cottages, and all the rest
belongs to the ancient world: the two harbours, north and south,
with a hundred flat yards or so between, with huge boulders and
foundations of the moles visible underwater, and the northern one,
for forty triremes, with two round towers at the entrance, one ruined
and one intact. There is an old caique askew with slanting mast on
the shore and fishermen hammering at it, and three caiques in the
deserted harbour, looking for sponges. And all inside, up two steep
slopes, like the lining to a crater, are the huge terraces of the old
town, a few rows of their great blocks and the untidy stones of
peasants above, and the streets and houses and temples now all small
stubble fields covered with stones and potsherds. We picked up a

horse's head and small bit of relief figure in terracotta, saw a marble metope used as a fence, and a long wall of marble fragments recently chopped up and still with sharp edges, cornices, Corinthian capitals. I would give anything to load one on the boat and carry it away.

The most beautiful statue was taken by Newton to the British Museum from the temple of Demeter. I walked there this morning – only the enclosure and blocks of the platform with an olive or two, under a smooth cliff face from which I suppose the blocks were cut. The theatre still has one corner, and its shape cupped in the hill; and from it a causeway goes up in three hairpin bends supported on walls, polygonal too. D. B. followed it and found the acropolis wall and a fortress on the hill behind with twenty-foot walls still standing. I stayed and pottered about and drew the harbour entrance, and saw the quays cut in the rock with steps.

Dear Jock, these letters get written in scraps of time and, anyway, I can't give you anything but a mass of details as it is too much to take in all at once. It is just like the first winter in the East, a whole new world pouring in; but here, it is the Greek world, our own origins, and therefore so deeply stirring.

FREYA

Caria [Loryma], 6 October 1952

I think this untidy letter may get off to you from Rhodes tomorrow. It is just across the way, about eight miles across a floor of sea. And here we are in a bay like a landlocked pool, with a north-west wind howling, and a fifth century BC fortress, hundreds of yards of wall of great bulging stones beautifully fitted, looking down on us from a low ridge of the sharpest limestone slabs and thorny bushes. All the human modern world is lost, but I don't mind just now, for I am living in something remote and enchanted. My goodness, it is witchcraft. We spent the morning so to say fishing, trailing a little bit of metal which no fish seems to appreciate; but it means trailing slowly under cliffs, by gulf and island, folded hills behind bays, flattened in sunrise or sunset like those pressed roses where every petal is there but the whole thing is flat. Hours and hours with never a house in sight.

The peninsula of Knidos is rust-coloured; it puts out great barren paws of rock, like sphinxes, with small waterless triangles of beaches, and lies as if made of metal; and the isthmus where the lands of Knidos began is only half a mile wide or very little more. The Knidians began to make a trench there to keep the Persians out, but they got tired of being cut with splinters of stone and asked Delphi if they were to go on. She said certainly not – if Zeus had wanted an island, he would have made one himself. So they gave themselves up to the Persians. We found the isthmus this morning and walked to look over at the other sea, through pines and hillsides of rosemary, broom, all the Mediterranean scrub; and a lovely view of pointed rocks and the one road with a bus surprisingly along it every day, for the people which is all this long stretch of loneliness contains.

Am feeling a little sick today!

Love, FREYA

Fethiye, 10 October 1952

DEAREST JOCK – We are now at Telmessos (modern Fethiye) and here again it is a vast harbour with islands before it and mountains beyond, and a red-roofed little town with caiques in the harbour. Though there is little left here, there are the tombs in the cliff, carved with Ionic columns, and stone sarcophagi, and a temple base or so used as foundation for somebody's house. It is an island which people abandoned in Charles Fellows's day because there were so many snakes; and, in the days of Cyrus, Croesus the King of Lydia sent to ask advice of the 'snake-men of Telmessos'.

I am going to post this now. Love always,

FREYA

Off Pamphylia, 21 October 1952

DEAREST JOCK – From Telmessos, if you look at the map, you will see us sailing round the southernmost points of Lycia, D. B. fishing (which I think waste of time), and I looking at Byzantine remains (which he thinks the same). As a matter of fact, I like the meditative part of fishing and he is becoming quite keen on sites. Who wouldn't, on tiny islands in a sea the colour of this one?

What a good way to learn history by going to see places. I feel far more intimate now with St Paul, having wondered what he felt as he saw his view dwindle away, such a wild romantic horizon of hills on hills. The sands have silted up round the Lycian tombs, leaving only their lids unhidden, and have made great dunes to choke the river harbour so that now one lands in a bend of the sea and has to walk forty minutes to the city site. Camels unload onto a platform of cement at the water's edge, like a picture by David Roberts or Lear, with a huge mountain background behind them.

Now we are here actually round the corner of Pamphylia, fierce wooded mountains with naked tops of stone, springing in one leap from the sea. The nomads still have most of this country, moving from summer to winter quarters. They were coming down yesterday, with carpets woven by themselves, laid on top of the baggage on the camels, and a cooking pot on top of all. That, too, was very like an old print, to see them and their black tents among the Lycian sarcophagi.

FREYA

from *Some Talk of Alexander: The Letters of Freya Stark*

Patrick Kinross made the same journey on the same *gulet* in 1953. This is his description of Marmaris:

Towards evening we sailed through the narrow channel which leads into the Gulf of Marmaris. The gulf is in effect a deep, secluded lagoon, a favourite anchorage of the British Mediterranean Fleet since the time of Sir Sidney Smith . . .

The small port of Marmaris lay compactly piled at the head of the gulf, around the towers and walls of a mediaeval Castle. Greek in aspect, its whitewashed houses, with red-tiled roofs and tall white chimneys, sea-blue shutters and vine-covered balconies, stood on firm foundations of mellowed golden stone. Along the harbour the insubstantial plastered houses were painted in a graceful confusion of clashing blues and chocolates and greys, with whitewashed windows and shutters in contrasting colours. Here and there even corrugated iron had been turned to decorative account. Used in

long vertical panels, painted green, it gave an elegant fluted look to
a facade. The streets were still cobbled, but there were sinister signs
of approaching prosperity. Pylons, not lamp-posts, awaited the
arrival of the electric light, while on the main square Atatürk was
up to his neck in gravel, part of the litter which arose from the
construction of a pier. In a Spor Kulübü the youth of Marmaris
played ping-pong; in a smoky coffee-house opposite their elders
played cards. From here we were removed by the local doctor, who
took us away to a bleaker, more refined establishment, further
down the quay. He was a native of Thrace, a far cry from Lycia. His
hair was wavy and fair, and he was proud of his costume – a pyjama
jacket, Glenurquhart tweed trousers and grey suede shoes.

FROM Europa Minor by Patrick Kinross

Despite these signs of development, Marmaris remained a small town
until the early 1980s. Its amazingly rapid, largely unplanned, expansion
from 1985–95, when its population jumped from 1,000 to 25,000, and
all the agricultural land behind the town (which had been covered in
orange trees) was built over, was tragic. But there was some benefit
from the tragedy, since the Ministry of Tourism, shocked by the sheer
speed with which it occurred, then tightened development regulations.

THE GREEK ISLANDS

In 1948 the Dodecanese islands became part of Greece (they had been
Italian colonies until 1943), and at that point all commercial or cultural
contact between the islands and the mainland ceased. As a result the
islands of the Dodecanese lived for a few decades in a highly isolated
and materially impoverished condition, which travel writers, at least,
found idyllic.

This is from an account of a year spent in Symi in the early 1960s by
William Travis:

. . . . in winter for weeks the island was without outside contact.
Fresh vegetables grew scarce and the stock of paraffin ran out. The
sea, lapping over the quay at the head of the bay, flooded all the
shops on the waterfront but this was of little concern for their

owners had long since moved to their winter quarters tucked away in the back streets. Not that their shops provided much for sardines, corned beef, tomato paste and poor quality pasta seemed the sum total of their dwindling stock. However, in spite of wind and loose tiles, rain-storms and leaks, poor provisions and poorer communications, we found that we still enjoyed our life on Symi. Four days in a row might be cold, sodden and miserable but the fifth would be a thing apart – sun-drenched, cloudless and still, with the smell of rain-revived thyme and sage aromatic in the nostrils and all the mountainside sprouting new plant life. And although to the outward eye the township was desolate and apparently abandoned, away in the back streets clustered on out-of-the-wind stone steps and jostling for position on sun-warmed porches the population went about their winter affairs with the women knitting, crocheting and sampling preserves and the men thronging the one-roomed tavernas where the air was thick with the fumes of sage-tea, fried sardines, and ouzo and where conversation and laughter drowned the noise of the funeral bells.

As suddenly as it came, winter went and warm westerlies brought with them lark-song and sunshine. Dwarf cyclamen carpeted the goat-paths, the first bees put in a hesitant appearance and, across the Doric channel, the snow-line daily receded upon the Anatolian peaks. The end of March found us back in the sea again, but even before then the town had come alive as we had never seen it before with furniture and the contents of chests and linen-cupboards piled up outside front doors and black-clad housewives busy scrubbing, mending, ironing and washing rugs. Why all this fuss, we asked. 'It's Lent', we were told which fact we had forgotten and the multiple rules governing the fast were explained to us.

During Lent all houses must be spring cleaned and every washable item within taken out and washed. The house must be repainted and re-whitewashed. New clothes must be made for the children and new cushion-covers and pillowcases embroidered. The churches must all be cleaned by the townswomen . . .

FROM *Bus Stop Symi* by William Travis

Mermaids Singing by Charmian Clift, an account of a year spent in Kalymnos in 1956, paints a similar picture. At this time Kalymnos was still a very poor island, and lived largely from its sponge-fishing fleet.

All summer long, while the boats are away, the town lies in a torpor of heat and idleness. Everyone who can goes to the other side of the island, to the little houses of Brosta or Merthies. If one has no house one erects a makeshift tent of striped rugs strung on bamboo poles. For the hot months Kalymnians live close to the sea on the fish they catch and the figs and prickly pears and grapes that grow around them and the sweet water from the wells. There is a charming unwritten law that any person, man, woman or child, may satisfy his hunger by taking what fruit he can eat from anybody's property, so long as he eats it there by the tree or the vine. He is only guilty of theft it he carries the fruit away in a basket or stuffed into his pocket to eat later.

During these months buying or selling are practically at a standstill. There will be no money coming in until the boats return late in autumn. There are no tourists to bring in a little summer revenue. Summer buying, pared down to the barest essentials, is almost all done on credit.

FROM *Mermaids Singing* by Charmian Clift

In many parts of the Turkish coast the first foreign visitors were hippies and young travellers in the 1960s and early 1970s. There was an inevitable culture clash, and occasionally things turned ugly. Jeremy Seal spent a summer in the early 1970s in a seaside village east of Antalya, which he calls 'Pomegranate'. He observes how Turkish villagers react to bikinis and free love:

It was hard to imagine a more achingly beautiful place than Pomegranate in the early seventies. The pioneering trickle of independent tourists certainly thought so. The locals, who took such scenic magnificence for granted, were struck instead by these visitors whose behaviour was quite as strange as their clothes, colourful and entirely absent below knee and elbow. In July and August, when the villagers were indulging in lengthy recesses from the heat of the day, these people could be seen pottering around the ruins of ancient temples and the amphitheatre, puzzling over fallen friezes before taking themselves off to undress – as well as men, women! – on the long beach that fringes the peninsular where Pomegranate stands. According to the sleepy but indignant village commentary that raised a cloud of drowsy wasps as it issued from beneath the shady vine trellises of homes and tea houses, the ruins had been there as long as anyone could remember and hardly merited exploring in the baking heat of high summer, while even the infidel Greeks in the old days, the oldest villagers readily confirmed, had never undressed on the beach.

Some Pomegranate families were prompted to clear spare rooms and offer them to the latest arrivals as pansiyon accommodation. The more enterprising among them even dared, having heard the practice was acceptable, to charge a few lira at the end of the visitors' stay.

But the first signs of trouble were not long in coming. Some visitors started to wander back from the beach in their bikinis and so caused grave offence among a profoundly traditional Muslim population . . . Signs in atrocious English and German – 'Bikini in village No' – were erected on street corners in an attempt to stem the offence. Unsurprisingly, these signs proved incomprehensible as much in concept as language to French visitors who had been largely brought up on nude sunbathing and doubtless thought slipping on a bikini for a jaunt through town might label them as puritan killjoys. As a result, several of them were stoned by incensed villagers.

Bruised and bemused, the French were driven back to the beach, but the influx of tourists was not discouraged. Pomegranate's twenty-five-bed capacity soon doubled, and doubled again, setting a pattern for the years to come. Pansiyon owners even started requisitioning the rough notice-boards which had recently railed against bikinis on which they might advertise their bed and breakfast rates. Suddenly, there was a new livelihood called turizm, predicated on the astounding discovery that foreigners seemed happy to pay for the things – accommodation, meals, and even visits to ruins – that the local people had always marked down under hospitality. It was not surprising then that Halil Yildirim should wake up early one spring morning as a young man and decide he no longer wanted to be a farmer.

FROM *A Fez of the Heart* by Jeremy Seal

Twenty years later Seal returned to Pomegranate, and was appalled by the completeness of the economic and cultural changes that had occurred and by the apparent ease of modern mass tourism's victory:

By the spring morning in 1992 when I arrived, it was obvious that there were very few farmers indeed left in Pomegranate . . . On the main street, the incursions of English and German had rendered Turkish a minority language. Turkish food had been replaced by 'handburgers', and even the ubiquitous doner kebab was being advertised as 'authentik Turkische cuisine', as if this staple of Turkish food could only hold its own by being touted as a gastronomic heritage experience. Here was the grilled red mallet, the lamp chops, even a distinctly unappetizing fried squit, something called stew of bot, bolloknese and cold drings. You could have your potatoes French freud regardless of psycho-Austrian objections. The music that drowned out the muezzin in the village's one mosque was Euro-pop. On the beach, serried ranks of oiled European breasts jiggled in the sun while the postcards on the nearby stands brazenly endorsed them with complementary images of topless girls and voluptuous buttocks ornamented with the briefest of G-strings above the bald statement: No Problem in Turkey.

One thing was clear: that underdressed Gallic retreat, a beachwards scuttle in a hail of traditionalist stones, had at some point been halted. The bikini signs had been taken down, the locals had come up with a new message in tidy English, and relaunched it on postcards as the slogan of a radically reinvented society, one that claimed to have gone from stonings to toplessness in twenty years. The retreat which had once seemed headlong was now exposed as a canny French feint; bikinis had established a bridgehead in town, and bared breasts were dug in on the beach . . .

FROM *A Fez of the Heart* by Jeremy Seal

June Haimoff, who became famous for her successful campaign to save İstuzu beach, the nesting ground of the loggerhead turtle (see Chapter Three), began cruising on the Turkish coast in the 1970s in her own *gulet*. She conveys how quickly the transformation occurs from 'unspoilt' traditional society to a society dominated and corrupted by modern commercial tourism:

Throughout the years we had watched with dismay the inexorable slide of Greece into mass tourism with resultant overcrowding and damage to tradition and nature. Gradually we spent more time in Turkey, then unspoilt and little frequented by tourists. The Turks are generally a warm race, welcoming to visitors. In due course we made friends along the magnificent coast and were invited by locals, like Asik Kaptan (love kaptan) a sponge fisherman, whose modest home stands in an almond grove in Selimiye, a hamlet on the Marmaris peninsula. His eyes, periwinkle blue, made a remarkable contrast to his mahogany tanned face. When we met in 1975 he spoke a smattering of German, having ferried in his boat the occasional German venturing here from the nearby shore, as Selimiye was then inaccessible by road. Asik, chuffed to meet a lady boat owner, was the first to christen me Kaptan June. He and I became friends and shared many a meal on his boat or mine or in his cottage with wife and children. Then a generous dish of almonds was always on the table. These, together with his own olives and olive oil were first class. With his smattering of German, my smidgeon of Turkish and plenty of hand signs we communicated pretty well.

Another family we visited frequently was that of Hussein, then a shepherd whose home was in the hills above N's island. We had met him some years before on our first visit to the (then) remote bay. No sooner had we anchored than he was signaling us to come ashore and, once on the beach, escorted us to his cottage half a mile away up a goat track which followed a dry riverbed where oleanders and giant plane trees grew. A steady buzzing of bees accompanied us; the air laden with the scent of coriander, oregano and thyme. At his two roomed home his wife Ayse made tea, whilst his daughters, Sengul and Nurten spread out the *sofra* and put out cushions for us to sit on the *köşk* under a fig tree. Apparently they all lived in one room, as the other was filled to the ceiling with large sacks of herbs. On this coast some of the local people still earn part of their living from gathering oregano, thyme, sage and bay leaves in the forest and sending them to Izmir for packaging and export. There was always an excellent breakfast at Hussein's; Ayse baked the bread, round flat loaves cooked on a sort of wok on an open fire. Tomatoes, onions, figs, grapes, medlars grew in their garden and they made their own honey, cheese and yoghurt. In winter they would retreat to the village high above their summer home; a one hour walk up a goat track. How we looked forward to these visits to Hussein and family. I shall never forget their kindness, the beauty of the setting and the scent of herbs enveloping all.

Today, twenty-five years later, a highway passes their door, it goes to the bay where Hussein and family have a restaurant and pension; they are not alone. The beach is plastered with restaurants, cafes, shops, kiosks, sun umbrellas and sun-beds. The hills facing N's island have been denuded of trees in order to build holiday villages and hotels. Signs abound on the beach, some advertising 'Full English breakfast served here'. I do not go there any more, preferring to remember it as it was in the days of authentic Turkish breakfasts shared with stress-free friends under a fig tree with the scent of herbs around us.

In one of the many marvelous bays in the gulf of Fehtiye we found another welcoming Turk, Mehmet, one of the first to offer any kind of catering on a still remote coastline. His 'restoran' was a lean-to three-sided shack overlooking a panoramic view to stun the senses. Like many 'businesses' in Turkey, it simply sprang up overnight on an otherwise uninhabited hillside accessible only by boat or donkey. Mehmet, an irrepressible entrepreneur, was the first to spot the potential of catering, in his cove, to visiting yachts. A large leap from his former occupation of goatherd, but Turks are amazingly versatile people, and so it was that we first became aware of Mehmet's presence when a cloud of chicken feathers floated towards us one morning as we prepared to drop anchor in this unfrequented spot. By the time we had finished anchoring,

Bouboulina lay in a bed of chicken feathers, from the shore a man was waving and calling to us, thus we became Mehmet's first customers . . . he had wrung the bird's neck on seeing our boat arrive. The meat was, of course, as tough as the proverbial boot, but fresh chips cooked over an open fire, roasted aubergines and peppers and some dark bread toasted, helped us swallow the chicken. Lashings of strong tea was offered 'on the house' and the price was ludicrous, something like one pound for the four of us. Mehmet's smile, his joy at our arrival and the sublime view sent us back to Bouboulina as happy as guests leaving a five star gourmet shrine. On future visits we were always greeted by chicken feathers floating their way towards us. As tourism developed, the lean-to became bigger and more solid. Today there is a large concrete restaurant able to accommodate a hundred people with a road leading to it from Fehtiye. Mehmet has a Mercedes and buys his chickens frozen from a supermarket. Prices have soared accordingly, we pass by on sailing trips remembering the 'good old days'.

FROM *Breakfasts with Kaptan June* by June Haimoff

Mary Lee Settle, an American writer, spent three idyllic years living in Bodrum in the early 1970s, and writes, 'I found there the greatest capacity for friendship I have ever known. It was in the genes of the Turkish people, so deep and so beyond individual choice that I have wondered ever since about its sources.' She had initially attempted to live in Kos, but she found it unfriendly and lonely. She was astonished at the contrast in Bodrum, where she immediately made friends and felt at home. She left Bodrum in 1975. Her return, sixteen years later, was painful:

I couldn't avoid going to Bodrum any longer. So after sixteen years of nostalgia and memory, it was time, if it would ever be. I went with one of my dearest American friends. I thought of him as imported friendship in case all my old friends were gone, or changed, or rich, or had forgotten me.

As we got nearer Bodrum, my worst fears were beginning to be realized. There was a constant traffic jam along the wide new paved road that ignored the ancient monuments so that vacation vans and cars and buses could speed into the town.

I recognized nothing as we drove in, not one landmark of the place I had known for three years. We turned into the main street along the Turkish harbor, and at last I saw something I knew – the little mosque beside the sea, with its slender minaret insignificant against the masts of foreign yachts.

Where there had been local *bakkals*, small groceries and food stores that stayed open half the night on hot nights in the old days when nobody could sleep, hotels and rich villas gleaming with new white paint and concrete stretched along the quays. There were offices for Avis, American Express, and Benetton; a private yacht club; a limo service; rug after rug after rug shop.

When we walked out along the wide elegant new quay, built over a shore where I used to watch the tide go in and out, I counted a hundred yachts from all over the world, nestled beside each other in the *liman* where once in high summer there might have been ten. There were no fishing boats, no sponge-diving boats among them.

All the way up to the walls of Halicarnassus, the empty hillside meadows were covered with holiday houses, all alike, that looked from a distance like white skulls. When I went to look for the ancient theater I found it, after a hard climb, beyond the new noisy highway, full of traffic, dangerous to cross.

It was Friday, but the *pazar* had moved away from the main square. That had been made into an informal parking space for taxis, parked nose to nose. They roared and sped and honked day and night up and down the narrow streets. I saw not one *dolmus*; any self-respecting camel would have scorned the place. There were no donkeys, no carts from the country. Bodrum had been completely mechanized.

There were no country people at the *pazar*. The beautiful vegetable market was organized and permanent, stretched under awnings along the main road into Bodrum. The display was as colorful as it had always been. But the booths in the clothing and hardware *pazar* were full of shoddy imitations of Western clothes and souvenirs for tourists.

It was no longer my sweet, kind, quiet town. It was, to me, a place that had been changed by invasion, as the cities I had seen in Anatolia had been changed and overlaid centuries ago. But this was twentieth-century invasion, Yenibodrum, New Bodrum. It is busy and shining and very, very rich, white as bone, too elegant for the country people I had known to live there any more.

They are all gone: the carpenter, the fishermen, the sponge divers, the dolmuses stuffed with country people. When I looked for the place where I had lived, I couldn't even recognize the street.

All the way along the Greek side of the town there were bars and hotels where there had been bakkals, fairly primitive lokantas, and small houses. Large charter boats clung together out at the end of a pier, some advertising belly dancers. The old Halikarnas Hotel on a point at the end of the bay had become a chic and noisy motel-cum-disco that I was told pulsed through the night.

. . . It seemed churlish to mourn. I stopped searching for what was gone and began to enjoy what was there – a new Bodrum, shining white in the sun.

FROM *Turkish Reflections* by Mary Lee Settle

CHAPTER SEVEN

Ottoman Episodes

For millennia upon millennia this coast has witnessed the rise and fall of Empires – be they Lydians, Persians, Athenians, Ptolemaic Egypt, Seleucid Syria, the Rhodians, Romans, Byzantines and Seljuks. Remnants of almost all these Empires linger on this coast, and sometimes intermingle. Recent history began in the fifteenth century when the Ottoman dynasty began to extend its rule from its heartland in north-west Turkey, gradually subsuming all their old neighbours, a cluster of Turkic Emirates, into its expanding Empire. The actual coastline remained a war zone for the Knights of St John of the Hospital preyed on the shipping as well as the settlements on the coast for some two hundred years of licensed piracy. So the Ottoman era over the southern Aegean only effectively began in 1522. This was the year that Sultan Süleyman the Magnificent finally forced the surrender of the Crusader Knights of St John in Rhodes, following an intensely fought siege that had lasted six months. With the departure of the Knights Turkish rule of this coast and of the Dodecanese islands was unchallenged and would remain so until the early twentieth century.

The Sovereign, Military and Hospitaller Order of St John had ruled Rhodes since 1309. Driven from Acre in 1291, their last foothold in the Holy Land, the Knights had retreated first to Cyprus, then seized Rhodes from a semi-independent Byzantine governor. From then until the early sixteenth century, the Knights of St John in Rhodes were the dominant naval power of the south-eastern Aegean. The knights ran their own sovereign, religious and aristocratic state. It was a slave-owning, slave-trading society, and its foreign policy was the incessant castigation of Islam.

The Knights operated a highly efficient navy, mainly galleys, with which they harassed non-Christian shipping. A network of outlying defences controlled by the Knights in Kalymnos, Kos, Leros, Nisyros, Tilos, and in the east Castellorizo (facing modern Ka), allowed them to control the coast. Bodrum Castle, begun in the 1450s, functioned as an armed lookout post, and could communicate with the castle on Kos. The knights would swoop on trading ships carrying timber south from the Black Sea, or spices from Arabia, or ships carrying honey, dried figs, and so on. The Ottomans viewed the Knights as little more than brigands and terrorists. This is clear from this Turkish description of the Knights by Mustafa Gelal-Zade, a Turkish diplomat-writer of the sixteenth century:

It was the determination of the Padishah, Father of the World and Conqueror of the Earth, to move against Buda, capital of the unhappy land of Hungary; but one sect of the accursed 'Firenghi', worst of the sons of terror, sent by Sheitan and noted for cunning and artifice, outcasts, accursed workers of iniquity, expert seamen and outstanding navigators, possessed great fortresses in all parts of the Mediterranean coast. In the straits and upon the islands inhabited by these obstinate vipers there were wide lands and strong forts in mountain and plain. These infidels were masters of much territory . . . and their Corsairs, noted for their energy and courage, attacked and cut the sea routes, causing great loss and suffering to peaceful merchants, capturing or destroying their ships and carrying the people off into slavery. Above all, the fortified city of Rhodes was a refuge for these accursed Franks. Its fortresses were without equal and its defences incomparable in all the earth, and here these souls destined for Eblis had their secure refuge whence they sent out their swift galleys to the hurt and loss of Islam, permitting no merchant or pilgrim ship to pass towards Egypt unharmed by their cannon, enslaving and putting chains upon the free and the innocent . . . How many children of the Prophet fall prisoner to the people of error? How many have chains put about their necks and gyves upon their ankles? How many thousands of the Faithful are forced to deny their Faith? How many virgins and young women? How many wives and infants? . . . Their malignity knows no end . . . The Sultans of the Jihad thought their conquest impossible . . . Mehmet Khan, now eternally in Paradise, may God illumine his tomb, sent the Grand Vezir Misac Pasha with valorous men . . . but they returned disconsolate. From that time [Rhodes] has increased in strength and confidence. It is the outpost of all the Infidel lands from whence come sustenance and treasure. The pride and the persistence in error of those evil men have closed and barred all the sea routes. Therefore, the Padishah, whose strength is of the Angels, the protected of God, the companion of Khidr, inspired and favoured by God . . . saw fit to conquer Rhodes . . . Once more the shout is raised whose echo fills the earth. The Lord of Time goes to war. Old and young raise your hands in prayer. Rejoice, for all is prepared . . . '

FROM *Assedio e conquista di Rodi nel 1522, secondo le relazioni edite e inedite dei* Turchi by E. Rossi

A first, unsuccessful, attempt had been made to capture Rhodes in 1480. Dynastic complexities distracted the Ottomans until 1522, when the young Sultan Suleyman the Magnificent landed an army of 100,000 men and again laid siege to Rhodes.

This is the Sultan's eve-of-siege letter of to the Grand Master of the Knights, of June 10th, 1522:

The Sultan Suleyman to Villiers de L'Isle Adam,
Grand Master of Rhodes, to his knights, and to the people at large.
Your monstrous injuries against my most afflicted people have aroused my pity and indignation. I command you, therefore, instantly to surrender the island and fortress of Rhodes, and I give you my gracious permission to depart in safety with the most precious of your effects; or if you desire to remain under my government, I shall not require of you any tribute, or do aught in diminution of your liberties, or against your religion. If you are wise, you will prefer friendship and peace to a cruel war. Since, if you are conquered, you will have to undergo all such miseries as are usually inflicted by those that are victorious, from which you will be protected neither by your own forces, nor by external aid, nor by the strength of your fortifications which I will overthrow to

their foundations. If, therefore, you prefer my friendship to war, there shall be neither fraud nor stratagem used against you. I swear this by the God of heaven, the Creator of the earth, by the four Evangelists, by the four thousand Prophets, who have descended from heaven, chief amongst whom stands Mahomet, most worthy to be worshipped; by the shades of my grandfather and father, and by my own sacred, august, and imperial head.

Quoted in *The Two Sieges of Rhodes* by Eric Brockman

There followed one of the great sieges of history, also one of the great symbolic battles between Christendom and Islam. Both sides showed extraordinary courage and tenacity, and the tiny defending force of a few hundred knights managed to withstand assault after assault and an intense bombardment from the Turkish cannons. But in December 1522, after six months the surviving Knights, exhausted and short of food, finally accepted terms and were permitted to leave Rhodes unmolested. The castle of St Peter in Bodrum was the very last piece of Asian soil to be lost by the crusaders. It surrendered in January 1523, shortly after the capitulation of Rhodes. By 1530 the Knights of St John were re-established in Malta, where they remain to this day.

*   *   *

The Ottomans ruled the Aegean for almost four centuries, and brought peace and a degree of security to a region that had not known it for a millennium. The secret of Ottoman government was its tolerance of minorities. Christians, Muslims, Jews and Armenians coexisted happily, and were permitted a degree of autonomy, providing they respected the military and taxation requirements of the Sultan in the capital. As a result the many different communities of the islands and of the towns lived quite peacefully together for many centuries.

From the late nineteenth century the peaceful coexistence between Greek and Turk that had existed since the cessation of the Crusades began to break down. In the larger islands – particularly in Crete and in Cyprus – Greeks and Turks began to fight. As Turkish power weakened, inter-communal tensions grew. Barry Unsworth's novel *Pascali's Island* captures this tension.

Between 1905 and 1910 Bodrum's population was virtually doubled by the arrival of Moslems driven out of Crete (in the mid-nineteenth century a third of the island was considered to be Muslim). In the 1960s the Turkish anthropologist Fatma Mansur interviewed some of the surviving 'Cretans' in Bodrum, and learnt their history:

One night in 1897, the Greeks attacked the Turks living in the villages of the Istiya district and it is said that three thousand Turks died that night. It is at that time that old Devlet Hanim had the lobes of her ears cut off because her attackers wanted her earrings. They thought that the little girl lying prone by the bodies of her parents was dead. Today, she is very old and can be seen in the streets of Bodrum, with her futa – the white and black cotton shawl worn by the Bodrum women – covering her mutilated ears.

This was not the first time that such massacres had occurred. Indeed the nineteenth century was punctuated by atrocities committed by both sides as Greece struggled to become independent from the Ottoman Empire.

All through the years, small bands of Greeks attacked Turks and vice-versa. But in 1897, the Greek resistance had been better organized by the Greek independence movement from the mainland, the Ethike Hetaireia, and the Ottoman commander was unable to control events. The survivors of the massacre left the villages and poured into the nearest towns, especially Kandya. There was another massacre. The Turks, terrified, having lost homes and cattle and with nowhere to go, attacked the Greeks, supported by the Turkish population of the town. Dervis Usta said that the Turks killed as many Greeks, if not more.

At this stage, the European powers stepped in. The French occupied Ispirlonga, the British Kandya and the Italians Hanya. Dervis's father was a cafe-owner and the cafe was next door to the prison. From that day on, there were two flags flying on the prison roof, and two sentinels by the prison gate, one Ottoman and one French. The French ordered the surrender of all weapons, but some of the Turks who were fishermen and seamen told Dervis's father and others that they should give their arms to them and that they would carry the arms into Anatolia, the motherland. At night, the armoury was broken into by the Ottoman officers and all the arms and ammunition were given to the seamen. When the French came in the morning, the Armoury stood open, its doors broken and its stores empty. Dervis's father and his brothers together with the other men were informed against and a search party of French soldiers came to the café to enquire. Not finding their men there, they came to his home and Dervis Usta remembers his mother opening the door and telling the French that she had not seen her husband for two days and nights. Dervis's father and his friends had fled to Bodrum in the night in the sailboat of another refugee. The journey was a hazard in those days, said Dervis, because there were no engines on the boats and people's lives depended upon the winds.

The French then declared that all the Turks who wanted to leave Crete could do so. Dervis Usta's family all left in a boat which was sailing that very day:

There were sixty-five families in the boat. After they started, the wind fell and they had to drop anchor in Kos harbour. They did that 'since Kos was Ottoman soil, just like Anatolia'. The leader of the Turkish community there prevailed upon them to stay in Kos, since he was intent upon increasing the size of his community. The families decided to stay and the man wrote to the Porte in Istanbul for credits to build them houses. When I asked Dervis Usta how many families settled in Kos during that period he said, 'Well now, let me see, three hundred houses were built and in those days there were six and eight people in one family'. This is how it happened that most of the Cretans who eventually settled in Bodrum arrived here via Kos.

In 1912, when the Italians took Kos along with other islands in the Dodecanese, the Cretan refugees came to Bodrum and began to make a new life for themselves. There were Greeks then still living in the quarter of Kumbahce, grouped around a largish church. 'Djange' Suleyman – so called because he changes money

for tourists – has a father who still remembers the arrival of the
Cretans. They all came, 'one boatful', about four hundred people,
and began to look for houses to live in. In those days the Cretans
lived all over town, wherever they could find a house for rent.

FROM Bodrum, a town in the Aegean by Fatma Mansur

*   *   *

In September 1922 the south Aegean was to witness an event that still
hangs like a shadow over the whole region. This was the burning of
Smyrna (now Izmir) and the death of many thousands of its Greeks and
Armenians in the flames. It was an event that shocked the world at the
time. For the nascent Turkish Republic it was something of a public-
relations disaster. But exactly what caused the fire is unknown. The
Turkish authorities at the time vehemently denied that the fire had been
deliberately started. But all accounts are highly partisan, particularly
when it comes to the question of who started the fire. The Turks blame
the Armenian and Greek communities for deliberately torching a city
they were abandoning. The Greeks and Armenians accuse the Turkish
army of deliberately setting fires. Foreign observers were divided.

The historical background leading up to the fire is highly complex,
for in the aftermath of World War One the victorious powers
attempted a wholesale break-up and redistribution of the Ottoman
Empire. The Italians occupied Antalya, and most of the south-west,
the French occupied Cilicia, the British and French together
garrisoned Istanbul. In the far south, France occupied the old Ottoman
province of Syria whilst Britain helped herself to Palestine, Jordan and
Iraq. Central Arabia and the Emirates along the Persian Gulf were to
be given their independence.

Meanwhile the Greek government, encouraged by Britain and
France, claimed the Mediterranean littoral of Asia Minor as part of
'Greater Greece', and landed an army in Izmir in 1919 and advanced
into Anatolia almost as far as Ankara. In August 1922 Mustafa Kemal,
the military commander who had heroically defended Gallipoli,
decisively routed the Greek army at the battle of Sakaraya river, just
outside. Pursued by the victorious Turks, the Greek armies retreated
to the coast, burning cities as they abandoned them.

The first units of Turkish army entered Smyrna on September 9th, and for a few days there was an uneasy calm as it took command of a city packed with terrified civilians. On September 14th the fire broke out. Something like half a million refugees fled to the quayside to escape the flames – an area a kilometre long and perhaps fifty metres wide. Here they found themselves trapped between the fire and the sea. Many jumped into the harbour to escape the flames and drowned. Izmir harbour was full of allied warships at the time, but their neutral status made them hesitant to intervene. Ten thousand civilians may have died in the disaster.

A few eye-witness accounts of this tragedy survive. This is by Captain Bertram Thesiger, an officer on HMS *King George V*:

Saturday 9 September 1922 – I landed this morning and walked to the railway station. The whole station yard and space between station and pier was a mass of people looting. Suddenly there was a sound of firing and a yell of 'the Turks'. The mob stampeded towards me pursued by about 400 Turkish cavalry slashing their swords about and firing pistols. I thought there was bound to be a slaughter but managed to get between the mob and the cavalry and hold up my hand and they all halted by order. The colonel in command having asked me who I was, asked me what I wanted. I then explained to him that the allies had taken over control of the town until the Turkish army was able to do so, and that if he went along the sea-front quietly there should be no danger and no firing. Whilst speaking to him a Greek was shot dead alongside me . . . I will leave out all other details.

Wednesday 13 September – As the Turks entered the town the refugees stampeded and many went overboard and were drowned. At first things were fairly orderly. The Turkish infantry arrived on Sunday and this afternoon landing parties were embarked. There was looting, rape and murder everywhere, most of it caused by the cheetehs, or irregulars. Many revolting and brutal things happened and murders were being committed all the time and the harbour was full of dead bodies.

Thursday 14 September – I never anticipated that this letter would be so full of absolute horrors as it will be. Yesterday afternoon the town was set on fire deliberately in three different places well inshore. There being a strong wind blowing towards the shore it soon spread. Our first job was to get off the remainder of the British refugees and this was done by about nine o'clock.

I am not clever enough to describe the scene during the night. Imagine a very large sea port town with very narrow streets and a row of houses facing the sea. On the road between the houses and the sea imagine a dense mass of humanity. Set the whole of this on fire about two streets from the sea and you have the situation about 9 p.m. About midnight the first flames broke through the front street, all the bundles in the street containing the clothes and worldly belongings of the refugees then caught fire. People started to jump into the sea to escape and the C-in-C made a signal to send boats to bring off anyone.

I went away in charge of our boats and made straight for the place where the fire had broken through. Many bundles of things had been thrown into the sea and bad luck made two sheets and a great coat get round my propeller which made me absolutely helpless. The boat drifted alongside the sea wall and my boat was rushed. We started to capsize when something happened; probably we rested on bundles on the bottom but we went no further. I drew my revolver but people were much too frightened to mind that in the least. In the end I shoved off a yard from the wall with boat hooks and got a pulling boat to tow me to the nearest destroyer where I cleared my propeller and carried on.

The noise was about the most horrible thing you can imagine. First we had the awful roar of burning then walls falling in and roofs, explosions of naphtha and other oils and occasionally ammunition and last and by far the worst continual screaming of the thousands on the front. One honestly could not hear oneself speak much less convey an order except by signs. Never in the history of the world can anything much worse have happened as the Turks made not the slightest attempt to save people in fact I gather they helped to burn them. I dread to think how many lives were lost and I only hope we are leaving here before tonight as tonight will be the same and the screams from the people on shore are awful. With the lot I brought off one man had had his throat cut and another was shot right through; they are still alive. The hospital was burnt down and all the wounded and patients cast loose.

The gratitude of the people for water was touching. It was all very difficult and the saddest thing I have ever had to do. The week has tried most people very much and many officers I have seen who have broken down at some of the sights.

If I have not written very clearly today forgive me but it has been a trying time and of course I had no sleep last night.

FROM the unpublished letters of Bertram Thesiger

Lieutenant Merrill, an American naval officer, returned from Constantinople on the USS *Edsall* at an hour before sunrise on September 14th. He found:

The entire city was ablaze and the harbour as light as day . . . thousands of homeless were surging back and forth along the blistering quay, panic-stricken to the point of insanity. The shrieks of women and children were painful to hear. In a frenzy they would throw themselves into the water, and some of them would reach the ship. The crowds along the quay were so thick and tried so desperately to close in abreast of the men-of-war anchorage, that the masses in the stifling center had nowhere to go but into the sea. Fortunately, the quay wall never got actually hot enough to roast these unfortunate people alive but the heat must have been terrific there to have been felt on the ship two hundred yards away. To add further to the confusion the packs belonging to these refugees, consisting mostly of carpets and clothing, caught, making a chain of bonfires the length of the street. Occasionally the pack on a horse's back would take fire and he would go charging through the crowd at breakneck speed, knocking right and left the Christian minorities; truly a 'fiery steed'.

The US headquarters at Smyrna theatre appeared like a large ball of fire. So hot was it in the street in front of this building that the four automobiles and two trucks parked at the door were burnt to cinders. Some of us saw a grim humour in the sign over the arched door in black letters two feet high. It was the name of the last movie shown: 'Le Tango de la Mort'.

Quoted in *Smyrna 1922* by Marjorie Housepian

Ward Price, a well-known journalist of his day, described the same scene from the deck of HMS *Iron Duke*:

What I see as I stand on the deck of the *Iron Duke* is an unbroken wall of fire, two miles long, in which twenty distinct volcanoes of raging flames are throwing up jagged, writhing tongues to a height of a hundred feet. Against the curtain of fire, which blocks out the sky, are silhouetted the towers of the Greek churches, the domes of the mosques, and the flat square roofs of the houses.

All Smyrna's warehouses, businesses, buildings, and European residences, and others behind them, burn like furious torches.

From this intensely glowing mass of yellow, orange and crimson fire pour up thick clotted coils of oily black smoke that hide the moon at its zenith.

The sea glows a deep copper-red. And worst of all from the densely packed mob of many thousands of refugees huddled on the narrow quay, between the advancing fiery death behind and the deep water in front, comes continuously such frantic screaming of sheer terror as can be heard miles away.

Added to this there is the frequent roar and crash of exploding ammunition stores, accompanied by the rattle of burning cartridges, which sounds like an intensive infantry action.

Picture a constant projection into a red-hot sky of gigantic incandescent balloons, burning oil spots in the Aegean, the air filled with nauseous smell, while parching mouths, cinders and sparks drift across us – and you can have but a glimmering of the scene of appalling and majestic destruction which we are watching.

FROM *Daily Mail*, September 1922

Over the following two years Greece and Turkey exchanged

minority populations on a vast scale. One and a half million Orthodox Greeks resident in Turkey moved to Greece, and some half a million Muslims resident in Greece returned to Turkey. There was great suffering on both sides.

The precise terms of this painful divorce were laid down in the bleak words of a convention signed at the Conference of Lausanne on January 30th, 1923:

> . . . There shall take place a compulsory exchange of Turkish nationals of the Greek Orthodox religion established in Turkish territory and of Greek nationals of the Muslim religion established in Greek territory. These persons shall not return to live in Turkey or Greece without the authorisation of the Turkish government or the Greek government respectively.

This was the world's first internationally ratified compulsory population exchange. It proved to be a watershed in the eastern Mediterranean, having far-reaching ramifications both for the new Turkish Republic, and for Greece, which had to absorb over a million refugees.

Today the Exchange is known as the 'Asia Minor Catastrophe' by the Greeks, while for Turks it tends to be viewed as an inevitable part of the peace process and the establishment of an independent nation state. However, in many parts of this coast the departure of the Greeks had a disastrous economic impact, and it would be many decades before prosperity returned.

Henry Morgenthau, an American financier who was sent as a US special representative to Athens in 1923, travelled by way of Salonika, and while there saw a ship carrying refugees from the Black Sea region, which had just sailed in:

> A more tragic sight could scarcely be imagined. I saw 7,000 people crowded in a ship that would have been taxed to normal capacity with 2,000. They were packed like sardines on the deck, a squirming, writhing mass of human misery. They had been at sea for four days. There had not been space to permit them to lie down to sleep; there had been no food to eat; there was not access to any toilet

facilities. For those four days and nights, many had stood upon the open deck, drenched by an autumn rain, pierced by the cold night wind, and blistered by the noonday sun. They came ashore in rags, hungry, sick, covered with vermin, hollow-eyed, exhaling the horrible odour of human filth – bowed with despair. And yet these old men and children and women only a few weeks before had been living at peace, in happy homes, useful and industrious citizens, comfortably housed and clothed, and fed with the fruits of contented labour.

FROM *I Was Sent to Athens* by Henry Morgenthau

It can be difficult to grasp the enormity of these events, and the scale of human suffering involved. This extract from a recent history of the Exchange of Populations conveys this:

For hundreds of thousands of people on both sides of the Aegean, the trauma of departure – of being deported, often in dire conditions, from a home village to which they were deeply attached – was compounded by the difficulty of adapting to their new country and deliberately forgetting most things that connected them to the old country. So if, when contemplating the physical environment of Turkey or Greece, we sense that we are in a place which has suffered a terrible shock or trauma whose effects are still being felt, that intuition is perfectly well founded.

It has been estimated that about 20 per cent of the population of Anatolia died violently during the last ten years of the Ottoman empire's existence: some 2.5 million Muslims, up to 800,000 Armenians and 300,000 Greeks. To put it another way, a third of the Christian population and one eighth of the Muslim population had been killed, making the Ottoman empire a far more rural, and Islamic place: its population was now at least 96 per cent Muslim, up from 80 per cent before the decade of mutual slaughter began. The population exchange marked a final, cold-blooded conclusion of the process whereby Anatolia became Muslim and the southern Balkans became mostly Christian.

It was not just the migrants themselves who were affected by this extraordinary episode in European history. It is hardly an exaggeration to say that the modern societies of Turkey and Greece were constituted by the population exchange; not only because of the newcomers that each country was obliged to absorb, but also (especially in the Turkish case) because of the population each state forfeited. For certain parts of Turkey, the departure of the Christians meant the loss of virtually all traders and entrepreneurs, as well as most professional people and skilled craftsmen. In those parts of central Anatolia where commercial life was once heavily dominated by Christians, there is still a sense that the local economy has never recovered.

Greece was affected more by an influx than by an exodus. In many of its northern regions, and in certain districts of Athens, the population is still overwhelmingly of 'Asia Minor' stock.

FROM *Twice a Stranger* by Bruce Clark

For an impression of the extreme suffering of the civilian population (of all religions and ethnic groups) in Anatolia in the period 1914–24 it is worth reading Louis de Bernières' novel *Birds without Wings*, which describes with great skill this traumatic and complex period of Turkish history. The novel is set in a mixed Greek-Muslim town of Eskibahce, about twenty miles from Fethiye before, during and after the First World War. The book conveys the horrific human implications for individuals and families of the decisions made by national governments.

Here de Bernières describes the forced resettlement of the Greek population of Eskibahce:

At first no one believed what the gendarmes were telling them, but it soon became apparent that this was no prank. Sergeant Osman's orders were to collect the entire Christian population of the town and march it to Telmessos [Fethiye], whence it would be transferred by ships to Greece. Sergeant Osman had been given no transport, no provisions and no money with which to accomplish this feat. It was not long before he was besieged by groups of Christians who were at the very edge of hysteria.

'What about my house?'

'Lock it up.'

'What about my animals?'

'Ask your neighbours to care for them. Sell them.'

'What about my mother? She's sick. What will become of her?'

'No one can be left behind.'

'What about my son? He's away for three days. What will become of him when he returns?'

'He will be sent after us.'

'What about my samovar? It is very valuable.'

'Don't bring anything you can't carry all the way to the sea. If you have any sense bring food and clothing.'

'Tomorrow I am supposed to be meeting someone to talk about some land.'

'It's cancelled.'

'What about my things? I haven't got a cart to carry them in.' Sergeant Osman would raise his hands to appeal for calm, repeating, 'Listen, all of you, in your new home you will get compensation to the exact value of everything you have lost. There will be an issue of certificates.'

'When? Where?'

'I don't know exactly. I expect it will get sorted out at Telmessos.'

'Where is Greece?'

'Over the sea. It's not far. Don't worry, you will be looked after by the Greeks and the Franks. They will find you new homes, as good as your old ones.'

'Are the Greeks Ottomans like us?'

'No, from now on you are Greeks; not Ottomans. And we are not Ottomans any more either, we are Turks.' The sergeant held out his hands and shrugged. 'And tomorrow, who knows? We might be something else, and you might be Negroes, and rabbits will become cats.'

In their houses the Christians attempted to deal with the bewildering and impossible task of working out what to take. There were some families who regularly took animals up to the yaylas in the summer months, and were accustomed to trekking away into the distance with all they could carry, but even so they had never had to do so under such conditions of haste and uncertainty.

Most people had been plunged quite suddenly into extreme states of emotion, and were completely confused. Some were shocked and silent, some hysterical and weeping, whilst others talked wildly of disobedience and defiance, of hiding until the gendarmes had gone, even as they obediently sorted through their possessions.

Some loaded themselves up only with food and water, and others deemed it better to take valuables that they could sell to raise cash, such as copper pots and dowry jewellery. Some sold their effects to their neighbours at knock-down rates, thinking that cash would be of more use than chattels. Some sorted out objects of sentimental value, and some looked, with greater or lesser irrationality, for things that may or may not turn out to be useful, such as small coils of rope, or the head of a hoe. It was one of those exceedingly rare occasions when blessed indeed are the poor, for by far the greater proportion of the people lived in such straitened circumstances that there were relatively few choices to make. These humble souls gathered what little they had into bundles, and foregathered in the meydan. Humbler even than them were the dozen beggars of Christian origin, who were alone in experiencing optimism in the place of despair. Some were mad, some retarded and some fugitive, but for all of them the hope of a new and better life in a new land was suddenly held out. They would follow the column of refugees, imploring alms from those who had nothing to give. Among their number was not to be found the Dog. He remained amid the tombs, removed from all considerations of race and religion by virtue of his speechlessness, his mutilation and his anchoritic life. Neither did any of the Christian prostitutes arrive from the brothel, being similarly removed from all considerations of race and religion by virtue of their profession.

Here, in the epilogue, he describes Eskibahce following the deportation of the Greek population:

All these events having transpired, and the Christians having been deported, the people that remained soon got into the new habit of referring to their former neighbours as Greeks. Certainly, it was to Greece that they had been deported, and they had become Greeks whether they had wanted it or not, even if their new compatriots often deprecated them as Turks. The word 'Ottoman' would fall into disuse and disrepute until such time as the inevitable revisions of later days, when the world would realise that the Ottoman Empire had been cosmopolitan and tolerant.

The population of Anatolia was in mourning. Ten years of war, in the Balkans, then against the Franks, then in the War of Independence against the Greeks, had left tens of thousands of widows and orphans, tens of thousands of parents without inheritors, tens of thousands of brotherless sisters. It was a people bereaved and worn out beyond endurance, and it would climb out of the pit of misery only because it would have the miraculous good luck to fall under the quirky but brilliant leadership of Mustafa Kemal, who had recently decreed that from now on everyone must have a surname, and that his own was Atatürk. It was bereaved also of those who had not died. Eskibahce was dying on its feet because not enough Greek Turks had arrived to fill the empty houses of the Turkish Greeks, and in any case they had brought virtually no wealth with them. Some of the abandoned houses were looted, especially those whose owners were reputed to have secreted treasure, but those whose owners had left keys and a trust of guardianship with their Muslim neighbours simply rotted slowly away against the return of their owners, until the timbers sagged, the roofs collapsed, the cisterns clogged, and the door jambs and window frames fell away from the walls. The wrought-iron gates of the two Christian ossuaries rusted and the few ribs and teeth that were left became the playthings of ghoulish little children.

Down at the entrance to the polis, the great pump house built in 1919 as an act of philanthropy by the garrulous merchant of Smyrna, Georgio P. Theodorou, broke down and fell into disuse, because there was no one left who knew how to repair it. Travellers emerging from the pines were no longer met by the joyful sound of cool running water, and their thirst was unslaked, their hands and faces unrefreshed.

Indeed, almost no one remained who knew how to get anything done. There had been such a clear division of labour between the former inhabitants that when the Christians left, the Muslims were reduced temporarily to helplessness. There was no pharmacist now, no doctor, no banker, no blacksmith, no shoemaker, no saddle-maker, no ironmonger, no paint-maker, no jeweller, no stone-mason, no tiler, no merchant, no spicer. The race that had pre-occupied itself solely with ruling, tilling and soldiering now found itself baulked and perplexed, without any obvious means of support.

There were only two artisans left, Iskander the Potter, much diminished by the terrible wound that he had inflicted upon his favourite son, and Mehmet the Tinsman . . .

FROM *Birds without Wings* by Louis de Bernières

*   *   *

Turkey was neutral in World War Two, but from 1943 the Dodec-anese islands were the scene of desperate fighting between the German and Allied armed forces.

Until September 1943 the islands were held by large Italian garrisons, increasingly bolstered by German units. On September 8th, 1943, when Mussolini's government fell, and a new Italian administration under Badoglio joined the Allies, declaring war on Germany on September 13th, the situation became extremely complex.

Kos surrendered to the British on September 15th, only to be recaptured on October 3rd, by a German invasion force dispatched from Naxos, which took 3,145 Italian prisoners and 1,388 British.

Between October 4th and 7th 103 captured Italian officers were shot in Kos, a massacre much smaller and less well known than that in Kephalonia at almost the same time (in which 9,700 men were shot, from a total garrison of 12,000).

This dispatch from the Commander of German Forces, South East Europe, of September 21st, 1943 (intercepted and deciphered by British Secret Service 'Ultra' and now in the PRO in London) reveals the intense bitterness of German feelings towards the Italian army at the time:

The following applies for behaviour towards Italian prisoners who have fought against us: Sentimental inhibitions of any sort on the part of the German soldier towards guerillas owing allegiance to Badoglio in the uniform of our former comrades in arms are completely out of place. Any one of these men who is fighting against German soldiers has sacrificed all rights to pity and must be treated with the severity deserved by a rabble that suddenly turns its weapons against its friends.

I expect this attitude to become general with all members of G.A.P. [Germany Forces, S-E Europe Command] without delay and that they will act accordingly.

FROM Public Record Office, Kew

In late October the German army moved on Leros, to the north of Kos, which was defended by 9,000 Italians and 6,000 British soldiers. Leros surrendered on November 16th after a three-day battle in which 8,500 Italians and 4,600 British were taken prisoner, and the Royal Navy lost almost a third of its Mediterranean fleet.

Through 1944 the newly-formed SBS (Special Boat Service) organised raids on the German-held Greek islands, operating from a ship called the *Tewfiq*, a 180-ton Levant schooner bought in Beirut. This was moored in the remote bays of north Bozburun, where there is still a bay named *Ingiliz Liman* (English Harbour) to this day.

David Sutherland, an SBS officer, recalls *Tewfiq* in his memoirs:

Climbing aboard *Tewfiq*, in which I was to spend the next six weeks, I was reminded of some piratical scene from *Treasure Island*, with contemporary arms, ammunition, equipment and noises for good measure. There was the homely smell of unwashed bodies, mixed with a whiff of garlic cooking in the galley. The quiet background noise of the ship's activities was overlaid by the raucous din from the petrol-driven patrol radio battery-chargers. The ship's large hold was filled with masses of men sleeping in hammocks and bunks. Forward of the hold was a large office used as an operation planning room, table in the middle, chairs around, walls covered with maps. There, too, was the terminal of our radio link with

RFHQ at Azzib, and the outside world. I pinched for myself a small panelled cabin with a comfortable bunk and fitted writing desk. It was two flights of steep, wooden stairs above the Ops Room. I insisted on having all the bits and pieces one needs for SBS operational planning such as maps, operational files, air photographs, moon charts, typewriters, magnifying glasses, pens, etc, to hand.

The Turkish authorities seem to have turned a blind eye to these irregular commandos living in remote bays. But on one occasion, on an expedition to get supplies, Sutherland found himself in the cells of Bodrum castle for the night:

The Turks provided two vital elements: secure anchorages hidden deep in Turkish Territorial waters for our base ships and an abundant supply of provisions – meat, vegetables, fruit, water, etc – to augment our rigid military diet. The place we used to get our supplies was the port of Bodrum, the ancient Halicarnassus . . .

It was a night passage with a slight swell from the south. I went to sleep . . . The next happening would be better described by Joseph Conrad than by me. There was a sudden crack as the caique keeled over. I was ejected from my bunk. Sea water rushed in, accompanied by the deadly noise of ship's timbers grinding against rocks. Quickly struggling to the surface, I saw we had missed the harbour entrance by about 10 metres. Andrea Londos, who had retained his Commander's cap untouched, stood there swearing. Some Turkish soldiers with fixed bayonets then appeared on the harbour wall above us to find out what was going on. Clearly we were a highly suspicious lot, so the Turks marched us to Bodrum Castle and locked us up there while they checked on our credentials. It was a bitterly cold night and we were shivering from our dousing in the sea. A sympathetic Turkish soldier spotted my teeth chattering and lit a warming fire from branches lying around the castle floor. As more branches were thrown on and shadows flickered on the castle walls, some of the Turkish soldiers began their local dances with incredible stamps, gyrations and leaps, and we began to sing in unison . . .

There was a lull in this jovial campfire singing and I heard the sound of horses' hooves at full gallop on the road leading towards us. Silence – then the castle door was opened and a young Turkish officer with a large black cloak and a curved sword appeared to say that we were free to leave. It was then three in the morning.

FROM *He Who Dares*, David Sutherland

Another SBS officer recalls discreet meetings with Turkish naval vessels:

Precautions were always taken by both Navy and SBS when lying-up in Turkish waters. A plan of defence was the first requirement when moving into a new anchorage. Depot ships were scattered and concealed by either natural or net camouflage. In deference to our Turkish hosts, landings on shore were restricted to the fulfilment of the natural needs. Excursions into the interior were absolutely forbidden. Not many people live along that lovely wooded coastline and the attitude of the local military posts appeared to be one of tactful ignorance of our presence. Sometimes, when curiosity concerning us became too great, or official business required transaction, a trim little motor launch flying the Star and Crescent would draw alongside, and an officer wearing the peculiar grey woollen uniform of the Republic would clamber up the gangway. A jar of special raki, conserved for these occasions, would be opened. The proceedings usually ended in a pig hunt and shooting competitions. Conversation was conducted in French. I had always thought the simple, unadorned English accent in that language the final philological monstrosity but the Turkish accent is worse.

Some forty anchorages had been reconnoitred between Castelrosso and the tip of Samos. Many of these were used as staging-posts, others only for fast surface craft who were patrolling some particular channel.

FROM *Raiders from the Sea* by John Lodwick

MORE RECENT EVENTS

Many travellers on this coast in the last fifty years have been surprised at the extreme vigilance of Turkish military command posts. In 1953 the writer Patrick Kinross was arrested while looking at the ruins of Patara. In Knidos he gets into conversation with the young soldiers at the guard posts and asks them who they think that they are guarding *against*:

> The account of our arrest at Patara diverted them, and they laughed scornfully at the folly of their colleagues. But suspicion of the foreigner was still deeply inbred in them. For whom, we asked them, were they keeping watch so studiously?
>
> 'For enemies,' they said, with a sweep of the arm towards the spectral forms of the Dodecanese Islands, opposite. 'For the Italians, for the Greeks . . . '
>
> 'But the Italians are there no more, and the Greeks are your allies.' They smiled incredulously and continued their watch.
>
> FROM *Europa Minor* by Patrick Kinross

CHAPTER EIGHT

Expeditions, Archaeologists and Discoveries

There were several officially-sponsored archaeological expeditions from Western nations to south-west Turkey in the nineteenth century. Their object was to remove sculpture and other discoveries to the museums of western Europe, something that seems very wrong to most people today. But at the time the organisers of these expeditions firmly believed that by transporting their discoveries home they were ensuring their preservation. This chapter looks at three such British expeditions.

CAPTAIN BEAUFORT'S EXPEDITION OF 1812–13

The first and in some ways most important expedition was not archaeological but cartographic. So little was known about the south Aegean and Mediterranean coasts of Turkey, that in 1811 the Hydrographical Office of the Royal Navy dispatched Captain Francis Beaufort to carry out an accurate survey of the coast. This took two seasons to complete and was published as *Karamania, or a brief description of the South Coast of Asia Minor and of the remains of Antiquity*. 'Karamania' was then a name for this coast, rather as 'Dalmatia' today still describes the eastern coast of the Adriatic. Apart from producing an accurate chart of the coast, Beaufort also accurately recorded the position of the classical sites along the coast, and managed to identify several of them.

In his preface Beaufort dwells on what he sees as the sad condition of the coast:

The name of Karamania is commonly applied by Europeans to that mountainous tract of country which forms the southern shore of Asia Minor. But however convenient such a general appellation may be as a general distinction it is neither used by the present inhabitants, nor is it recognised at the seat of Government. A kingdom of that name did indeed once exist, it comprised the ancient provinces of Lycia, Pamphylia and the two Cilicias with parts of Caria and Phrygia, and was so called from Karaman, the chieftain by whom it was founded . . .

The names and boundaries of those ancient provinces are also entirely obliterated, and the limits, even of the present states, cannot be ascertained with any precision. Sheltered from all effectual control of the Porte by the great barrier of Mt Taurus, the half independent and turbulent pashas amongst whom they are parcelled are engaged in constant petty hostilities with each other.

Thus groaning under the worst kind of despotism, this unfortunate country has been a continued scene of anarchy, rapine and contention – her former cities deserted, her fertile valleys untilled and her rivers and harbours idle. Perhaps nothing can present a more striking picture of the pervading sloth and misery than the hardly credible fact that on this extensive line of coast, which stretches along a sea abounding with fish, the inhabitants do not possess a single boat.

The allurements of a visit to a country in such a state of civil degradation are certainly small, when contrasted with the risk of venturing among those jealous and discordant tribes. Nevertheless, it does appear somewhat strange that, while the spirit of modern discovery had explored the most remote extremities of the globe, and while the political convulsions of Europe had forced the enterprising traveller into other continents, this portion of the Mediterranean shores should have remained undescribed and almost unknown. For beside its tempting proximity to the borders of Europe and its easiness of access, this once flourishing region seems to have eminent claims to attention . . . it was once the seat of learning and riches, and theatre to some of the most celebrated events that history unfolds . . .

At a few of the western ports, it's true, some recent travellers had touched ... but of the remainder of the great range of country, the only accounts extant were those left by the ancient geographers and there were no nautical descriptions of the coast nor any charts whatsoever by which the mariner could steer.

FROM *Karamania*
by Captain Francis Beaufort

To map the coast Beaufort used a series of running surveys, in which headlands were fixed by back-and-forward bearings from known positions of his ship, while the details on the shore were fixed from a team of boats led by Beaufort himself. Under his leadership, his crew of two lieutenants, master, sundry midshipmen and the ship's doctor – whom Beaufort considered 'a better surveyor than ship's surgeon' – worked well together. It was a punishing regime, Beaufort breakfasting 'often by candlelight, always by 5' and working until sunset or later if the 'evening breeze did not lull until 8 or 9'.

He was a keen and knowledgeable antiquarian, one reason why he was given the assignment. In making an accurate chart of the coast, he also managed to locate and identify many ancient cities, as described by classical authors such as Pliny and Strabo.

Visiting Phaselis in Lycia, he describes his excitement at discovering an un-plundered tomb, which he then proceeds to break open:

There are several sarcophagi in Phaselis but none of their inscriptions were legible and excepting one, they had all been opened: this had escaped the general fate, having been concealed by a thick covering of earth, which as it lay close to the shore, the surf had partly removed; thus leaving one end of it exposed to view.

Elated with the discovery we eagerly proceeded to explore its contents. While the necessary implements were collected, our imaginations were on the stretch and urns of coins, or ancient weapons at least were expected to reward our labours. At length the tools arrived. The ponderous lid was raised and the bones of a single skeleton were discovered, and nothing more. They were strong and firm and did not undergo any immediate change from exposure to the air; the skeleton was of the middle size, was placed with the face up, and the head to the northwest.

The sea had broken into a mausoleum that stands near the aqueduct and two large sarcophagi which lay on the beach appeared to have been washed out by its violence. They were of the whitest marble and of very neat workmanship. The lids or roofs of the sarcophagi on this coast are all formed of a single stone and are generally shaped like a gothic arch. These, however, were flat. On each was a recumbent human figure in low relief. The sides of both of them were richly ornamented, one with wreaths of flowers and fruit, the other with a funeral procession and a chase, in which the figures of the boar, the rhinoceros and the elephant were manifest. Neither of them have any inscriptions. As they lay on a gravel beach exposed to the swell the sharper parts of the sculpture had at the period of our first visit already suffered from the attrition of the pebbles; but on our return the following year we were astonished at the rapidity with which the work of destruction had advanced. The more delicate parts were utterly effaced and the whole was so bruised and disfigured as to be hardly recognisable. Even the huge blocks of marble were turned over or broken into fragments.

A few weeks later Beaufort rescued the young Charles Cockerell (best remembered as the architect of the Ashmolean Museum in Oxford):

At Avova we had the satisfaction of meeting Mr Cockerell, who had been induced by our report to explore the antiquities of these desolate regions. He had hired a small Greek vessel, and had already coasted part of Lycia. Those who have experienced the filth and other miseries of such a mode of conveyance, and who know the dangers that await an unprotected European among these tribes of uncivilised Mahommedans, can alone appreciate the ardour which could lead to such an enterprise. I succeeded in persuading him to remove to His Majesty's ship, in which he might pursue his researches with less hazard and with some degree of comfort. The alarm felt by his crew on seeing the frigate had been excessive. Had she been a Turkish man-of-war, they were sure of being pillaged under the pretext of exacting a present; if a Barbary cruiser, the youngest men would have been forcibly seized for recruits, and the rest plundered; and even if she had been a Greek merchant-ship, their security would still have been precarious; for when one of these large Greek polaccas meets even her own countrymen in small vessels and in unfrequented places she often compels them to assist in loading her, or arbitrarily takes their cargoes at her own prices.

Cockerell's journal describes the same meeting:

April 28th – We weighed anchor early, but there was no wind as yet, and we had rowed for some hours when we became aware of a large sail coming up on a breeze. As I scanned her I had little doubt she would be the Salsette or the Frederiksteen; but my poor captain was very much frightened, and when he saw her send a boat to board a small vessel before us, he desired his sons to hide his money in the ballast. It was not long, however, before I made out with my glass the red cross, and then I was able to set his mind at rest. When our little caique came alongside, we must have been a shabby sight; but Captain Beaufort bade me heartily welcome and gave me so cordial a shake of the hand as I can never forget. He said he had hunted for me all along the coast, and pressed me to take a cruise with him, rather than go on travelling in this hazardous fashion in the caique. The offer was tantalising; but, as I was not sure if I should feel at my ease, I only promised to stay a few days to begin with.

FROM *Travels in Southern Europe & The Levant*
by Charles Cockerell

Some weeks later, on June 20th, Captain Beaufort was wounded and one of his midshipmen killed while exploring and surveying further east along the Mediterranean coast near Iskenderun.

CHARLES FELLOWS AND THE XANTHUS EXPEDITIONS
OF 1842 AND 1844

Charles Fellows was an enterprising gentleman-scholar, who made three visits to Turkey between 1838 and 1844 and is now famous for making the city of Xanthus in Lycia familiar to the world and organising the removal of a large part of it to the British Museum. Most modern guidebooks talk about Fellows 'stripping' the site. But he seems to have acted out of a wish to protect the monuments, as much as a wish to enrich the British Museum. And by the standards of his age his methods were careful and responsible. He describes his first impressions of Xanthus in the journal of his first visit, in 1838:

> It was noon before we had found . . . the frontier village of Koonik. When taking the riding horses, we started to see the ruins of the city of Xanthus, which lay at about two miles' distance, upon or overhanging the river of that name. The other horses were to wait our return. We had no sooner entered the place of tombs, than objects of such high interest to the antiquarian, sculptor, and artist appeared, that I determined to send for the baggage, and pitch my tent here for the night.
>
> *April 19th* – It is now noon, and I regret that I have not had time, and do not possess sufficient talent, to examine completely the objects here, which alone afford inducement to the man of taste to visit this country, even from distant England. The remains appear to be all of the same date, and that a very early one. The walls are many of them Cyclopean: The language of the in-numerable and very perfect inscriptions is like the Phoenician or Etruscan, and the beautiful tombs in the rocks, on the side of the entrance of one of which is the following inscription, are also of a very early date.
>
> The elegant designs evince the talent of the Greeks, and the highly poetical subjects of the bas-reliefs, the temples, friezes, and tombs, some of them blending in one figure the forms of many, probably to describe its attributes, are also of Greek character. The ruins are wholly of temples, tombs, triumphal arches, walls, and a theatre. The site is extremely romantic, upon beautiful hills; some

crowned with rocks, others rising perpendicularly from the river, which is seen winding its way down from the woody uplands, while beyond in the extreme distance are the snowy mountains in which it rises. On the west the view is bounded by the picturesquely formed but bare range of Mount Cragus, and on the east by the mountain chain extending to Patara. A rich plain, with its meandering river, carries the eye to the horizon of the sea towards the south-west.

The city has not the appearance of having been very large, but its remains show that it was highly ornamented, particularly the tombs, two of which I have put in my sketchbook somewhat in detail, as well as some other sculptures. I did not find any well-formed Greek letters; in an inscription over a gateway, and on one or two architectural stones, the Greek alphabet was used, but not the pure letters. There is no trace of the Roman or the Christian age, and yet there are points, such as the costume in the bas-relief, the attitude and appearance of groups of figures, that reminded me of the times of the Crusades and of the Romans.

I have attempted a sketch of the most beautiful of the tombs, and I add the description by pen to make my drawing more intelligible. It is a sarcophagus, entirely of white marble, standing on the side of a hill rich with wild shrubs, – the distant mountains, of the silvery grey peculiar to marble rocks, forming the background . . .

FROM *Journal Written in Asia Minor* by Charles Fellows

The following year, accompanied by a young architect and a draughtsman, he made a much more thorough, almost systematic, search for ruined cities in Lycia and Caria, the old Roman provinces to the south of Smyrna. On this expedition he managed to locate twenty-four of the thirty-six cities in those provinces mentioned by Pliny the Elder in his *Naturalis Historia* of AD 77 – an impressive achievement.

The publication of his journals caused such interest that in 1842 HMS *Beacon*, accompanied by Lieutenant Spratt, was sent to bring various monuments and tombs back to the British Museum.

A *firman*, or permission to excavate and remove, had first to be obtained from the Turkish government, known as the Porte. Even at this time, this was no very easy matter. The Ambassador applied for a *firman* in Constantinople, and they were not always granted. It is interesting to reproduce the correspondence for the *firman* for Xanthus:

A letter from the H.H. the Grand Vizir to Hadji Ali Pasha,
Governor of Rhodes, dated 155th Sheoval 1257 (29th Nov. 1841)
[After the usual titles] – The British embassy has represented by tairer [a note in Turkish] that there are some antiquities consisting in sculptured stones, lying down, and of no use, at a place near the village of Koonik, in the District of Marmoriss, which is one of the dependencies of Rhodes, and not far from the sea-shore; and has requested that the antiques aforesaid should be given to the British Government, for the purpose of putting them in the Museum. The British Embassy has in the meantime represented, that the distinguished Captain Graves has been ordered by the British Government to embark those stones and to carry them to England; and that as he is going himself to the spot a letter was asked in his behalf, that your Excellency may give him every assistance on this occasion.

The Sublime Porte is interested in granting such demands, in consequence of the sincere friendship existing between the two Governments. If, therefore, the antiquities above mentioned are lying down here and there, and are of no use, Your Excellency shall make no objection to the Captain's taking them away and carrying them on board; and to that effect you will be pleased to appoint one or two of your attendants to accompany him. Should any great obstacle exist in giving them, you will write him on the subject, that we may do what is necessary.

Such are the Sultan's commands, in conformity to which you will act; and, consequently, I write and forward to Your Excellency the present dispatch.

L. Mehemed Riouf S.

QUOTED IN *Travels and Researches in Asia Minor*
by Sir Charles Fellows

Lieutenant Thomas Spratt, co-author (with the naturalist Dr E. Forbes) of *Travels in Lycia* (1847) gives a vivid description of the excavations at Xanthus:

> Whilst we were there, these sculptures were daily dug out of the earth, and brought once more to view. The search for them was intensely exciting; and, in the enthusiasm of the moment, our admiration of their art was, perhaps, a little beyond their merits. As each block of marble was uncovered, and the earth carefully brushed away from its surface, the form of some fair amazon or stricken warrior, of an eastern king or a besieged castle became revealed, and gave rise to many a pleasant discussion as to the sculptor's art therein displayed, or the story in the history of the ancient Xanthians therein represented – conversations which all who took part in will ever look back upon as among the most delightful in their lives. Often, after the work of the day was over and the night had closed in, when we had gathered round the log fire in the comfortable Turkish cottage which formed the headquarters of the party, we were accustomed to sally forth, torch in hand, Charles Fellows as *cicerone*, to cast a midnight look of admiration on some spirited battle scene or headless Venus, which had been the great prize of the morning's work.

However, when Spratt revisits Xanthus in early March, a certain guilt about the removal of these antiquities is clear:

> Xanthus was once more our point of rendezvous on the departure of the *Beacon*, and our little party, having bade adieu to all friends on shipboard, took up its quarters among the ruins. The lively scene of the last two months, the busy group of active English sailors, and wondering crowd of turbaned natives, had changed; and Xanthus was almost as desolate and lonely as when first discovered. Not, however, the same, for its proud monuments had been despoiled of their ornaments, and its long-buried treasures brought to light. On the platform before our habitation lay between seventy and eighty huge cases, containing the relics of its ancient grandeur, destined to adorn the national Museum of a distant land, – one which, when

Xanthus flourished, was yet more wild and barbarous than the land of the Xanthians is now.

FROM *Travels in Lycia* by T. Spratt and E. Forbes

Fellows seems to have tried hard to limit the damage inflicted on the sculptures in the naval removal works, as his description of the removal of the Horse Tomb seems to show:

Xanthus, February 1844

The gunner informed me one morning at half-past eight o'clock, that they were going to pull down Horse Tomb. I begged that he would delay for an hour, as I wished to mark with lines and numbers the various cracks and stones upon the middle story, and to map them accurately, as I felt sure it would fall in pieces as soon as the weight of the top was removed. This I did, and left the men to proceed with this monument also, for the removal of which I had suggested plans, differing altogether from those now adopted. My feelings were the same as with respect to the Harpy Tomb, and I did not interfere, except to request them to clear away previously all stones from around, and afterwards to preserve any fragment which might fall. The means adopted appeared to me to be more sailor-like than scientific; the men placed slings and cord over the top, which probably weighed ten tons, and making blocks fast to the neighbouring rocks, pulled the top off. As I anticipated, the centre fell in pieces, but the sculptured parts did not receive more injury than they probably would have done from a more scientific operation. The whole may be easily restored, and will again form one of the most elegant and interesting monuments I have ever seen. The several parts of this tomb are so heavy that it is necessary they should be cut: I have therefore marked with black paint the lines for the saw, in order that the sculpture should not be injured. This will reduce the weight of the various parts so that they may be packed in cases . . .

Travels and Researches in Asia Minor by Sir Charles Fellows

Although Fellows was the first European to rediscover Pinara, by far the best description of that city is in Lieutenant Spratt's *Travels in*

Lycia. It is difficult, reading his description, not to feel the excitement of the young man, knowing that he is one of the first Europeans to set eyes on the ruins of this magnificent city:

> The next day was devoted to visiting the ruins of Pinara. Our expectations had been greatly raised respecting this wonderful city, by the account of it which we had received from Mr Hoskyn, who had told us that it was the finest of all those in the valley of the Xanthus; and the little sketch given by its discoverer, had also excited our curiosity, but the reality far exceeded both the report and the picture. At about a quarter of an hour's walk from the village, we suddenly came upon a magnificent view of the ancient city, seated in a rocky recess of Mount Cragus. A stupendous tower of rock, faced by a perpendicular precipice, perforated with a thousand tombs, and crowned by ruined fortifications, rose out of a deep ravine which was thronged with ruins and sarcophagi, and intersected by ridges bearing the more important edifices. Dark precipitous mountains of the grandest outlines overhung the whole. After gazing with astonishment at this wondrous scene, we plunged among the maze of ruins, making a hurried ramble through them, so as to become acquainted with the localities of the site, intending to pay future visits for the purpose of more minute exploration. We first visited a fine theatre, excavated in the side of a woody hill, fronting the city. The Lycian theatres are invariably so placed as to command a grand prospect, or when by the seaside, a broad expanse of ocean. For a scene of rocky magnificence none of them could vie with the theatre of Pinara. Opposite the theatre are the remains of a building of much later times, with Ionic columns, some of which are double, and have the fluting grooved in a coating of cement. Close by are several very fine arch-lidded tombs, with Lycian inscriptions; above is the lower acropolis, a long ridge of buildings, many of them of Cyclopean architecture. Among them is a small theatre, or odeum, and a gigantic portal, shattered apparently by an earthquake. We then ascended to the base of the rock of the greater acropolis, finding on our way a remarkable group of sarcophagi. They are arranged so as to form a square round an enormous central

sarcophagus, with a pedestal-formed summit. This sarcophagus was the largest we met with in Lycia. Its interior is remarkable, the sides being surrounded by a projecting ledge or shelf. The tombs of the square bear no inscriptions, but are peculiarly ornamented, the cement which covers their sides being scored so as to represent the appearance of a regularly-built stone wall, exactly as we sometimes see on plastered houses at home. The stone at Pinara, though hard and durable, being a conglomerate, is not favourable for inscriptions; and the ancient inhabitants seem to have been in the habit of coating it with a fine mortar, or cement, and on that carving the letters. We ascended the acropolis rock by the only pass, a steep and difficult path cut on its side.

On its level but sloping summit we found the remains of many fortifications and cisterns, not, however of the most ancient architecture. Such parts of the margin as were in any way accessible, were strongly defended by walls. On the highest part of the summit is an isolated fortification, or stronghold, furnished with tanks, and surrounded by a ditch. The view from this is very grand, whether upward among the gloomy gorges of Anticragus, or forward over the fertile plains of the Xanthus, and the snowy ridges of Massicytus. The tombs which perforate the perpendicular face of this gigantic rock, are oblong holes, occasionally with a semi-circular top. They lie mostly irregularly arranged, but occasionally form perpendicular rows. There are no traces of panels or doors to their entrances. They must have been excavated by workmen suspended from the summit. They are now inaccessible, and are the dwelling-places of eagles.

FROM *Travels in Lycia* by T. Spratt and E. Forbes

THE EXPEDITION TO BODRUM AND KNIDOS OF 1856

In 1856 Charles Newton led an official British expedition to excavate Bodrum and Knidos. This was financed by the Foreign Office and supported by the British Museum. This was the first archaeological expedition to be photographed.

The main object of the expedition was to locate and excavate the

site of the famous Mausoleum of Halicarnassus, one of the Seven
Ancient Wonders. Since the eighteenth century antiquarians had
realised that Bodrum was the ancient Halicarnassus, and site of the
Mausoleum. However, the Mausoleum, although a vast structure,
(perhaps fifty metres high, if you believe Pliny's description) had
completely disappeared. For in the fifteenth century the Knights of St
John in Rhodes had plundered the Mausoleum, using it as a quarry
with which to build Bodrum Castle.

Since Britain and Turkey had recently been allies in the Crimean
War, the ambassador in Constantinople, Sir Stratford de Redcliffe,
had little difficulty in obtaining an official permit or *firman* for these
excavations. HMS *Supply*, with one hundred men on board, and all
the equipment needed for an archaeological excavation, arrived in
Bodrum in November 1856.

It was not until the following May, and after several false starts, that
Newton was certain he had located its site. His journal entry shows
more relief than jubilation:

Budrum, April 10, 1857

After months of anxiety and weary labour I am at length able to say
that the main object of the expedition is fulfilled, for the site of the
Mausoleum is no longer a matter of uncertainty. The manner of
its discovery was thus. In the centre of the town of Budrum, just
above the konak of Salik Bey, is, or rather was, a site distinguished
by nothing very particular, except the fact that in several places
pieces of large Ionic columns of the finest Parian marble were still
lying about on the surface. Examining the site more closely, the
practised eye might observe a certain artificial irregularity of
ground, such as is the case where ruins have been thrown about
and afterwards buried under the natural accumulation of the soil.
The site was covered with houses and little plots of ground divided
by modern stone walls. In several places were drums of fluted
columns about 3 feet 6 inches in diameter, and of the purest white
marble, and on a close inspection of the walls of the houses
and gardens, I perceived that here and there fragments of Ionic
architecture of great beauty were built into the masonry . . . I

decided therefore on digging here. The ground was divided into a number of little plots, each a separate owner. After a great deal of trouble, I obtained leave from one of them to dig a strip of ground, the one half of his field.

It was on the 1st of January in this year that I first broke ground on this memorable site. After a few spadefuls had been thrown up, I examined the character of the soil. It was a loose black mould, full of small splinters of fine white marble and rubble. The whole appearance of this and the absence of stratification in it, suggested the notion that it was a recent accumulation, such as might have taken place in the 400 years which have elapsed since the building of the castle of Budrum by the Knights. The fragments of marble were evidently from some Ionic building. I collected them with the greatest care. After a short time a mutilated leg turned up: this evidently from a frieze. I began to have vague hopes. More bits of sculpture appeared – always legs and scraps of frieze, till at last I got a piece of foot with the moulding of the frieze remaining. I at once recognized this to be the moulding of the frieze from the Castle, which Lord Stratford obtained for the British Museum in 1846.

About the same time that I made this discovery, I happened to be examining a wall near where I was digging, and found that a battered fragment of a marble lion formed one of the foundation stones. From that day I had no doubt that the site of the Mausoleum was found.

Strange as it may seem to you, the moment of making this great discovery was not at all one of great joy and exultation. I cast a wistful eye on the site covered with houses and plots of garden land, each belonging to a separate proprietor, and asked myself how will it be possible to buy all these people out. The presence of a ship of war, too, made the process of negotiation all the more difficult, for there was no concealing from the officers and sailors the fact that the site of the Mausoleum had been discovered; and the intelligence could hardly be communicated to a whole ship's company as a profound secret. Fortunately, at that time, no one attached to the expedition, except myself, could speak three words of Turkish; still the proprietors of the houses very soon got an inkling that the Consul had found something very wonderful – the konak of some Padishah who lived 2,000 years ago. They regulated their tactics accordingly.

FROM *Travels & Discoveries in the Levant*
by Charles Newton

The excavations continued for almost two years. The greatest discoveries of the excavation were the horse and rider from the quadriga at the top of the Mausoleum and the oversize statues assumed to be of Mausolus and Artemisia, his sister-wife. These can now be seen in the British Museum.

Newton also coveted various marble lions and a frieze from the Mausoleum that he had identified in the walls of Bodrum castle. He sought to obtain official permission to remove these, but the Turkish governor sensibly decided to have them removed before this *firman* arrived from Istanbul.

However, the *firman* did arrive, and just before the governor's caique, already loaded with the marbles, had left the harbour. The following incident says a lot about high-handed European attitudes at the time:

While we were making these discoveries on the site of the Mausoleum, we were anxiously waiting for the *firman* empowering me to take possession of the lions which I had discovered in the Castle last year. Unavoidable delays prevented the granting of this document; and in the mean time the Commandant of the Castle suddenly received orders from the Turkish Minister of War to remove the lions from the walls and send them to Constantinople. He lost no time in putting this order in execution, and before many days had elapsed two of the finest lions were extracted from the walls. It was not a pleasant sight for us to see this operation, performed under our very eyes, after we had brought spars for scaffolding and all manner of means and appliances for the express purpose; however, I gulped down my mortification as well as I could and despatched two letters, one by sea, the other by a swift overland runner, to Smyrna, to apprise Lord Stratford that the Turkish Minister of War was trying to steal a march on us. My messenger sped on night and day; and the Commandant pushed on with his work no less expeditiously. Two more lions were soon dug out of the walls. The extraction of two of my eye teeth could not have given me so great a pang. When the Commandant had removed four lions, he paid a formal visit to my diggings, accompanied by all the principal Turks in Budrum.

'You have found nothing but little fragments, I see,' he said, with an air of triumph. At that time we were digging up small fragments of lions' tails, with an occasional leg or hind-quarter, but no heads. I endured his civil impertinence for about a quarter of an hour, till at last my inward chafing found vent in a strong expression or two in English, addressed to Captain Towsey. The Turks did not understand what I had said; but guessed from the expression of my countenance what was passing in my mind, and withdrew with many ironical compliments. That same day, the lions having been duly swathed in raw sheepskins, were placed on board a caique to be sent over to Kos, where they were to be transhipped by steamer to Constantinople. I had a photograph made of two of them, and took a last fond look at these precious remains of the school of Scopas. The caique, the Commandant informed me, was to sail that night, and I went to bed sick at heart. It was the end of a great hope.

At 4 a.m. the next morning I was suddenly roused from my sleep by the voice of a midshipman from the Gorgon. 'The Swallow is come in from Constantinople, and the officer of the watch thinks that the *firman* is on board.' I had had so many disappointments about the *firman*, that I received this news with sceptical indifference, and doggedly fell asleep again: At 6 a.m. another messenger from the Gorgon woke me up. 'The captain wants to see you immediately.' I hurried on board, and found Towsey pacing the quarter-deck impatiently, his gig alongside, ready manned.

'Why have you been so long?' he said, 'the *firman* is come.'

'Of what use is the *firman* now?' I answered, very sulkily; 'the lions are gone.'

'The caique is still in the harbour,' he said, 'waiting for a fair wind to come out, and we are yet in time.'

I jumped into the boat without a word more: a few vigorous strokes brought us into the harbour. The captain of the caique was drawing in his little mooring lines in a lazy, sleepy sort of way.

On the pier-head stood the doctor of the Quarantine, an Italian, who took great interest in our diggings.

'Don't let that caique go,' I cried out; 'I have a *firman* for the lions.'

'It is all right,' he replied; 'I have his papers and he cannot leave without my signature.'

We walked straight into the Castle, and asked to see the Commandant. Very much astonished he was at so early a visit from the Captain of the ship of war and the Consul. He had evidently just emerged from his yorgan, and his nargileh was hardly lit . . . After hastily wishing him good morning, I put the *firman* into his hand with that air of cool satisfaction with which a whist-player trumps an ace on the first round. Turks are seldom astonished; but my friend the Commandant was really discomposed. He read the *firman* through several times. The document was duly signed and sealed; the wording of this writ of habeas corpus was so precise that there was no evading it. The lions were to be delivered to me whether still in the walls or already embarked. Suddenly a bright thought struck the Commandant.

'The *firman*,' quoth he 'makes mention of lions, *aslanlar*; but the animals in the walls of the Castle are leopards, *caplanlar*.'

'Come, come, my friend,' I said, '*aslanlar* or *caplanlar*, you know very well what are the beasts meant by the *firman*, and where to find them. I claim those beasts, and no others.'

'But,' said the Commandant, suddenly shifting the ground of his objections, 'who is to pay me for the expenses I have incurred? The allowance made to me by the Porte is so small that the outlay for removing the lions has been made in a great measure out of my own pocket.'

'Make your mind quite easy on that subject,' I said; 'I am ordered to pay all the expenses incurred.'

'And the caique, who is to pay that?'

'I pay the caique too.'

The lions were forthwith handed over to me, and the Commandant reimbursed.

In consideration of the trouble he had had, and the courteous and obliging manner in which he had behaved, I presented him with a handsome gratuity over and above his expenses. He was so touched with my generosity, that he let me take a leopard's head not specified in the *firman*. This was set in a battlement over the gateway leading into the Castle, and probably came from the Mausoleum. It is on a smaller scale than the lions, and much decayed, but in a good style.

FROM *Travels & Discoveries in the Levant*
by Charles Newton

In December 1857 Newton and about a dozen of his party moved to Knidos, the ruined ancient city at the end of the Datça peninsula. Here he hoped for some spectacular discoveries – 'considering the great celebrity of Knidos in antiquity and the magnificence of the architectural remains which cover the site there is great probability that fine sculpture and interesting inscriptions would be found under the mass of super-incumbent ruins,' he wrote to the Foreign Secretary.

Life was very uncomfortable. They lived in military huts that had been sent from the Crimea, but without their stoves. Unfortunately, this was a winter of particular severity, as Newton's despatches explain:

Ruins of Knidos, March 10, 1858
The winter here since our arrival has been one of extraordinary severity, and from time to time a Crimean north wind sweeping with relentless fury over the naked promontory where we are encamped, split the half-inch planking of our huts, and penetrated the very marrow of our bones. We have no stoves, and the nights have been so cold, that I have sometimes felt tempted to take refuge in the tent where our little flock of sheep are folded to protect them from the jackals, who howl round our encampment all night. This year the wolves have been driven by hunger to the very end of this peninsula, and have devoured two horses within two hours' distance of this place.

FROM FO Papers, Public Record Office, Kew

To his great disappointment, the excavations at Knidos initially yielded little. But in early summer he found the famous Knidos Lion.

Ruins of Knidos, July 2, 1858

It is pleasant to be able to announce the remarkable discovery which we have recently made here. At the distance of about three miles south of Knidos the coast throws out a bold headland, lying opposite Cape Crio, and distant from it about three miles. On the summit of a cliff which forms part of this headland, Mr Pullan observed the ruins of an ancient tomb. On the bare rock below this tomb lay the long-sought lion.

He is truly a magnificent beast, measuring ten feet in length and six feet in height, and cut out of one block of Pentelic marble. He lay on his side, his nose buried in the ground. His forepaws and lower jaw have been broken off, probably when he fell. The side which has been exposed to the weather is much worn, and has assimilated so much in colour to the surrounding rock, that when I showed him to the inhabitants of the district and asked why they had never pointed out to me where he lay, they told me that they had often seen a great rock lying there, but had never perceived that it represented a lion till I told them so. On examining the ruins of the tomb, I find that it has been a square basement, surrounded by a Doric peristyle with engaged columns, and surmounted by a pyramid.

To the east of this tomb the ground slopes gradually. The upper part of the declivity is strewn with architectural ruins. The lion lies a little below these. It is evident from its position relative to the tomb, that it must have originally surmounted the pyramid. It may have been thrown down by an earthquake, and must have fallen in one solid mass, probably pitching forward on the forepaws, which have been united to the body by a joint, and all trace of which has now disappeared.

On making this great discovery, I proceeded at once to pitch my tent on the spot, and to transport from Knidos sheers, ropes, blocks, timber, and all necessary means and appliances for raising, packing, and embarking our colossal prize. The sheers having been carefully adjusted over him, he was turned over without any difficulty, mounting slowly and majestically in the air, as if a Michael Angelo had said to him, 'Arise!'

. . . After raising the lion by the sheers, we lowered him into a case suitable for his dimension, which was bolted together with iron rods.

Once in the case, he was blocked up and secured in every possible way, so as to prevent all movement or friction . . . The next thing was to drag him slowly down a newly made road, which we had cut zigzag down the mountain-side to the sea. The case was placed on a sledge made of the strongest materials and hauled for three days by a hundred Turks . . .

At last we got the lion down to the edge of the cliff, whence he was to be hoisted onto a raft by a pair of sheers . . . Even this last operation was not unattended with some anxiety; for the lion weighed about 11 tons . . .

FROM *Travels & Discoveries in the Levant*
by Charles Newton

Newton's expedition sent back 385 cases of excavated material, from Bodrum, Knidos and Branchidae, near Didyma. The huge scale of his removals now seems horrendous. But Newton would have considered such scruples misguided. He sincerely believed that he was protecting these objects.

You can still visit the site of the Mausoleum today. It lies within a walled enclosure right in the heart of old Bodrum. Though there is not a great deal to see (Newton himself described it as a 'desolate-looking spot, of which the idea is finer than the reality') the little that remains is of great interest. The site of the lion's discovery and the windswept tomb on which it once presided, can also be visited. You can either walk from the Knidos road (it is about 2 kilometres from the road across rough landscape) or visit by boat, though getting ashore is not very easy. The sledge road built to transfer the great beast down to the sea is still quite clearly visible. Like the site of the Mausoleum, it is strangely atmospheric.

The Historical Appendices

The publishers have specially commissioned two historical essays that appear in print for the first time under the protective cover of Rupert Scott's *Turkish Coast: through writers' eyes*. Dr Ffiona Gilmore Eaves has written on daily life in the ancient cities of the Turkish shore. She is a lecturer who combines intimate knowledge of the archaeological remains with an awareness of a wider literary culture to reinvigorate the dusty ruins of our shared past. In this essay, the temples, agora, oracles, shrines and gymnasia of the ancient cities of Lycia and Caria are filled once more with the passionate and discordant hum of humanity. The second essay, by Barnaby Rogerson, takes the reader on a quick gallop through the very ancient history of Turkey in order to focus attention on the achievements of the indigenous culture of Lycia. It is hoped to later expand this section, with freshly commissioned historical essays on the Byzantine and Seljuk periods which will appear in future editions of the *Turkish Coast*. In the interests of fluency, footnotes and sources have been deliberately omitted.

Ffiona Gilmore Eaves was educated in Winchester, where she started digging as part of the major series of excavations in the town. She took a double first in Archaeology and Anthropology at Newnham College, Cambridge. Her doctoral research on the Eufrasian basilica at Porec was carried out at the University of Nottingham while she was working in adult education. She is co-author of *Retrieving the Record: a century of archaeology at Porec*, published by the University of Zagreb. She speaks Croatian, and is an enthusiastic participant in the music and dance of the Balkans and Turkey. She would like to thank her husband Laurence Eaves for his encouragement, and is grateful to her friends Rosy Phelps and the late Louise Millard for sharing hours of enjoyment exploring the byways and backwoods of the Turkish coast.

Barnaby Rogerson has written guidebooks to Istanbul, Cyprus, Morocco, Tunisia and Libya, a history of North Africa, a biography of the Prophet Muhammad, a history of the first four Caliphs (*The Heirs of the Prophet Muhammad*) and most recently *The Last Crusade*, a history of the worldwide conflict between Muslim and Christian states between 1415 and 1580. He also runs Eland Publishing with his wife, Rose Baring, who with her daughters, Molly and Hannah, has joined in many happy trips along the coast and into the mountains and valleys of Lycia and Caria.

Daily Life in the Ancient Cities
FFIONA GILMORE EAVES

THE NECROPOLIS
City of the dead

The dead are the first to extend a welcome to travellers to an ancient city.

Since burial within the town was prohibited by law and morally repugnant (a source of discord between Christians and their pagan neighbours in the later Empire), both inhumations and cremations took place outside the walls, preferably as close as possible, and often along the roads leading into the town.

Wealthy Lycians of the fourth century BC were buried in elaborate rock-cut chambers, some pillared like temple facades (which you can see at Caunos and Fethiye), others resembling log cabins. But most sarcophagi were displayed above ground. This may reflect the extraordinary difficulty of digging a burial vault in rocky terrain, for instance at Termessos, but it also emphasises the role of the tomb as an indicator of wealth and status. As Trimalchio, the creation of satirist Petronius Arbiter at the time of Nero, says:

> It's a big mistake to have nice houses just for when you're alive and not worry about the one we have to live in for much longer.

The traveller struggling up the steep path to the city of Termessos would be very conscious of the city of the dead on the other side of the gorge, a jumble of sarcophagi and rock-cut tombs, dominating the view. At Patara on the plain, burials accompany the road in a more sedate line. Sarcophagi with the occupant's life-history mingle with tombs with benches, equipped with fixtures for placing flowers or other gifts, while some support an awning of some sort, so that families visiting the dead could eat a commemorative meal in comfort, and pour a little wine or milk through an aperture into the tomb for the missing member to enjoy. One or two older Lycian sarcophagi lie just within the boundaries of the town, but this is only because that boundary must have been pushed outward, perhaps at a time when the burials were ancient enough to be regarded as part of the town's history, rather than sore thumbs.

ARCHES AND ENTRANCE GATES

If tombs indicated the status of an individual and his family, walls and gates spoke for the standing of the city, as well as defending it in the hazardous times of the fifth to first century BC. Sometimes they spoke too loudly. Diogenes of Sinope, the Cynic philosopher, visiting Myndus and noting the disproportionate size of the gates to the population, commented 'Oh men of Myndus, I urge you to shut the city gates, as your town might leave from them.'

Nothing could be more grandiloquent than the main gate of Perge. The tall circular towers of about 200 BC would have been visible for miles across the flat plain. They flanked an entrance of a type found in several of the larger cities of Asia Minor, a walled courtyard leading to an inner gate. Originally defensive, entrapping enemy troops who had managed to batter down the outer gate, this courtyard was embellished around 120 AD, in the time of Hadrian, with fourteen statues and a marble-veneered, two-storeyed triple arch where the inner gate would have stood.

Though none of the statues from this courtyard survive, the inscriptions indicate the dedicatees, and illuminate the social networks which underpinned life in the cities under the Roman Empire and the bonds which linked them to Rome. The honorific arch was home to the usual array of emperors from Nerva to Hadrian, with their wives and relatives; a display of loyalty on the part of a local family in the person of Plancia Magna. Fifteen inscriptions throughout the city refer to statues dedicated by her, or to her. These gave the opportunity to advertise her social status – priestess of Artemis and of the Mother of the Gods, demiurgos (a high civic office), priestess of the cult of the Emperors – and to associate the name of the Plancii with the imperial family. The statues in the courtyard linked the Plancii with another important element in the mythology of the city: its founders (*ktistai*). The 'founder' of a city could be a historical person, a legendary figure, or an honorific title. Plancia Magna associated her family with seven mythological heroes from the time of the Trojan Wars, including Calchas son of Thestor of Argos (a seer). Besides linking the Plancii dynasty with the heroic age, she was providing the city with the credentials it needed for entry into Hadrian's newly instituted Panhelleneia, festivities designed to unite the Greek-speaking cities of the empire in the consciousness of their past and culture. And to ensure that Latin speakers, incomers such as the Plancii themselves, were at home in the city, all the inscriptions were in Latin as well as Greek.

Other cities honoured emperors or their representatives with a single arch thrown across the main approach road, to celebrate benefits received or tacitly solicit future favours. Vespasian is named at Xanthos; the governor Metellus Modestus warranted an arch with niches for busts of his whole family at Patara. The approach to a town was a history lesson and, particularly under the Roman Empire, a celebration of its benefactors.

THE AGORA
'A place set apart in the middle of the city'
In the fifth century BC, Herodotus put these disparaging words into the mouth of the Persian king Cyrus about the workings of civic democracy:

> I never yet feared the kind of men who have a place set apart in the middle of the city in which they get together and tell one another lies under oath.

Two salient points stand out: the agora lay at the heart of the city, and was synonymous with democracy. Another is implicit: it was 'a place', not a series of buildings, far less a planned unit. A trend towards monumentalisation of simple 'places', to underline their functions and to differentiate them, produced many of the fine buildings and complexes that are now such a feature of the cities. The development of the Letoon near Xanthos, from a holy spring surrounded by a sacred grove, to a religious precinct with walls, stoas, three temples and a nymphaeum, is a prime example. The same trend produced the splendid rectangular walled agora of Perge and the multiple agoras of Miletus and Xanthos. Not all the ancient cities went as far down the road as that, however.

Originally, most of the life of the city – religious, civic, marketing – was played out in and around the agora. All that was needed was a flat open area somewhere, not rigidly, near the centre, preferably with access to water. Here citizens met, argued, listened to a speaker, watched religious events and civic processions. Where there were people, there might be a customer, so traders moved in, market stalls were set up, selling meat, fish and other commodities. A comic poet of the fourth century BC, Eubolus, listed some of them:

> You will find everything sold together in the same place in Athens: figs, witnesses to summons, bunches of grapes, turnips, pears . . . givers of evidence, roses, medlars . . . lawsuits, puddings, irises, lambs, water-clocks, laws, indictments.

'How many things I do not need!' Socrates mused, passing all this merchandise.

Some moralists found it degrading that the agora should become the home of idleness, gossip, and dubious transactions: Aristophanes makes Demosthenes castigate a sausage-seller as 'a cheeky rascal from the agora'.

Over the centuries, specific types of building developed to accommodate these activities, and by the third century BC many agoras had been refurbished and the messy market-places swept away to a new site. Priene is one of the best sites for seeing this phase, and for imagining the scene of the busy agora, though some of the features discovered by the excavators are hard to make out now. The city was built on a series of terraces scooped out from the hillside. The open space of the agora takes up the entire width of one of these, with associated buildings taking their place on the next terrace up. Seventy-five by thirty-five metres, it was surrounded by a peristyle or colonnade, giving shelter from sun and rain, on three sides. At the centre was a large altar, dedicated to Hermes, patron of commerce, though the market was hived off to an adjacent square when the agora was smartened up. Massive crowds would have assembled at news of a sacrifice here, hoping to taste some of the meat as well as attending the spectacle. A stone dais or two nearby lifted visiting speakers, philosophers or politicians above the level of the crowd. A canopy above would dignify the speaker and help to reflect his words. In front, excavations unearthed twelve blocks of stone with letters carved on them, which have been interpreted as markers for fitting the poles of an awning, most welcome to city fathers sitting through long speeches or ceremonies.

Small rooms – shops or offices – backed the peristyle, but on the open side of the agora an extraordinary collection of stonework, statue bases and exedrae, vied for the attention of the passer-by. The exedra is one of those mysterious architectural terms that crops up again and again in technical descriptions of the ancient world. It defies any concise interpretation because of its varying scale and many different uses. At its simplest it is a semi-circular stone wall, varying from waist-high to a half-dome, which acts as a focal point. Incorporated within a building, it forms an apse, giving dignity in a Roman basilica to a judge or speaker, or in a Christian one to the altar. Free-standing and fitted with a bench, it can commemorate the donor (indeed, sometimes act as a tomb) while inviting the passer-by to sit down. Bronze statues, whose footprints can be seen on at least one of the bases, helped to make this area a delightful place to sit and talk, or to reminisce about the past glories of the city.

A stoa runs the entire length of the upper side of the agora. The stoa is another multi-purpose building, adding to the sophistication of the agora by providing a monumentalised promenade, meeting-place and shopping mall. The front was open to the delightful breezes which in summer carried some freshness to the stone-paved square. A row of columns (two in this particular stoa, giving it double width) supported the roof, which also rested on a wall at the back, frequently incorporating a row of small rooms used as shops and offices. Here citizens and visitors could promenade, enjoying the view and meeting friends, as did Socrates in the Athenian agora:

So once seeing him sitting in the Stoa of Zeus Eleutherios, apparently at leisure, I went up and sat beside him, asking, 'Why are you sitting here, Ischomachus?

The stoa could serve as a free lecture room: philosophers held forth to their disciples, and the Stoic school derived their name from such a use. Diogenes of Sinope, founder of the Cynic school and famous for carrying his disdain of the material world to the length of living in a wooden tub, once said to a friend 'Athens has given me a home in the Stoa of Zeus.' And the stoa could also be used for the administration of justice. Socrates again:

Now I must present myself at the stoa of the Basileus to answer the indictment which Meletos has brought against me.

In many of these respects, the stoa served the same variety of functions as the Roman basilica. But it had another aspect, as art gallery or museum, celebrating communal history and upholding civic pride, as revealed by Pausanias's description of the Painted Stoa at Athens:

This colonnade has first of all the Athenians on it, drawn up . . . in the Argolid against the Spartans. This is not a painting of the full event, the rage of battle, or particular deeds of daring, but the first moments of a battle as the armies come to grips . . . On the middle part of the wall, Theseus and his Athenians are fighting the Amazons . . . Next to the Amazons, the Greeks have just taken Troy . . . The last part of the painting is the men who fought at Marathon . . . There are bronze shields there, some inscribed as coming from the Skionaians and their allies, some others smeared over with pitch, so that time and verdigris will not consume them.

Holes in the columns of Priene's stoa may have taken pegs to hang such ornamentation, perhaps painted portraits or trophies.

From the stoa you could walk into another pair of new and specialised civic buildings, the bouleuterion and the prytaneion. These reflect the visible working of the constitution of an ancient city. This was composed of the citizen body, the ekklesia which would typically include all adult males except foreign residents, with some minimal property or tax-paying qualification. From this body (often sub-divided into a dozen tribes or clans) a council (boule) was chosen, which was the main governing body of the city. The well-preserved bouleuterion or council chamber at Priene consists of an almost square building (twenty by twenty-one metres) with sixteen tiers of seating. Pillar bases attest to the fact that this building was roofed, unlike the theatre which it resembles in miniature. So the building is designed for councillors to see and hear a speaker taking the floor, or a ceremony at the altar in the middle of the floor, a prelude to every sitting of the council. The seating capacity of the building, thought to be over six hundred, raises problems of interpretation however. Could the council really comprise so many members? George Bean argued that the building actually held the ekklesia: six hundred or so enfranchised citizens could suggest a fourth-century BC population of around three thousand. Others think it was built much later, around 150 BC, and that a council of over six hundred is quite conceivable: the equivalent building at Miletus would seat well over a thousand.

The bouleuterion forms a very recognizable type. One on the agora at Termessos again seats around six hundred in about eighteen rows. There are intimations of grandeur here. The walls were once covered with a mosaic of coloured marble, while inscriptions on the walls listed the winners of the city's games, from horse-racing and races in armour to wrestling. The city fathers of Termessos were particularly keen on the latter sport: inscriptions in the town to victors in contests sponsored by wealthy citizens frequently mention wrestling, and this seems to have been a regional preference in the province of Pisidia.

When the council was not sitting, it's likely that the building was used for other purposes requiring the same facilities for listening and seeing. Hence these buildings sometimes go by the name of Odeon, the usual Roman word for small concert or recital halls. Perhaps Eucharistos of Patara, whose epitaph tells us that he 'successfully read the poems of Philistion in the theatre' would have found it easier on the voice to read to a more select audience in the bouleuterion.

Next to the bouleuterion in Priene stands the prytaneion. This conjunction is again quite common. A smaller meeting place was needed for committee work, and this was combined with the imperative for an honourable setting for the 'inextinguishable and immovable flame' of the goddess Hestia (equivalent of the Roman Vesta), guardian of the hearth, both domestic and civic. Processions would set out from here, passing through the long stoa, to the agora, perhaps to rekindle or repurify the hearths of the citizens. One may be reminded of the Easter ceremony that precedes the 'Scoppio del Carro' in Florence, when the new flame, kindled with relics of the Crusade, is brought to the cathedral and householders reach out to light their candle and take it home, or of the ritual which still takes place in the Holy Sepulchre in Jerusalem and throughout the Greek Orthodox world.

A possible ceremonial hearth was found in Priene's prytaneion, which otherwise looks like an ordinary peristyle house, small rooms assembled around a central courtyard. Indeed it had a more domestic function as well. Officers of the boule and visiting dignitaries were usually entitled to dine there, and this privilege was also extended as a reward to citizens who had brought honour on their town, either in political affairs or by winning a prize in athletics or other games. A column shaft in one of the rooms bore an inscription (damaged) illustrating this habit, and the civic pride with which it was linked:

> The most brilliant city (polis) of the Ionian citizens of Priene and the most powerful council (boule) and the most august Synhedrin of the elders in accordance with the things frequently received in accounts ... have honoured Marcus Aurelius Tatianus, the market official ... the president of the festal assembly for the city's goddess Athena, the presiding officer of the goddess, the chief president, and the crowned president of the senate (boularchon). May you prosper.

The latest types of agora, dating from the period of the Roman Empire, are very much more formal, losing touch with the concept of a civic meeting-place. The well-preserved example at Perge cuts brutally across the line of the earlier town wall as part of a late-second century scheme which created a massive new public space in front of the old city gate. Four conjoined stoa with shops, forming a rigid square of seventy-six by seventy-six metres, isolate the inner courtyard from the life of the town. Perhaps this might be better known as a macellum, a Roman market: all other civic life has been removed from it. Or almost all: a gaming table fitted into one of the porticos suggests that idlers could still find a place to pass the time away.

THE BATHS
'With swimming-pools and additional ornamentation'

The ancient city of Perge burst out of its original bounds in the late second and third centuries AD because more and more space was required for public buildings in the Roman style, like the macellum mentioned above, numerous monumental fountains and nymphaea, but above all to provide the space required for the new public baths. Bathing was not a new habit: the second century BC baths at Priene are a rare survival of baths in the Greek style, a simple affair of large stone basins with cold water flowing through them, troughs for foot washing, and a slabbed floor for the bather to stand on. Forming one corner of the gymnasium, and adjacent to the stadium, the single medium-sized room must have been used by the schoolboys who engraved their names in the lecture hall two rooms away. 'The place of Phileas, son of Metrodoros': this formula is repeated seven hundred or so times: generations of eighteen- to twenty-one-year-olds sat on the benches in the lecture hall, oiled themselves with olive oil, covered themselves with fine sand to avoid slipping if they were wrestling, boxed and raced and finally, well-bonded if exhausted, scraped themselves down and headed for the baths.

This simplicity was very different from the Roman style of bathing, with its progression through apodyterium (changing-room), tepidarium (warm room), caldarium (hot room); opportunities for massage, various options of heated rooms such as the laconicum (hot dry room) and sauna; followed by brisk immersion in the frigidarium (cold room, usually with a plunge pool – the natatio) to close the pores. Those with a serious interest in their health or figure could precede the more pleasurable aspects of bathing with brisk physical exercise in the palaestra or exercise yard. This sequence, with its emphasis on sweating for health, depended on the invention of central heating with the hypocaust system in the first century BC, as well as on copious amounts of water supplied by aqueducts (the one from Kalkan to Patara fed four large baths complexes). Its origin in the Roman rather than the Greek world is evident in the naming of the parts, all Latin except for the changing-room, which already existed. As time passed, baths also became more opulent and spacious. As Lucian describes it so vividly,

> On entering, one is received into a public hall of good size, with ample accommodation for servants and attendants. On the left are the lounging-rooms . . . attractive, brightly lit retreats. Then besides them a hall, larger than need be for the purposes of a bath, but necessary for the reception of richer persons. Next, capacious locker-rooms to undress in . . . with a very high and brilliantly lighted hall between them, in which are three swimming-pools of cold water; it is finished in Laconian marble, and has two statues of white marble in the ancient style, one of Hygeia, the other of Aesculapius.
>
> On leaving this hall, you come into another which is slightly warmed . . . it has an apse on each side. Next to it, on the right, is a very bright hall, nicely fitted up for massage, which has on each side an entrance decorated with Phrygian marble, and receives those who come in from the exercising floor. Then near this is another hall . . . in which one can stand or sit with comfort, linger without danger, and stroll about with profit . . . Next comes the hot corridor . . . The hall beyond it is very beautiful, full of abundant light . . . It contains three tubs.
>
> When you have bathed, you need not go back through the same rooms, but can go direct to the cold room through a slightly warmed chamber . . . Moreover, it is beautified with all other marks of thoughtfulness – with two toilets, many exits, and two devices for telling time, a water clock that makes a bellowing sound and a sundial.

Few of the public baths of Asia Minor could quite match up to the number and magnificence of the rooms described by Lucian – except perhaps the baths of Vedius in Ephesus. But then Ephesus was a quite exceptional city, its wealth derived from its harbour: 'the city, because of its advantageous situation in other respects, grows daily, and is the largest emporium in Asia this side of the Taurus' (Strabo). The baths of other cities in Asia Minor generally consisted of a row of three or four parallel halls, with a few ancillary rooms. But the light pouring into Lucian's ideal baths must have streamed through huge south-facing windows as can still be seen at Tlos, at Patara, Perge and many other cities. Their builders and patrons clearly agreed with Seneca, writing at the time of Nero:

> The old baths were confined and dark; our ancestors thought themselves warm only when it was not light. Today we describe as 'baths where you moulder' those which are not so laid out that from beginning to end of the day they are flooded with sunlight through large windows; we want to be tanned by the sun, at the same time as being washed, and to have a long view, from the bath, over the countryside and sea.

These hugely expensive and prestigious buildings could be erected through a mixture of private and public funding. They were often helped by Imperial gifts, for visiting Emperors or their representative governors saw this as a way of winning hearts and boosting confidence. The younger Pliny, holding a special commission in the province of Bithynia and Pontus (north-western Turkey) to enquire into the political and financial affairs of the towns, which had arraigned two successive governors, wrote to the emperor Trajan:

> The public bath at Prusa, Sir, is old and dilapidated, and the people are very anxious for it to be rebuilt. My own opinion is that you could suitably grant their petition. There will be money available for building it, first from the sums I have begun to call in from private individuals, and secondly because the people are prepared to apply to building the bath the grants they usually make towards financing the distribution of olive oil. This is, moreover, a scheme which is worthy of the town's prestige and the splendour of your reign.

Vespasian, an emperor who travelled extensively through Asia Minor, may also have had ideas of kick-starting the economy of Patara when he repaired the aqueduct that brought water to the town as a prelude to refurbishing the Harbour Baths and another complex near the theatre which bears the inscription:

> The bath was built . . . by Flavius Vespasianus . . . during the time of the military governor Sextus Marcus Priscus, by using the funds collected from the people and with the contributions of the (military unit), together with swimming-pools and additional ornamentation.

But the 'additional ornamentation' and novelties of one age become stale in a later century, and a pattern of holes in the walls tells of the marble veneer so beloved of Lucian being affixed to the walls at a later date, even to the extent of obscuring the founder's inscription.

The stunning array of statues from Perge's South Bath, now in Antalya Museum, brings home the extent to which the baths had usurped the role of social and cultural centre from the agora. Opening off the north side of the palaestra was a long hall, named by the excavators after Claudios Peison, whose name appears on plinths or more prominently on the shield held by Aphrodite: not of course as artist, as it was almost unknown for artists to sign their works at this period, but as dedicator and sponsor. This gallery housed at least thirty-two statues, many of high quality and extraordinary technical skill. The figure of a dancer, draperies whirling, is cut from two different marbles so that her skin appears white, while her clothing and hair are black. Other capacious rooms in the baths could cater for ceremonies of the Imperial cult (another way of bonding the disparate cities of the Empire to Rome).

The image of refinement or at least luxury evoked by the huge but silent halls, the marble veneer, the statues, should be balanced with Seneca's account, even if it is that of a critic of contemporary mores, of a chunk of city life when the baths were in full swing.

> I live over a bathing establishment. Picture to yourself now the assortment of voices, the sound of which is enough to sicken one. When the stronger fellows are exercising and swinging heavy lead

weights in their hands, when they are working hard or pretending to be working hard, I hear their groans; and whenever they release their pent-up breath, I hear their hissing and jarring breathing. When I have to do with a lazy fellow who is content with a cheap rub-down, I hear the slap of the hand pummelling his shoulders, changing its sound as the hand is laid on flat or curved. If now a professional ball-player comes along and begins to keep score, I am done for. Add to this the arrest of a brawler or a thief, and the fellow who always likes to hear his own voice in the bath, and those who jump in the pool with a mighty splash as they hit the water. In addition to those voices which are, if nothing else, natural, imagine the hair-plucker keeping up a constant chatter in his thin and strident voice, to attract more attention, and never silent except when he is plucking armpits and making the customer yell instead of yelling himself. It disgusts me to enumerate the varied cries of the sausage dealer and the confectioner and of all the pedlars of the cook shops, hawking their wares, each with his own peculiar intonation.

THE THEATRE
'So the whole city . . . rushed into the theatre with one accord'

A theatre was a prerequisite for any civilised classical city. Drama had evolved from religious festivals, and theatre and religion continued to be closely linked. Altars are often found in the orchestra; and every performance would be prefaced by ceremonies here or in shrines of Dionysos which were often sited close by. Attendance at the theatre was a mark of citizenship, an occasion for weaving together the strands of the citizen body into a strong thread.

The earliest theatres consisted simply of a grassy bank with a view of a flat, more or less circular, area – the orchestra. Here the members of the chorus, usually fifteen, sang and danced. The two or three actors also performed in the orchestra, though some scholars believe they may have stood on a low dais or platform. Gradually the skene evolved, a building backing the orchestra, of wood on stone foundations. Its flat wooden roof could serve for scenes on a rooftop, or for heaven. The two or three rooms it contained could be used for storage or dressing.

But these first simple theatres would seem old-fashioned and a disgrace to the city in the course of time, and were replaced by more complex stone-built structures, leaving little if any trace of their predecessors. Priene is one of the few cities whose theatre was not substantially rebuilt under the Roman empire, and so perfectly illustrates a small-town theatre of the fourth to second centuries BC that it is commonly cited as a set-piece example. Spectators sat in forty-seven rows of stone benches (cavea) set into the steep slope of the mountain but, as nature had not provided a semi-circle, supported at the sides by retaining walls (analemmata). These rows were divided roughly in the middle by a gangway, the diazoma, which served not only to help circulation to seats, but also to divide the classes. Smarter people sat in the lower rows, where there are traces of what in Roman theatres became known as the bisellium, a space twice as wide as was generally allowed, where in Roman times a slave would place his master's folding stool. Originally the front row consisted of a shaped stone bench (prohedria) with a back for additional comfort and to keep the feet of those in the row behind from nudging the great and the good. Even this, however, was judged insufficient to honour the most distinguished guests. Around 200 BC five marble armchairs were inserted into the bench, complete with skeuomorphic carved legs with lions'-claw feet, carved armrests, and a curved back which would fit snugly around an average citizen but would hardly allow for extreme girth. Inscriptions record that the chairs were dedicated to the god Dionysos by Nysios, son of Diphilos.

The audience looked down on a horse-shoe shaped orchestra, partly enfolded by the rows of seating. From the third century BC it was backed by a proskenion, a low stone pavilion with a flat top. How this was used has been much debated. Was it a backdrop, with the traditional three doors for exits and entrances and flaps with painted scenery in between? Or was the flat top intended as a stage for the actors? If the latter, what were the doors for, and did the spectators in the prohedria develop a crick in the neck?

All agree that by the mid-second century staging conventions were changing to accommodate a different form of drama, New Comedy. The importance of the chorus and thus the orchestra had dwindled, and spectators expected to see actors on a stage (logeion), which could be formed by the roof of the old proskenion, backed by a two-storey skene (stage building), through which exits and entrances could be made. This stage was nevertheless narrow, a platform for declamation rather than for action. At this time, a new set of prohedria was constructed in the fifth row, now recognised to be the optimum viewpoint. Under the Roman Empire, Priene's stage building was moved back to allow the width of the stage to be doubled, and a shaft for the operation of the *deus ex machina* was included in the new construction.

Standardised masks made it instantly obvious to the audience which stock character was represented: in New Comedy, little of which actually survives, the genial or cross old man, the slave, the young man in love, the pimp, the courtesan, played out family relationships, love interest and cases of mistaken identity. Such masks were hugely popular motifs in many art forms, including frescoes and mosaics in the Roman period, and can be seen decorating the arched entrance to the theatre adjacent to the Letoon, exquisitely carved on blocks from the decoration of the scene building at Myra, and staring open-mouthed from a frieze in Perge.

Like most of a city's public buildings, theatres were ornamented with statues. Apollodorus and Thrasybulus, prominent citizens of Priene, achieved this signal honour. The bronzes that represented them have long gone, leaving only footprints in the stone; set well apart, they indicate that the statues struck poses of dramatic motion. Less expected is the presence at the other end of the prohedria, on the top of a pedestal, of hollows that drained the water from a clepsydra (literally water-thief) near one end. This early, and for a long time only, form of clock was used mostly in the council chamber or law court to curb the length of speeches. Not the sands, but the water of time, ran out of a standard-sized vessel. This reinforces the suggestion that the theatre, seating an estimated five thousand, would be a natural meeting-place for the ekklesia, the assembly of the 'people of Priene', to whom, coupled with Zeus Olympios, the sculptor Klearchos, 'wearer of the wreath' (i.e. crowned winner at some contest), proudly dedicated his works.

The theatre continued to be the place that the people turned to, indeed rushed to, when they felt threatened and needed to debate their course of action. In the first century of the Roman Empire, the theatre of Ephesus (which dates back to the third century BC) was in the process of being redeveloped to become the massive 24,000-seater that can be seen today. Scaffolding may have covered the stage building as the proscenion was enlarged, and a recent commentator imagines the workmen watching open-mouthed as an unexpected drama unfolded with the arrival of St Paul, the disciple of Christ.

> For a certain man named Demetrius, a silversmith, who made silver shrines of Diana, brought no small profit to his craftsmen. He called them together . . . and said 'Men, you know that we have our prosperity by this trade . . . not only at Ephesus, but throughout almost all Asia, this Paul has persuaded and turned away many people, saying that they are not gods which are made with our hands. So not only is this trade of ours in danger of falling into disrepute, but also the temple of the great goddess Diana may be despised and her magnificence destroyed . . . ' And when they heard, they were full of wrath and cried out, saying 'Great is Diana of the Ephesians!' So the whole city was filled with confusion, and rushed into the theatre with one accord . . . And when Paul wanted to go in to the people, the disciples would not allow him . . . Some therefore cried one thing and some another, for the assembly was confused, and most of them did not know why they had come together.

Roman Imperial authority deeply mistrusted any unauthorised meeting: this might be assessed as a riot or an incipient rebellion and the city accordingly punished. The city clerk took to the stage to try to defuse the situation.

> And when the city clerk had quieted the crowd, he said: 'Men of Ephesus, what man is there who does not know that the city of the Ephesians is temple guardian of the great goddess Diana, and of the image which fell down from Zeus? Therefore, since these things cannot be denied, you ought to be quiet and do nothing rashly . . .

Therefore, if Demetrius and his fellow craftsmen have a case against anyone, the courts are open and there are the proconsuls . . . But if you have any other inquiry to make, it shall be determined in the lawful assembly. For we are in danger of being called in question for today's uproar, there being no reason which we may give to account for this disorderly gathering.

The difference between the Greek and the Roman theatre is neatly expressed by Vitruvius, author of *On architecture*, a handbook on city planning plus builder's manual of the time of Augustus.

When the forum [the Roman term for an agora] is placed, a spot as healthy as possible is to be chosen for the theatre, for the exhibition of games on festival days of the immortal gods . . . For the spectators, with their wives and children, delighted with the entertainment, and the pores of their bodies being opened by the pleasure they enjoy, are easily affected by the air . . . The building should be so contrived that a line drawn from the first to the last step should touch the front angle of the tops of all the seats; in which case the voice meets with no impediment . . .

The platform has to be made deeper than that of the Greeks, because all our artists perform on the stage, while the orchestra contains the places reserved for the seats of senators. The height of this platform must be not more than five feet, in order that those who sit in the orchestra may be able to see the performance of all the actors.

The seats on which the spectators sit are not to be less than twenty inches in height, nor more than twenty-two; their width must not be more than two feet and a half, nor less than two feet.

The 'scaena' [stage building] itself displays the following scheme. In the centre are double doors decorated like those of a royal palace. At the right and left are the doors of the guest chambers. Beyond are spaces provided for decoration – places that the Greeks called 'periaktoi', because in these places are triangular pieces of machinery which revolve, each having three decorated faces. When the play is to be changed, or when gods enter to the accompaniment of a clap of thunder, these may be revolved and present a face differently decorated. Beyond these places are the projecting wings which afford entrances to the stage, one from the forum, and the other from abroad.

. . . The Greeks have a roomier orchestra, and a 'scaena' set further back, as well as a stage of less depth. They call this the 'logeion', for the reason that there the tragic and comic actors perform on the stage, while other artists give their performance in the entire orchestra. The height of the 'logeion' ought not to be less than ten feet nor more than twelve.

The spectacularly well-preserved Roman theatre at Aspendos bears out Vitruvius's description and adds further archaeological proof of the concern for audibility in these large areas. Scarring the stonework of the towers on either side of the stage is a sloping line, remnant of the wooden roof which rested at its lower end on the wall of the scene-building, and projected upwards and outwards over the stage to reflect the actors' words even to the gallery at the top of the theatre: the same height as the roof of the stage, as Vitruvius also recommended.

Many of the 'Roman' theatres of Asia Minor are in reality adaptations of existing theatres, using the slope of the hill in the Greek manner. Such a method of building would make great savings in cost. While larger cities, or those who had a patron with access to the emperor, might hope for imperial funding, others depended on their own resources or hoped for benefactors, particularly for adding the trimmings. But there could be problems as revealed in this report sent by governor Pliny to the Emperor Trajan.

The theatre at Nicaea, Sir, is more than half built but it is still unfinished and has already cost more than ten million sesterces, or so I am told – I have not yet examined the accounts. I am afraid it may be money wasted. The building is sinking and showing immense cracks, either because the soil is damp and soft or the stone used was poor and friable. We shall certainly have to consider whether it is to be finished or abandoned, or even demolished, as the foundations and substructure intended to hold up the building may have cost a lot but look none too solid to me. There are many additions to the theatre promised by private individuals, such as a colonnade on either side and a gallery above the auditorium, but all these are now held up by the stoppage of work . . .

Such individual patrons, indeed a whole theatrically-minded dynasty, were on hand at Patara. Theatre-goers queueing at the entrance could read an inscription, now half-sunk in the sand which has engulfed the city, proudly stating that

Velia Procula of Patara enriched the proskenion constructed by her father Q Velius Titianus of Patara from the base with statues, decorations, marble carvings . . . in honour of the gods of the city of Patara, and in honour of the emperor Antoninus Pius . . .

Another inscription tells us that the Velii had paid for the eleventh row of seating in the upper cavea, and an awning over the auditorium. The awning (velum) must have contributed greatly to the comfort of spectators at long performances. Inscriptions attest to repairs in the third century AD to the one at Ephesus, and at Priene and many other sites one can see the bases of posts that held up some kind of awning or parasol. Two rows of corbels projecting from the back wall of the theatre at Aspendos form the seating for a series of masts, keeping taut the ropes on which the awning could be rolled out. This system is more familiar from amphitheatres, and mentioned as an enticement to draw in the crowds: '*Vela erint*' promised the painted slogans at Pompeii.

Greek theatres had a seating capacity well above that of any theatres or opera houses until very recently. La Scala of Milan seats 3,600, the Paris Opera 2,156, and the Capitol in New York (when it first opened its doors in 1919) seated 5,327. But the ancient theatres at Priene and Miletus could seat more than 5,000, though it must be admitted that calculations of seating capacity in ancient times depend on how tightly you think people can be squeezed on a bench. Forty centimetres per person, one measure frequently used, is not an over-generous space for larger citizens. Under the Roman Empire, however, theatres were built with a much greater seating capacity: estimates of the crowds at Aspendos have been given as 15,000, though in recent times as many as 20,000 have squeezed in for genuinely popular events such as

Turkish wrestling and singing. Most existing theatres were enlarged, doubling or trebling the numbers that could be catered for: Miletus grew from an estimated 5,300 to 15,000; while the theatre at Ephesus received a third cavea (and a third storey to the scene building to match it in height) so that it could eventually accommodate 24,000.

The seating plan of the theatre presented a microcosm of society. In some Greek theatres, spectators sat according to their voting tribes, but the front seats were always accorded to the dignitaries of the town. In the fifth century BC women did not attend the theatre, except for hetairai, educated courtesans, who might sit in prominent places and give their opinions as confidently as the rest, but from the fourth century onwards this rule may have been relaxed. In the Roman Empire, the divisions of the cavea again reflected the social classes, the highest sitting in the lower cavea and vice versa. Boxes for high-ranking spectators, sponsors, even priestesses, were arranged above the arches that now spanned the parodoi, formerly unroofed entrances to the orchestra. Women were now allowed to attend at least some performances, generally segregated from the men, although as the poet Ovid remarked that men who sit behind a woman in the theatre should take care that their knees do not bruise her shoulders, this cannot always have been the case. Slaves might be allowed to sit in the rows at the very top of the auditorium.

What did the spectators in these huge theatres see and hear? Very little, one might think, unless they possessed acute hearing and excellent eyesight. Testing acoustics in the ruins of a theatre is hardly representative: unless the audience was preternaturally quiet, there would be a considerable volume of background noise. Sounding vessels built in below the seating, as Vitruvius suggests, might have helped, and it's claimed that the masks that actors wore, their grotesque open mouths 'fit to swallow the audience' as Lucian remarked, improved the projection of their voices. Nevertheless, in Italy at least, the type of theatrical diet on offer changed dramatically in the first few centuries AD. How much this was due to the constraints of performing in an arena where nuances would be indistinguishable to the majority of the spectators, and how much it is a product of social or moral change, is debatable, nor do we know whether the provinces were more conservative in this respect. If they followed the fashions of Rome, though, productions on the stage were mainly mime, a slice of everyday life with plenty of bawdiness and even obscenity to salt it, and pantomime, a form of posturing or ballet relying on one main performer, who could become the pop star of his age. 'Paris, sweet darling', 'Paris, pearl of the stage', gushed the graffiti of Pompeii.

However, in the western part of the empire the popularity of any kind of stage performance was eclipsed by the contests of the arena and circus. Pliny, sniffy and self-righteous, complained:

> . . . It surprises me . . . that so many thousands of adult men should have such a childish passion for watching galloping horses and drivers standing in chariots, over and over again . . . Such is the popularity and importance of a worthless shirt [the colours of a racing stable] – I don't mean with the crowd, which is worth less than the shirt, but with certain serious individuals. When I think how this futile, tedious, monotonous business can keep them sitting endlessly in their seats, I take pleasure in the fact that their pleasure is not mine.

SACRED SHRINES
'What the law obliges not to introduce into the hieron and the temenos'
Coastal Turkey is rich in the remains of major sanctuaries, what we could call pilgrimage shrines. This is no accident: travel by sea was easier than travel by land. The Letoon, the ritual heart of Lycia, lay close to the sea, and it mirrored the historical and political preeminence of the city of Xanthos a few miles inland. Here Apollo, his sister Artemis and mother Leto were worshipped, and games in their honour drew crowds and competitors from all over the eastern Mediterranean.

Gently wrapped in silt as the river Xanthos, trapped by sand-dunes, deposited its alluvial burden, the Letoon offered its French excavators a treasure trove: three temples, a nymphaeum, a sacred way lined with statue bases and ending in an exedra, all enclosed within a stout wall. Lined on the inner side with stoa, this delimited the temenos, the holy

area surrounding the temple. A theatre, doubtless also part of the
religious complex, stood just outside the temenos. Above all, thousands
of inscriptions survived, transforming our understanding of this site.

> What the law obliges not to introduce into the hieron and the
> temenos; arms, petasia, kausia, fibula, bronze, gold, rings plated
> with gold, and all equipment except clothing and shoes, which one
> wears; neither to camp in the stoa, except for those who are offering
> a sacrifice.

Like the statutes of a medieval fair, the sacred law attempts to
forestall the kinds of trouble that occur when crowds gather. The
petasia and kausia, a broad-brimmed hat and a kind of beret basque,
were the type of head-gear characteristic of the military, and therefore
inappropriate in the hieron, sanctuary. The fibula, a kind of cloak-pin,
closed the chlamys, a short cloak also with military connotations. But
it could also be used as a dress-pin, and in desperation as a lethal
weapon: a story ran that Athenian women had thus dispatched the one
survivor of a raid in which all their husbands had been killed, and had
been forced thereafter to wear the Ionian chiton, fastened with draw-
strings.

Pilgrims, pedlars and loafers might all congregate in the stoa for
shelter and warmth. The law tries to protect the true pilgrim who is
allowed to camp here in order to prepare his sacrifice, and eat the
remains afterwards (considerable quantities of bones were excavated).
Other inscriptions show the authorities worried about cleaning and
above all about fire, and rightly so, since a text commemorating a
benefactor much celebrated in Lycia, Opramoas of Rhodiapolis, says
that he financed reconstruction of 'the double and single stoa of the
sanctuary of Leto, which had been burnt down'.

Inscriptions reveal the Letoon as the cult headquarters of the Lycian
League, a federation of city-states of the area. Perhaps delegates from
Tlos, Patara, Pinara, Myra, Olympus, regularly processed here from
Xanthos, entering the shrine on the Sacred Way through imposing
gates (propylaea) to offer sacrifices. But every five years a tent city
would have emerged outside the site as competitors and spectators
came from all over Lycia, from Ephesus and Pergamon, even from

Argos and Alexandria, for the Romaia Letoia, a competitive festival in honour of Roma and Leto: a tactful synthesis of the goddess who had always protected Lycia with the newer but powerful deity personifying Rome.

The contests were of two kinds, artistic and physical. Music was represented by the aulos (often translated as flute, but more like a clarinet or oboe) and the cithara (lyre). But there were far more classes in the 'gymnastic' contests, with the long run, stade and double stade, running in armour (races were otherwise run naked), boxing, wrestling and pankration (a combination of boxing, wrestling and strangling). For many of the events, there were age categories: children (where suitable), 'beardless' and men. Even more exciting than pankration, where you might if lucky see one of the contestants twist his opponent's foot out of its socket or break his fingers, were the horse races. The categories here were for foals and adult horses: riding, biga and quadriga (two- and four-horse chariot). An inscription names Peitho of Ephesus, a woman, as a contestant in the biga race, but she would be the owner rather than the driver.

The name of your city was as important as your own, but more susceptible to change. A winner was proclaimed by a herald, saluted by a trumpeter, and then asked by the agonothete (organiser of the games) which city he crowned. The answer brought glory to a city, and some were prepared to give citizenship to those who could not otherwise claim it, and, it was alleged, to those who could be bribed to forget their real citizenship. So the child Athenodoros won his category in the Nemean games, 'crowned' the city of Ephesus where he had lived as an outsider lacking citizen's rights, and was given full citizenship on his return. Peitho, on the other hand, was already a citizen of Ephesus, but chose to dedicate her crown to the city of Apollonia, where perhaps she had business interests, in order to gain citizenship there too. But Pausanias, an early travel writer of the second century AD, discussing past Olympic history, indicates that a successful athlete might be suborned by a powerful head of state:

Astylos of Kroton . . . won the running race at Olympia three times in succession and scored victories in the two-lap race as well. Because in his last two victories he proclaimed himself a Syracusan to please Hieron son of Deinomenes, the people of Kroton decreed that his house should be a prison and they destroyed his portrait in the sanctuary of Lakinian Hera.

Some inscriptions indicate that the winner could not keep his crown or wreath, or other sacred objects given as prizes. The agonothete might declare 'I placed the crown on the altar of Roma', meaning that the event had been declared sacred. Herodotus records the scandalous behaviour of a fellow citizen of Halicarnassus (Bodrum):

> It used to be customary at the games of Triopian Apollo to give bronze tripods as prizes, and the winners were not allowed to take them away, but were required to dedicate them on the spot to the god. This ancient custom was openly defied by a Halicarnassian called Agasides, who, after winning his tripod, took it home and hung it up on the wall of his house. In punishment for this offence the five cities of Lindus, Ialyssus, Camirus, Kos and Knidos [members of a federation known as the Dorian hexapolis] excluded Halicarnassus [which was the sixth] from the temple privileges.

Occasionally, the crowns given in the Romaia were dedicated to the gods because no-one was adjudged good enough to claim them, in fact they were 'whistled off the stage'. One of these was the children's poetry category, and one can imagine this embarrassing debacle taking place in the theatre near the Letoon, relatives applauding furiously but unable to stem the tide.

Hadrian endowed the sanctuary with a nymphaeum, a grandiose water feature much beloved in the Roman Empire where it often distributed, with a plethora of basins and as much plashing and splashing as possible, the water brought to the town by aqueduct. Hadrian's gift to the Letoon consisted of a pool which trapped the rising spring waters to mirror marble apses and statuary around its rim. In distant centuries Lycian votaries had placed terracotta figurines of a goddess by such a spring: Hadrian's contribution was the last link in the long development of the site. Eventually rising water levels would submerge the lowest levels of the temples and began the decline of the sanctuary after a lifespan of a thousand years, and the end of the games. Nevertheless the half-buried temples retained their numinous atmosphere, for in the fifth century AD it was felt necessary to build a church on the site, to dispel its magic.

THE ORACLES
'Apollo's holy groves'

Farmers, ship-captains, merchants, emperors, generals and governors all sought to discern the divine will or prosper from knowing something of the future. They learned this from the fall of dice before the tomb of an ancestor, the flight of birds as viewed from a temple sanctuary, or the chanting of a sibyl. A powerful place was assigned to the seers, the 'prophets' or diviners who could interpret the mystery of divine favour. Should you take arms against a powerful opponent? Should you sell your farm, marry, travel overseas? Where are your stolen ear-rings, and who is putting the evil eye on your daughter? Several well-known oracular shrines along the Turkish coast could give you an answer, albeit an ambiguous one. The lord Apollo spoke through his sibyl or seer, and at one shrine even through the movements of sacred fish.

Didyma had not only a local, but an international reputation. King Croesus of Lydia consulted the Branchidae, priests of the temple here, before his ill-fated campaign against the Persians, though Herodotus tells us that it was Delphi's famous advice 'if Croesus attacked the Persians, he would destroy a great empire' of which he chose to take cognizance. Later, the oracle of the Branchidae foretold a victory of Alexander the Great, who had given generously to revive the cult after its long decline following the Persian wars; and it warned one of his successors, Seleucus I, another major benefactor, 'Be in no hurry to reach Europe: for you, Asia is far better'. He ignored this advice, and was assassinated on setting foot in Greece.

As rebuilt on the grandest scale from the third century BC onwards, Didyma outshone even Delphi. The architects were Paeonius of Ephesus and Daphnis of Miletus (the nearby city), who had worked on the temple of Artemis at Ephesus, accounted one of the seven wonders of the world. The plan echoes the cult. An open space for the sacred spring, the sacred laurel (Apollo's tree), the altar and cult statue, is the basic requirement, taking us back to the earliest days of worship here. This was surrounded by towering walls seventy feet high, and outside these a double colonnade was constructed on the most imposing and ostentatious scale.

The suppliant entered the temenos from the Sacred Way from Miletus and entered a forecourt with a platform for offerings, stoa, and statues. A large circular altar stood on the axis of the building, and after purifying himself with water from a sacred well, the questioner offered a sacrifice. Water from the well was sprinkled on an animal, usually a goat; if it reacted by jerking its head and trembling, the god was present, and the animal's blood and horns could join the pile of ashes from the sacred fire.

Once Apollo's favour had been ensured, the enquirer climbed a monumental stairway of fourteen steps, passed through a forest of massive columns, and found himself in a long pronaos (porch) with columns four abreast, where he could present his question for transmission to the oracle. He could not even look into the sacred courtyard where the prophetess would make her answer, his way being barred by a cross-hall that stood high above the floor of the pronaos. This hall is thought by many scholars to have been the chresmographeion attested by inscriptions, where the oracular words of Apollo's mouthpiece were turned into verse and noted down for the temple archive. A window onto the pronaos allowed the awaited response to be pronounced to the questioner.

Apollo's medium was a woman chosen, curiously it may seem, not for her prophetic skills or even her family connections, but annually by 'lot' (possibly a pre-arranged short-list) from the eligible women of Miletus. The techniques used to induce inspiration (or enthousiasm, god-within-ness) centred on the sacred spring, according to a late source, Iamblichus (fourth century AD). The soothsayer might hold a staff 'given by a certain god', wet her feet or the hem of her robe in water, or inhale the vapour from the water. Possibly more effective was the stipulation that she should live in the sanctuary, and abstain from food for three days before prophesying.

Claros, in the territory of Colophon, lies on the coast not far from Ephesus, and here too the clientele came from far and wide, leaving inscriptions to record their presence. What is impressive here is the evidence for civic delegations, and the distance they travelled. From Crete they came; from Corinth; Olbia, on the Black Sea; as well as other parts of Asia Minor. Frequently they set up commemorative texts when they got home, and these extend the bounds of Clarian Apollo's worshippers to Algeria, Dalmatia and even Rome.

Inscribed blocks from Hierapolis (Pamukkale) tell a story that is probably typical of many. Impelled by an outbreak of plague, a group of townspeople had sought advice from Apollo. He told them that the cause was the anger of mother Earth. They were advised to set up at the city gates images of Clarian Apollo 'shooting from afar with his holy arrows'. Then, when 'the evil powers have been appeased . . . boys and girls [should] go together to Claros, with hecatombs and glad libations'. Recent excavations at Claros have uncovered four rows of stone blocks with hooks attached: enough to tether the hundred animals needed for the massive sacrifice of the hecatomb.

Boys and girls constituted choirs who approached the sanctuary along the Sacred Way, chanting paeans of thanksgiving to Apollo. Their names are recorded everywhere, columns and exedrae that once supported bronze statues of satisfied customers becoming covered in spindly incisions. The first contact, when a city sought advice, was a graver occasion. When Alexander the Great was moved to re-found the city of Smyrna 'from a vision he had in his sleep' when hunting on Mount Pagos, the anxious city fathers sent ambassadors to ask at Claros what their position was, and the god answered with this prophecy:

> You shall live three and four times happy
> At Pagos, across the sacred Meles.

The ambassadors found within the temenos of Apollo at least two temples, one to Artemis and one to Apollo. The seat of the oracle was beneath the latter. A tortuous route leads to two chambers, vaulted and hardly high enough for a man to stand – again, engendering humility. Directly below the statue of Apollo, the inner chamber held a large basin of water, where the prophet sought inspiration. The outer chamber is thought to have been for other servants of the god rather than for suppliants: a thespiode, who rendered the oracle into verse, and secretaries, are mentioned in inscriptions.

Tacitus gives a description of the procedure when relating the visit of Germanicus in 18 AD. (The oracle scored a melancholy bull's-eye, warning the imperial visitor of his approaching end – he died, poisoned, the next year.)

> There is no woman there as at Delphi . . . rather a priest, after hearing merely the number and names of the clients, goes down into a cave; there he drinks from a secret fountain and, though generally illiterate, issues responses in verse concerning the various matters in the consultants' minds.

There is a fair degree of concordance with the archaeological and other textual evidence, if we assume that by 'cave' Tacitus means the dark, underground chamber in the temple. Pliny also mentions 'a pool in the cave of Clarian Apollo' adding the piquant detail 'a draught of which inspires wonderful oracles, but shortens the life of the drinker'. Little wonder that here as at Didyma the prophet only worked a shift of one year.

Literary and archaeological sources support each other too in bringing to life one of the most curious means of divination in the ancient world. In the rag-bag of fact and wildest fiction that makes up the elder Pliny's Natural History, the encyclopaedist enters only this one example of oracular fish, even after accepting tales of Syracusan eels that wear ear rings, and Syrian fish that obey the voice of temple ministers.

> But at Myra in Lycia at the fountain of Apollo whom they call Surius, the fish, summoned three times on the pipe, come to give their augury. If they tear the pieces of meat thrown to them, this is good for the client, if they wave it away with their tails, it is bad.

Plutarch, once a priest of Delphi and therefore an authority on oracular responses, adds that the diviners sit to watch the fish as they would birds of omen, and decide the augury according to fixed rules or common sense, observing how the fish twist and turn, pursuing or fleeing from one another. But the fullest account, and one which locates the oracle more precisely, comes from Polycharmus.

> When they come to the sea, where there is a grove of Apollo by the shore, on which is the whirlpool on the sand, the clients present themselves holding two wooden spits, on each of which are ten pieces of roast meat. The priest takes his seat in silence by the grove, while the client throws the spits into the whirlpool and watches what happens . . . the pool fills with sea-water, and a multitude of fish appear as if by magic, and of a size to cause alarm. The prophet announces the species of the fish and the client accordingly receives his answer from the priest.

The remnants of a temple, now engulfed in a marsh, can be made out at the foot of the hill identified as Surion. The sulphurous streams that emanate from the base of the cliff could well have produced vortices as they met fresh water, suggesting a whirlpool. But the identification of the site rests on more certain, epigraphic, evidence. A precipitous stairway of rock-cut steps can, with difficulty, be traced up the stony hillside. Half-way up is a rock-cut chair. Here perhaps the priest paused in his ascent to or descent from the plateau, where a tiny acropolis and a selection of Lycian tombs evidence some kind of settlement. Carved in the rock face are a series of skeuomorphic stelai cataloguing 'the priests of Apollo at Surion', and thereby forming a definite link between the archaeological remains and the ancient writings.

Oracles were the subject of a particularly vicious attack as edicts against pagan practices thundered down from the imperial court at Constantinople in the reign of Theodosius I. A pronouncement of 385 AD ordered that

> No man shall have the effrontery to encourage vain hopes by the inspection of entrails, or to attempt to learn the future by the detestable consultation of oracles.

The grove of Apollo must have vanished then, but a large basilica ostentatiously sited at the foot of the cliff suggests that here too, as at the Letoon, Christian adversaries found it necessary to counter the lingering fame of the deity.

THE GAMES

Didyma came alive every four years for festivities honouring Apollo in much the same way as the games at the Letoon honoured his mother, with contests in oratory, music and drama as well as races.

Where did such events take place? Some, it seems, were at nearby Miletus, though surprisingly, ancient sources suggest that the dramatic contests were not held in the fine theatre there but at Didyma. So far no theatre has been found in the sanctuary, though by no means the whole temenos has been explored. What has been found, however, is a stadium for running races. Seven tiers of benches were raised, parallel with the south wall of the temple and at a distance of thirteen metres. A little to the east, in the forecourt, lay two rows of stone blocks with perforations. Similar blocks at Priene have been interpreted as a starting-sill. The 'track' delimited by these features is short and narrow, but might reach to a half-stade: the stade, measuring around 184 metres, giving its name to the stadium. Spectators sat not only on the benches, but on the stepped base of the temple, where they scratched their names: two hundred or so have been found, most closely packed at the east end where the best view was to be had of the start, and perhaps the finish.

The stadium at Priene is of the standard length. Its seating relies, like the early theatre, on a natural bank, this time supplied by terracing, available only on one side of the track. The holes drilled into the starting block are thought to have enabled a rope to be kept taut in front of the runners until it was dropped by a race official, allowing all the contestants a fair start. The stadium at Perge, built in the heyday of the city under the Roman Empire, is more monumental, with seating built up on barrel-vaults in the manner of a Roman theatre. Here the festivals were held in the name of Artemis, patron of the city, and crowds of 12,000 or more were evidently anticipated. The silversmith Nikias, whose name was scratched in one of the vaults, was one of many shopkeepers who would hope to profit from this occasion, in the same way that the silversmiths of Ephesus owed their prosperity to the crowds who visited the temple of Ephesian Artemis or Diana.

The contestant in running, long-jump, wrestling and other sports was nude (gymnos). The gymnasium where he practised was another essential feature of Greek towns, attracting some opprobrium from Roman writers. Varro, pontificating in the first century BC on the time-worn theme of the superiority of the countryman over the city dweller, wrote:

> They so divided the year that they attended to their town affairs only on the ninth days [i.e. market days] and dwelt in the country on the remaining seven. So long as they kept up this practice they attained both objects – keeping their land most productive by cultivation, and themselves enjoying better health, and not requiring the citified gymnasia of the Greeks.

Gymnasia were still being built, or rebuilt, under the Roman Empire. Pliny, investigating events in Bithynia for the emperor Trajan, wrote to him for advice:

> The citizens of Nicaea have also started to rebuild their gymnasium (which was destroyed by fire before my arrival) on a much larger and more extensive scale than before. They have already spent a large sum, which may be to little purpose, for the buildings are badly planned and too scattered. Moreover, an architect – admittedly a rival of the one who drew up the designs – has given the opinion that the walls cannot support the superstructure in spite of being twenty-two feet thick, as the rubble core has no facing of brick.

Trajan replied:

> These poor Greeks all love a gymnasium, so perhaps they were too ambitious in their plans . . . They will have to be content with one which suits their real needs.

The games preferred by Trajan were those held in the amphitheatre. In celebration of his triumph over the Dacians

> he gave spectacles on one hundred and twenty three days, in the course of which some eleven thousand animals, both wild and tame, were slaughtered, and ten thousand gladiators fought.

In Asia Minor, sponsors of gladiatorial games had to make do with adapted premises. At Perge, the hemispherical end of the stadium was converted late in its life by throwing out a wall across the track to obtain a more or less rounded area, probably for use as an arena. But it is in the theatres that clearer signs of such adaptation and use can be observed. The lower tiers of seats were generally removed, and a parapet was added around the orchestra to separate the spectators from the bloody events to be played out there. At Ephesus, the iron railing which had been sufficient to separate orchestra from cavea was replaced by a wall two metres high, on the principle that it was better to lose a few rows of seating than the dignitaries who sat in them. The theatre at Miletus shows the same phenomenon, with low doorways in the wall where beasts could be let out into the orchestra, now become an arena, or wounded *venatores* (hunters) given shelter.

With the gradual triumph of Christianity came a series of edicts outlawing many of these events, though it's clear that the first of these, Constantine's outlawing of gladiatorial combat in 325, was disregarded for most of the fourth century. Gladiatorial games, with their terrible connotations of Christian martyrdoms, were banned from around 400, but the slaughter of animals aroused less moral indignation and continued in the eastern provinces. The last Olympic games, tainted for Theodosius I by their dedication to a pagan god, were held in 393, but familiarity with athletics and the stadium moulded the minds and language of anyone from the eastern provinces so that Christian writing, permeated with metaphors derived from the gymnasium, perpetuated their ethos.

> I have fought the good fight; I have completed the course [dromos, a road or track]; I have kept the faith. What remains is for me to be awarded the crown [stephanos: the winner's wreath] of righteousness, which the Lord will convey to me on that day, being a righteous judge . . .

Ancient Lycia 'The First Republic'

BARNABY ROGERSON

History begins with the Flood. For at the end of the last Ice Age Northern Asia, North America and Europe was released from the grip of a vast glacial super-continent, releasing torrential rivers, changing the weather for the wetter, which produced a dramatic rise in sea level. This was the period when such islands as Britain, Cyprus, Sicily and Sardinia were cut off from the mainland and 'foam-born from the sea'. It was also the time when the surging waters of the Mediterranean cut their way through the mountains of Spain and Morocco to meet the Atlantic in the far west. In the East they sliced a passage through Anatolia, cutting the Dardanelles and the Bosphorus channels so that a floodtide of water drowned a vast agricultural plateau to create the Black Sea. This environmental catastrophe was repeated in the south, where the rains, monster-rivers and rising sea drowned another fertile, low-lying coastal plateau to create the Persian Gulf. Civilization seems to have been kick-started by this double catastrophe as the refugees fled inland and were forced to rapidly create new forms of subsistence. So that in the highlands of Turkish Anatolia a worldwide revolution was fostered, as the old wild grasses gleaned by hunter-gatherers were now farmed as crops of wheat and barley. The wild animals of these hills were gradually domesticated by gifts of fodder and transformed into meek herds of sheep and goats. The fact that grain could be safely stored for many years allowed this agricultural revolution to endure and prosper. Porridge and pottery were soon followed by bread and beer. There could be not turning of the clock back once these inventions became widespread.

The process by which these inventions were spread is still not fully understood though each new archaeological dig into the early settlements of central Anatolia seems to extend by another thousand years the chronicle of our Neolithic civilization. From these excavations we can however watch mankind's cultural evolution as the crude circular huts of the first hamlets grow into tightly packed villages of rectangular houses out of which emerge the first walled cities. Courtyard-like house-shrines evolve into temples and palaces, the architectural mirror to the advance of high-priests into a form of Kingship. By the time that Bronze was being smelted the first Empires had been formed. They were at first based on the triumph of a single city which sat beside one of the ever-flowing great rivers which watered an agricultural hinterland, be it in China, Egypt, Mesopotamia, Syria, India or Anatolia.

The Empire that ruled over central Anatolia from around 2000 to 1000 BC is known as the Hittite. Their walled fortresses and sanctuaries have been well excavated, and so we can now look at the faces of many of their Kings and their deities which were carved from an enduring – if undeniably abrasive – black volcanic stone. The Hittites, like most agricultural Empire-builders, worshipped an all-powerful mother-goddess, ruler of the earth, life and death who was associated with a number of male consorts. Two of the most important of her lovers were Tesub and Habat who were envisaged as sky gods, associated with the sun, moon and the storm-clouds, whose role was to fertilise the great mother with rain, semen and sacrificial blood. We see these Gods depicted as warrior-monarchs, bearing thunderbolts, war-axes and spears, as they stand on the backs of sacrificial bulls. Nothing of the Hittite language survives (though it is known to have been Indo-Aryan) but we can yet read much about them for they were locked in a super-power rivalry with their neighbours, the Assyrian Empire of Mesopotamia and that Empire of Egypt which was ruled by Rameses II. From the writings of their enemies we know that the Hittites managed to extend their authority over south-west Turkey. The Lukka, as the people of Lycia were known, were conquered by the Hittite King Suppiluliamus but it seems clear that they subsequently rebelled and recovered their liberty. Later the ships of the Lycians began to raid the Syrian and Egyptian coasts. For they are listed amongst the component elements of the sea-peoples (that international fleet of pirate-settlers) that very nearly brought down the old Bronze Age Empires around 1200 BC. This was the period when the sea peoples were established on the coast of Palestine – as the Philistines – while other sea-peoples were planted in central Italy where they created the Etruscan federation.

The spiritual capital of the Lycians, where they worshipped the mother goddess and her consorts was Tlos, whose ruins can still be found tucked away in a high mountain valley through which the sacred Xanthus river flows. The ancient Lycians were an extraordinarily enlightened people. For they governed themselves in federations of twelve cities that met to elect a leader (the Lycian Lysiarch), a federal treasurer, lesser officials and a board of judges. The number twelve has a strong relationship to the sacred, for not only are the hours of the day assessed into units of twelve but so is the solar year. This allowed for an easy division of responsibilities, for each unit within a twelve-strong federation could take responsibility for a central shrine and exercise the priestly powers for a lunar month before passing both the power and the expense on to a neighbour. But not all cities can be equal so the Lycian federation later created a constitutional adaptation which ranked their influence into either one, two or three votes at the federal assembly depending on their wealth and population. Local magistrates and officials were elected by each individual city who continued to govern their own affairs but agreed to abide with the decision of the federal assembly on all matters to do with peace, war and foreign affairs. The formal name they gave themselves was the Termilae even though the rest of the world knew them as Lycia. But they were clearly used to double standards, for in something of a similar manner, they continued to trace their ancestry, names and cousin-age through their mothers and grandmothers but also maintained a separate paternal identity for political life and formal inscriptions. The Lycians had their own language and their own alphabet which seems to have been a halfway house between Greek and the original Phoenician alphabet. They tolerated, and even welcomed, the presence of foreigners in their land. However, the bustling trading ports that were established on the Lycian shore such as Miletus (which had a strong connection to Crete) and Phaselis (which had an even stronger link with nearby Rhodes) were treated as independent city-states allied to Lycia rather than as intimate members of the league. The Etruscans were aware of their ancient link to their Asian homeland and maintained many of the traditions of Lycia, such as their own celebrated league of twelve federated cities. The Lycians were recorded by Homer as coming to the aid of Troy, their generals Sarpedon and Glaucus fighting against the invading fleet of Menelaus and Agamemnon. Yet clearly the Lycians also felt some innate kinship with the Greeks, for those most Hellenic of all the deities, Apollo and his virgin sister Artemis, were born on Lycian soil (at the sanctuary of Letoon) while one of the gods' most celebrated temple-oracles was also sited in Lycia (at Didyma – a brood sister to Delhi and Delos).

The Lycians managed to maintain their independence against the emerging Anatolian super-power of Lydia (based on the city of Sardes) though they were forced to concede a dependent and tributary alliance in 540 bc when a Persian army under general Harpagus pushed its way into their mountains. Providing the Lycians paid the annual tribute and sent regiments to join the Persian Emperor when he went to war, they were left to run their affairs under the ancient traditions of their federation. The Persian yoke proved light enough that the Lycian federation refused to ally themselves with a dynamic new state that was being created by a dissident governor. For Mausolos the satrap (the governor of the region) tried to create his own dynastic kingdom from a fusion of Greek and Anatolian cultures. The monster tomb that his sister-wife Artemisia created for the two of them seems to have been a product of genuine grief and also commemorated their father and grandfather (Hyssaldomus and Hecatomnos) who had ruled as proud satraps of this most western part of the Persian Empire.

In 333 Alexander the Great, on his way to confront the army of the Persian Empire at Ipsus, marched his army through the Lycian mountains. Having first destroyed the power of the city of Halli-carnassus he was everywhere greeted as a liberator, and offered golden crowns as the restorer of Lycian freedom. It was this victory march, which passed through some thirty cities including Telmessus, Pinara, Tlos, Xanthus and Phaselis, which Freya Stark had such fun tracing back in the 1950s. After Alexander's death, the Lycian federation passed under the suzerainity of the Ptolemaic dynasty of Egypt. The Ptolemies were great codifiers of the constitutions of the various city-states over which they ruled and it was during this period that the Lycian language (and alphabet) was at last superseded by the lingua franca of Greek which was in common use from Afghanistan to Sicily. Towards the end of the second century BC, Lycia found itself unwittingly on the disputed frontier between the Seleucids (another one of the dynasties founded by one of Alexander's generals) and the Ptolemies. This rivalry allowed Rome to start meddling in the high politics of Asia, and the Lycian federation found itself locked in a tenacious struggle to retain independence against Rhodes – the chosen regional ally of Rome – which was then at the height of her maritime power. But the ancient freedoms of the Lycian League were maintained and so they remained immune from the chaos of the Asian revolt against Rome and the brutal destruction inflicted during the Mithridatic wars. It was a curious irony of history that those who most valued the Republican freedoms of Rome (and who murdered Julius Caesar in 44 BC to preserve them) were to be responsible for the end of the freedom of Lycia. For it was the Roman republican army led by Brutus and Cassius that invaded the territory of the Lycian League and in 42 BC encircled the ancient city of Xanthus. The Xanthians did not surrender but chose to burn down the surrounding farmhouses and prosperous suburbs rather than let them fall into the hands of the enemy. They encircled their city in a moat and earthen wall, and when driven from these defences fell back on the temple-studded citadel. When this too was stormed by the disciplined legions, the Xanthians gathered all their possessions on great communal fires, slaughtered their unresisting families and then finally cast themselves on to the flames. Plutarch records the story of a Lycian mother hanging from a noose with her dead child slung around her neck, a burning torch strapped to her arm with which she intended to set fire to her house. They preferred death to the loss of their ancient liberties.

Later that year Brutus and Cassius were themselves destroyed at the battle of Philippi by the army of Antony and Octavian. In the share-out of the Roman empire that followed this victory, Antony received all the provinces of the East. He delighted in reversing the actions of his Republican enemies by restoring the ancient liberties of Lycia. So when he visited the Lycian Federation he came ashore as an honoured guest and a liberator, while in the rest of the eastern Mediterranean he was saluted as ruler and a latter-day Dionysus (and a highly unpopular one who insisted on collecting an 'accession' donative rated at ten years' worth of tax). According to a cherished local legend it was during this time that the Lycian League prepared the island of Cedreae for the arrival of Queen Cleopatra to meet Antony on neutral territory. To make their honoured guest feel welcome they transported galleys full of the golden sand of Egypt which was strewn on the shore of Cedreae so that Cleopatra would feel at home. It worked, Antony and Cleopatra loved the sandy beach and the temporary escape from their royal cares. They sailed south together to rule their joint dominions from Alexandria.

After Octavian had buried them both Lycia became just another province within the Roman Empire. Romance was over but replaced by good governance, which saw the region's population grow to exceed 200,000 divided amongst some thirty flourishing towns and cities. But the legend of ancient liberties lived on, a role model that was cherished by both the ideologues of the French Revolution and another tide of sea-peoples transplanted on to a foreign shore, the United States of America – even if the numerology of thirteen rebel colonies does not quite match the sacred twelve of Lycia.

Acknowledgements

We would like to thank all of the authors for making this collection possible by allowing us to use their material, and gratefully acknowledge permission to reprint copyright material as follows:

Jane Bean for permission to use extracts from the works of George Bean, *Lycian Turkey* and *Turkey Beyond the Maeander*, Bogazici University Press for permission to use an extract from *Life's Episodes: Discovering Ottoman Architecture* by Godfrey Goodwin, Brill NV for permission to quote from *Bodrum: A Town in the Aegean* by Fatma Mansur, Tom Brosnahan for permission to quote from his book *Bright Sun, Strong Tea*, Claire Glazebrook for permission to use an extract from *Journey to Kars* by Philip Glazebrook, Granta for permission to use the extract from *Twice a Stranger* by Bruce Clark, Arcadia for permission to use an extract from *Dinner of Herbs* by Carla Grissman, June Haimoff for permission to use extract from her books *Kaptan June and the Turtles* and *Breakfasts with Kaptan June*, HarperCollins Publishers for permission to publish the extract from Mary Lee Settle's *Turkish Reflections*, Michael Kalafatis and the University Press of New England for the right to use an extract from *The Bellstone* by Michael Kalafatis, John Murray for permission to quote from *Ionia: A Quest* by Freya Stark, The Orion Publishing Group for permission to use the extract from Thomas Pakenham's *Remarkable Trees of the World*, Pen & Sword Books Ltd. for permission to quote from *He Who Dared* by David Sutherland, Princeton University Press for permission to use an extract from *The Ancient Mariners* by Lionel Casson, The Random House Group for permission for the extract from *Birds Without Wings* by Louis de Bernière, Michael Russell Publishing for permission to quote from the letters of Freya Stark, Jeremy Seal for permission to use an extract from his book *A Fez of the Heart*, and Sheil

Land Associates Ltd for permission to use an extract from *The Ulysses Voyage* by Tim Severin.

Every effort has been made to trace or contact copyright holders. The publishers would be pleased to rectify any omissions brought to their notice at the earliest opportunity

Works & Writers mentioned in the text

Antipater of Sidon, A Description of the Seven Wonders

Apollonius of Rhodes, *The Voyage of Argo* (2nd or 3rd century BC)

Arundell, Rev. Francis, *A Visit to the Seven Churches of Asia*, J. Rodwell, 1828

Bean, George E, article in *Illustrated London News* November 7th 1953

Bean George E, *Turkey Beyond the Maeander*, Ernest Benn, 1971

Bean, George E, *Lycian Turkey*, Ernest Benn, 1978

Bean, George E, *Turkey's Southern Shore*, Ernest Benn, 1979

Beaufort, Captain Francis, *Karamania*, R. Hunter, 1917

Blanch, Lesley, *From Wilder Shores*, John Murray, 1989

Bradford, Ernle, *The Companion Guide to the Greek Islands*, Collins, 1963

Brockman, Eric, *The Two Sieges of Rhodes*, John Murray, 1969

Brosnahan, Tom, *Turkey on $5 a Day*, Frommer, 1971

Byfield, Andy, 'Arums and Aristolochias' *Cornucopia*, 2001

Byron, Lord, *The Poetical Works of Lord Byron*, John Murray, 1854

Casson, Lionel, *The Ancient Mariners*, Gollancz, 1959

Casson, Lionel, *Travel in the Ancient World*, Allen and Unwin, 1974

Chandler, Richard, *Travels in Asia Minor 1764-5*, edited by Edith Clay, British Museum Press, 1971

Charlemont, James Caulfeild, *The Travels of Lord Charlemont in Greece and Turkey*, 1749. Reprinted 1984, A. G. Leventis Foundation, edited by W. B. Stanford

Clark, Bruce, *Twice a Stranger*, Granta Books, 2006

Clarke, Dr Edward D., *Travels in Various Countries of Europe, Asia and Africa*, T. Cadell and W. Davies, 1817

Clift, Charmian, *Mermaids Singing*, Michael Joseph, 1958

Cockerell, Charles, *Travels in Southern Europe & The Levant*, Longmans, Green and Co., 1903

Courtney, Nicholas, *Gale Force 10: The Life and Legacy of Admiral Beaufort*, Headline, 2002

Davis, P. H., *A Journey in S-W Anatolia, part 2* Journal of the RHS, December 1948

De Bernières, Louis, *Birds Without Wings*, Secker and Warburg, 2004

Fellows, Charles, *Journal written during an excursion in Asia Minor*, John Murray, 1839

Fellows, Charles, *An Account of Discoveries in Lycia*, John Murray, 1841

Freely, John, *The Western Shores of Turkey*, John Murray, 1988

Grissmann, Carla, *Dinner of Herbs*, Arcadia, 2001

Haimoff, June, *Kaptan June and the Turtles*, Janus, 1997

Haimoff, June, *Breakfasts with Kaptan June*, Janus, 2005

Homer, *The Odyssey*, translated by J. W. McKail in *The Oxford Book of Greek Verse in Translation*, 1938

Hope, Thomas, *Anastasius*, 1821, reprinted Baudry's Foreign Library, 1831

Hesiod, 'Sailing Weather', in *Works and Days – Oxford Book of Greek Verse in Translation*, 1938

Kabaağaçlı, Cevat Şakir, *Mavi Sürgün (The Blue Exile)*, 1961

Kalafatas, Michael, *The Bellstone*, University of New England Press, 2003

Kinglake, William, *Eothen*, John Ollivier, 1845

Kinross, Patrick, *Europa Minor*, John Murray, 1953

Lodwick, John, *Raiders from the Sea*, Green Hill, 1990

Lucian of Samosata, *Works*, Loeb Classical Library

Makal, Mahmoud, *A Village in Anatolia*, Valentine Press, 1954

Mansur, Fatma, *Bodrum: A Town in the Aegean*, Brill, 1971

Maranz, George, in *The American Weekly*, September 5th, 1937

Merrill, Lieutenant, quoted in *The Smyrna Affair* by Marjorie Housepian, Harcourt Brace Jovanovic, 1988

Moorehead, Caroline (ed.), *Some Talk of Alexander*, Letters of Freya Stark Vol VII (1952–7), Michael Russell, 1982

Murray's Handbook for Travellers in Turkey, John Murray, 1854

Newton, Charles, *Travels & Discoveries in the Levant*, John Murray, 1861

Orga, Irfan, *The Caravan Moves On*, Martin Secker & Warburg, 1958

Orga, Irfan, *Turkish Cooking*, Duckworth, 1958

Pakenham, Thomas, *Remarkable Trees of the World*, Weidenfeld and Nicolson, 2002

Phelan, Nancy, *Welcome the Wayfarer*, St Martin's Press 1965

Pierce, Joe, *Life in a Turkish Village*, Holt, Rinehart and Winston, 1964

Pliny the Elder, *Naturalis Historia*

Polycharmus, *A History of Lycia*

Price, Ward, in *Daily Mail*, September 1922

Rogerson, Barnaby, 'The Lycian Shore', *Cornucopia*, 1996

Rossi, E, *Assedio e conquista di Rodi nel 1522 secondo le relazioni edite e inedite dei Turchi*, Rome 1927

Selous, Frederick C., *Sport & Travel, East & West*, Longmans, Green, 1900

Sibthorp, Dr John, Excerpts from his travel journals, quoted from *The Magnificent Flora Graeca*, Stephen Harris, Oxford University Press, 2007

Seal, Jeremy, *A Fez of the Heart*, Picador, 1995

Settle, Mary Lee, *Turkish Reflections*, HarperCollins, 1991

Severin, Tim, *The Ullysses Voyage*, Hutchinson, 1987

Sewell, Brian, *South from Ephesus*, Century, 1988

Spratt, Lt, T.A.B., R.N., F.G.S. and Prof. E. Forbes F.R.S., *Travels in Lycia* (1847) Vol. 1

Stark, Freya, *Ionia, A Quest*, John Murray, 1952

—— *Alexander's Path*, John Murray, 1954,

—— *The Lycian Shore*, John Murray, 1956

Sutherland, David, *He Who Dares*, Leo Cooper, 1998

Thesiger, Captain Bertram, unpublished journals, National Maritime Museum, Greenwich

Throckmorton, Peter, 'Thirty-three centuries under the sea' *National Geographic*, May 1960

Travis, William, *Bus Stop Symi*, Rapp and Whiting, 1970

Wharton, Edith, *The Cruise of the Vanadis*, Bloomsbury, 2004